MW01657029

Max and the Musicians

Jack Cazal is a sometime lawyer and all-time music fan. He splits his time between Devon, in the South-West of England, and Périgord, in the South-West of France. Jack supports the notion that all bureaucratic and political red tape should be used exclusively to gift wrap bureaucrats and politicians and not wasted on the undeserving general public.

"I lie, sorry, like, this book tremendously!"
A former Prime Minister

"Wonderfully erudite and sophisticated prose."
Reader of another book

"A gloriously light and frothy musical confection."
Attila the Hun

Max and the Musicians

JACK CAZAL

MEADWOODCREATIVE
TORQUAY

Published by MeadwoodCreative
www.meadwoodcreative.com

Copyright ©Jack Cazal 2023
The right of Jack Cazal to be identified as the author of this work has been asserted by him in accordance with the Copyright, Designs and Patents Act 1988.

This book is a work of fiction

ISBN 978-1-7393098-0-0 – Hardback
ISBN 978-1-7393098-1-7 – Paperback

Typeset in Garamond by Elaine Sharples

To Fiona – for her peerless support and encouragement

ACKNOWLEDGEMENTS

This book arises out of a lifelong love of music and musicians and was great fun to write. I started putting finger to keyboard in December 2019, with the idea of Max forming a band with a group of eccentric outsiders. However, my original plot was completely hijacked by the early, and completely unexpected, appearance of one RW. Once present in the story, RW dug his heels in and simply refused to go away! The story was completed in October 2020.

Close readers of the text will note that RW, and certain other supporting characters in the book, appear to have names that are remarkably similar to those of real musicians, actors, and presenters. I would therefore like to make it clear that although this might, just possibly, be completely true, both the personalities and all actions of name-sake characters portrayed in the book are entirely of my own wild invention; they are meant to be affectionately tongue-in-cheek, and should not be taken in any way to depict how such characters might behave in real life. In real life, these characters may not be nearly as amusing, charming, well-rounded, or indeed sane as portrayed in the book.

Finally, I would like to thank my editor, Debra Riggle, for her professionalism and sense of humour – apologies for all those song and album titles! – and to confirm that responsibility for any errors, omissions, or indeed anything at all that may be amiss or remiss, rests entirely with the government.

The café sat towards the right-hand end of a rough stone beach, looking out over Mead Bay. It was to be found down a sloping path from the sea road, which ran along the base of a tree-covered hillside of persistently disintegrating shale.

Across the road and set back diagonally from the café, was a stunning Regency Crescent, painted uniformly in cream. With its manicured sloping lawns, pool and tennis courts, it presented a wonderful distraction for boats in the bay, of which there were never very many.

A small, central section of the Crescent still remained as a hotel, but the vast majority of the building had now become expensive time share apartments. A faded blue plaque adorned the wall of one of the ground floor apartments to record that Charles Darwin had spent six weeks there on holiday. The décor in the hotel suggested that it was contemporaneous with his visit.

The café was a functional, rectangular-shaped, white building with a flat, pitch roof. It had two large serving hatches, one on the path side for doling out ice cream in summer and the other, facing onto the railed concrete terrace above the beach, for taking food orders and serving up teas and coffees.

The terrace in front of the café was partially shaded by a fixed, flat-roofed portico supported by steel poles, the latter now wrapped around with rope from top to bottom in a practical and not altogether unclever attempt to disguise the rampaging rust. It would not be too long before the ropes would be the only thing keeping the poles together.

An inside seating area had been tacked onto the end of the café some years back, accessed by an external side door. As the café remained open all year round, this made a great deal of sense. It was also a good place to chat to the beach café staff on their break, as an internal door led directly to the kitchen area.

The café had no official name but was known affectionately as Sharkies after a shark-fin-shaped rock that projected some twenty feet from the sea, four hundred metres offshore.

It was eleven o'clock in the morning, and Max was sitting in the shade of the portico at a pedestal table for two, his feet dangling beneath him, occasionally kicking back against the wall of the café. This was his favoured spot for reading and for people-watching.

To his left, Max could keep an eye on the punters queueing for food and drink, whilst surveying in front of him the varying types of humanity and caninity that circled around the foldable, high-gloss, steel tables lining the whole length of the terrace.

It was a Sunday in mid-May, and the whole bay was sparkling with the kind of weather that the brochures usually made up. Out of main season it may have been, but the heat had tempted a rag bag of partially fossilised locals, accompanied by their moth-eaten dogs, to venture out and take the air. Meanwhile, a smattering of younger souls, presumably self-employed or, like Max, unemployed, made up the numbers.

A small, attractive, blonde woman in early middle age caught Max's attention. Despite the heat, she was dressed all in black, with a grey scarf around her neck. The clothes were stylish, and the black contrasted starkly with her very pale skin, a skin which was showing signs of moisture from the heat. She was seated at a table for two, under a small awning at the far end of the terrace where steps led down to two long rows of gaudily painted concrete beach huts. The woman was demonstrably attempting to make herself invisible, and therefore, not succeeding.

Max stood up and, leaving his book and sunglasses on the table to establish ownership, edged towards the woman under the pretence of finding a good spot to take photos of the view with his iPhone. A book sat open in front of her with the intriguing name of *How to Travel Without Arriving*. The woman coughed nervously as Max approached and apologised for getting in his way, which she wasn't. Her voice had a pleasant Oceanic lilt to it but with a noticeable uplift to the end of her sentence, as if asking a question that required validation.

Max took this as his entrée and made a reference to the weather, the view and the niceness of the café, in that order. Hardly inventive stuff, but the accompanying warm smile succeeded in establishing a connection with the woman, which led in turn to him asking textbook follow-ups about where she came from and what she was doing here.

With some accompanying coughs, Jessica, a New Zealander it

transpired, told Max in her questioning, self-doubting voice that she was on enforced vacation from her job as a press writer for a Viennese-based film company. Apparently, a routine check by HR revealed that she had only taken six days holiday in the past three years, and they were determined that she should now take at least three months off. Whereas most people in Max's acquaintance would have sold their souls to an investment bank for such an opportunity, it was clear that Jessica was very unhappy about it. Indeed, the tone of her voice suddenly, and markedly, changed so that her questioning tone now came across as more of a forthright challenge to anyone to disagree with her.

"I mean, it's crazy, right? It's not as if I haven't been anywhere. I've been to six different countries in the past three years."

Max calculated that this meant one day in each country and said so.

"Well, sure. I mean, I don't like to hang around too long and outstay my welcome. And it's not like I'm not busy or something. I've always got lots of errands to do and stuff, right?"

A bit of subtle probing by Max established that Jessica was single and lived in a small studio apartment in downtown Vienna, near her widowed father, an Austrian by birth. Max began to wonder if Jessica was having him on but continued by asking about how she had chosen a beautiful but down-at-heel seaside town in the South of England for her involuntary break.

"Well, there's a Mead Bay in Saskatchewan I visited for an afternoon about ten years ago that was very nice, and then there's the sea and lots of places to walk here. Also, the hotel will allow me to book on a daily basis. It costs a lot more but gives me flexibility."

"So, you're planning on visiting other parts of the UK?"

"No, not really."

Max began to feel that he was losing his grip on this conversation and brought it back to safer ground by asking Jessica if she'd like another coffee.

"Thanks, yes, but I can't stay very long as I have some errands to do."

Max wondered what errands were possible in the town. Feeding seagulls perhaps? Or helping repatriate Northerners back to where they came from? Still, as he had absolutely no errands to carry out, a further thirty minutes or so spent not doing them, while sharing a coffee with an attractively strange woman, was more than welcome. In fact, Max found the woman's questioning speech patterns quite soothing, as all he needed to do was say yes or no occasionally, while admiring the view.

"See you around?" the woman lobbed in casually, and somewhat unexpectedly, as they rose to head their separate ways.

"That would be great! My name's Max," he said, realising with surprise that he had not already told her his life story. This was something he was apt to do at the drop of a hat with strangers on the basis that, as it was usually the last conversation he would have with them, why not tell everything?

Outwardly confident Max, in reality, had all the natural self-confidence of the queen's personal guillotine tester, and this might have gone some way to explaining his single status. Calm, cheery and motivated when employed, indeed highly confident when having lots of responsibility, completely unforeseeable redundancy had left him, after two years of no interviews, with his underlying angst in full bloom. Combined with the black hole of his self-esteem, Max was also very, very, very, very angry. He would often dream of the pleasure to be had in cracking open champagne on the occasion of learning that anyone he felt to blame for his predicament had suffered some serious illness or permanent incapacity, been disgraced, or died. Max wished for this very much. All of the time. It kept him sane.

"Will you be around tomorrow?"

This seemed to create uncertainty in Jessica. Max could see her wondering about the need to commit to being at one place at a given moment in time.

"Maybe around four for a coffee?" she answered.

He took that as being as fixed as possible and headed up the 151 steps behind the café to the road where he lived.

***

Tired by reading at home with his feet up on the coffee table, Max decided to return to the café at teatime for a change of scene. He chose the shortest and lightest of the three books that he was reading, *The Hitch-Hiker's Guide to the Galaxy*, and sauntered lazily along the road and down the path.

The top part of the path took him through a stone arch and down steps that meandered in a lazy S shape, lined closely on each side by wild bushes. The path then gave onto a flat piece of ground that was part of a permanently empty car park, with markedly beautiful views of the bay through a filtering of wind-blasted pine trees, before winding steeply down more rail-lined steps to the road above the beach. In the spring and summer, wildflowers were in abundance on this top stretch of the path, and butterflies flitted and danced like they actually meant it.

Looking up to the arched entrance from the car park, the upper path looked secluded, and even a touch magical. Although Max was not a believer in fantasy, except in books, he had always felt that if fairies did exist, or that if man could communicate directly with nature, it would be here. However, that being said, he was also convinced that humans were not half as smart as they thought they were (the continuing existence of Millennials sprang to mind here) and that many other-worldly things might be possible to explain scientifically, if you just changed the science. He was sure famous keyboard player turned perma-smiling scientist, Brian Cox, would agree with him. But was Brian really real, though, or just a bad dream?

Someone, a fat person, had snaffled Max's usual seat under the portico, and he gazed around for a place to sit, having bought a hot buttered tea cake this afternoon as well as tea.

He wasn't the only one looking for space. A slightly harassed looking mother with dishevelled hair and a food-stained Muse T-shirt, dragging two fractious, snivelly ice-cream- dripping pre-schoolers, was also looking for a resting place. She had spotted a table for four occupied only by a lone middle-aged male and made a beeline for it.

The man was wearing a triumvirate of slightly unfashionable glasses, clothes and shoes. He had receding, mousy coloured hair with flecks of grey that showed prominently where slight hair wings protruded over his ears, a bright red, round face with a pointed nose and an air of total serenity. He had carefully laid out a large map across the entire top of the table, using the café`s only remaining condiments to hold down the edges. He had placed his coat over the arm of one chair, his rucksack on another, and his battered Panama hat on a third. *Probably in his mid-40s,* Max thought, *but spiritually from the 1940s.*

The harassed mother made her approach and hovered by the table. Map Man ignored her studiously. She made some remark to him about it being busy down here. He responded in a firm teacher-like way, with unmistakeable, public-school tones, that it was indeed and that is was important to plan your arrival at a time most likely to secure a place. He advised the mother, based on his observations of the past four days, to arrive around three o'clock like he had. Having imparted these words of wisdom, he returned to his map.

The mother, irritated, made a concerted fuss over one of her grizzling offspring, saying out loud how tired they looked and how that nasty cold would only get better with some rest. Map Man raised his gaze at this point to agree wholeheartedly with the mother's expressed point of view and added that he could advise on a particular type of children's medicine that was unusually good as well as cheap. He would check on Google what it was. The mother, in a raised and sarcastic voice, told him not to bother himself.

The intended barb not connecting in the slightest, Map Man insisted it was not a problem at all, and that he was only too glad to help. He then took a measured five minutes to connect with the internet, and another two to write out the medicine details conscientiously, adding some bonus advice about the value of buying two for one, and presented it to the mother.

Broken, dejected, and with distraught kids standing in expanding ice-cream puddles, she distractedly thanked him and slunk off to wonder about her sad life.

Satisfied with his good deed, Map Man looked around him benevolently.

Max caught his eye and was immediately invited to sit down.

"I heard you speaking to the girl at the counter and thought you must be local," the man said.

"Well, yes, I know the area well from childhood and am temporarily stranded here while looking for work. I have a house near here, but until recently I was based in Paris."

"Me, too," said Map Man, smiling warmly.

"Max," said Max.

"William," said Map Man.

"Yes, I got made redundant and slunk back here to regroup. Unfortunately, Mead Bay is not a great place to look for work from. Every time I go to London it costs me a hundred quid for a non-refundable cheap ticket, and half the time I find the person I've gone to have coffee with cancels at the last moment because they've got something better to do. On top of that, First Great Western is the worst train company on the network. The seats of the new trains are like rock, and they've got rid of the buffet car. Now you have a rolling trolley that rarely makes it to you at all, and I can't tell you how many times there's no hot drinks available because the boiler is not working. It's quite clear that the imbeciles who run the company have never been on a train in their lives. What's worse is that the reasons always given for these changes are that 'We have been listening to our customers.' No they haven`t. I haven't heard one single report of a First Great Western executive team member being killed by having a fridge dropped on their head from 10,000 feet."

William listened calmly and observed that Max seemed a bit out of sorts.

"It's the unemployment," he went on. "Two years of nothingness is enough to drive anyone crazy. Not that I am crazy, though, it's just that I've had time to realise that nearly everyone else is."

"I'm not working either at the moment," said William. "I used to work for Gamblers Bank, but since the crash of 2008, they've been cutting back on legal compliance staff like me. 'Non-core' they call us. I was stressed for a time, but now I've discovered that contract work topped up by insurance-related state benefits is a pretty good deal. I had twenty years working full time, so my pension will be fine. I just need to manage the gap." He paused. "Really, though, I see myself as an artist."

He picked up a handful of A4 size paper sheets and handed them to Max.

"You specialise in bar codes?"

"Abstract. I find that art is all about perception, about understanding and being in tune with people and the world around you."

"This brown section here?" asked Max.

"The sand."

"And the blue one?"

"The sea."

"And the white bit is the sky, right?"

"Seagulls."

"Very interesting," said Max. "You kind of cut out all the distractions, some might even say the defining details, of real life."

"Exactly. I think there is a particular kind of ability required for this kind of painting."

"Undoubtedly. Have you ever thought about expanding into portraits?"

"Well, yes, actually. My first professional commission was from a Spanish woman who wanted me to paint a picture of her daughter, as a present."

"How did that happen?"

"I was at a wine tasting in Barcelona, and we were both tasting the same wine. She mentioned that the bottle label was a great piece of art, and I took the opportunity to mention that I was an artist. She was interested, so I showed her some pictures on my iPhone."

"And she commissioned you to paint her daughter? Did she make any comment about your style, or whether her daughter was attractive or, er, not?"

"No, actually, although the photos I showed her were of my father's paintings. He's quite a talented amateur."

"Ah, yes, I see."

"But I did mention that my interests are currently more abstract than the photos I showed her."

"Indeed. How did the painting go?"

"I took a lot of care over this, as it was a first commission. Practised a lot to get the flesh tones right, as I've noticed that many artists slip up on this."

"And the painting session?"

"Went very well. I'm a gentleman, so it was a bit awkward raising the question of nudity, but once we got over that, it was fine."

"She had no issues with the nudity?"

"No, she's Spanish, and they're always naked."

"Are they? I thought that was the Swedish?"

"Ah, yes, maybe you're right. Anyway, I took off my own clothes just to make her feel comfortable."

"That was extremely kind of you. Do you have a photo of the painting?"

"Yes, certainly."

William scrolled through his iPhone for some time before proudly handing it over to Max.

"Wow, that's quite remarkable!" Max exclaimed, nodding admiringly. "And what is the brown colour covering the bottom half of the canvas?"

"Pubic hair."

"Gosh, really, that much? I mean, could you actually see the girl? And the green? Her eyes?"

"Her nipples."

"Incredible, and were they really that saucer shape, too?"

"Well, there is a bit of artistic licence. I had her sit with her back to me."

"Good that the nudity wasn't wasted at all. I notice that the rest of the painting, apart from the brown and green swathes, is a sort of pinky-purple."

"The skin was a bit difficult to master in the end, but I think I captured the spirit of the girl."

There were a few seconds silence while Max gathered his thoughts. "And did the painting go down well?"

"I'm sure it did. But there's a sad twist here. The daughter's house burnt down shortly afterwards. Apparently, she had left the painting too close to an open fire, and whoomph! Luckily, I had got the mother to sign a contract guaranteeing my IP rights in the work, so I am planning a T-shirt run with her daughter's name on it. Do you paint?"

"Oh, no, I've got absolutely no talent in that direction, or at least so I used to think. No, I'm more of a singer-songwriter."

"What do you play?"

"Nothing really. I strum the guitar badly. I only learned enough chords to write songs, and I haven't felt inspired to write for the last twenty years. What I really need is to meet someone who also writes songs as a kind of inspiration. I mean, there are loads of brilliant musicians out there who just regurgitate other people's stuff. Pub open-mic nights are filled with them. But that has never interested me."

"What style do you favour?"

"I suppose rock-blues with some punk spirit thrown in. Needs to have a bit of meaning and reality. Nowadays, songs never have any bloody lyrics, nor tunes either. When I was in my clubbing days..."

"Seal clubbing?" William asked, interrupting with a self-satisfied chuckle.

"... you used to go to dance to songs that you liked that also happened to be danceable, and you could sing along with them, too."

At this point, Max broke out into song.

"*Slowly walking down the hall, faster than a cannon ball....* Genius."

"The Smiths?"

"Close, Oasis. Anyway, nowadays, when you go to a club, there's no tune or lyrics, just thudding noises..."

"Like the clubbing of seals?"

"...and your ribs start to vibrate. There was a time you couldn't hear the bass properly on records, but now it's the whole frigging record!" Max paused to re-charge his disdain. "Maybe you and I should put on a show together? Your art and my music and lyrics. A bit edgy. *I want to be a toilet, flushed with excess, I want to throw up baby, all over your gingham dress.*"

"I like it. The gingham bit adds class. Oasis?"

"No, one of mine."

"Really good. We should definitely talk some more."

Max and William exchanged email details, and Max asked what brought him to Mead Bay.

"A stroke of luck really. I discovered this great deal at the hotel behind the beach, The Darwin. If you pay for three month's stay, they give you free massages and a 20% discount off all materials at the local art shop. The owner is a keen painter, and that's how I discovered the hotel online. I'm in between contracts at the moment and thought it was a good opportunity to do some painting. Plus, there's some really good golf down here."

"But what about the authorities in France?"

"No problem at all. I make lots of job applications to keep them happy, and I help my counsellor with her English."

"How?"

"Well, I noticed that she made a lot of mistakes in English and had a vehree Frrrench accent, so I made some suggestions as to how she could improve."

"She didn't exactly ask you for help then?"

"No, I thought I would take the initiative. The French can be a bit touchy about their English skills."

"I'm surprised that she doesn't speak French with you."

"I offered, but she said she prefers to stick to English."

"Good, your French, is it?"

"Getting better. I've been in Paris for fifteen years now and am about to apply for French nationality, so I've been brushing up. The thing is that you only really need key words in any language to get your communication across. I always do my research before I need to speak French to anyone for a job interview or with the authorities. I rehearse topics and then stick to them."

"Very resourceful. What happens if the person changes the subject?"

"I've found that nodding seriously and/or laughing and then continuing right on with my spiel usually wins them over in the end. There have been one or two sticky moments, but in those situations, I throw in a few additional words of German and Spanish that I've learned, and that seems to impress them."

"I'd love to be there. Look, I've got to head off in a moment, but let's keep in touch."

At this point, they both picked up their empty mugs and returned them to the café serving counter. A smiley, in a sort of desperate way, tall girl with long, tied-back, dark hair, intellectual glasses and a Lionel Richie shirt, took their mugs and thanked them.

"That's sooo kind of you," she said. "Normally people just leave everything on the tables, and then the seagulls take over. And if it's not the seagulls, then it's the wasps, and I'm very busy, and I feel so guilty if I can't clear up before new people sit down," she said in one breath. "And Glen's not much help, lovely though he is, because he has to do the cooking and can't be running around after me."

At this point, a comfortably built man with a bright, cheery face, post-designer stubble, decked out in spectacular harlequin trousers and wearing a Peter Hook designer-range 'Hacienda' bandana, waved from behind a frying pan of sausages.

"Don't mind Cee," he bellowed, in an accent that Max placed as being well north of Taunton. "Not everyone can be a cheery chops like me."

"Back to your sausages, Glen," said William, in a potentially over matey tone. "And would that be a Broommie accent?" he added, giving his best attempt.

Glen flinched painfully, like he had sat on a startlingly over-sized needle.

"You must be joking! Burnley born and bred and proud of it!"

"That's where Black Sabbath come from isn't it?"

"You're having me on! They're from Birmingham. I know that both towns begin with a B, but that's as close it gets."

"Who are Black Sabbath?" asked Cee.

"Don't you start!" said Glen.

"They're a famous rock band," intoned Max. "Founded in 1968 and seen as the originators of heavy metal. Sold hundreds of millions of records and only recently retired. I saw them on their farewell tour in Paris."

"And I was there for the very last concert in Birmingham at the NEC!" exclaimed Glen joyfully. "Brilliant, it was."

"Do you two know everything?" Cee asked.

"Yes," replied Glen and Max together.

"Any famous musicians from Burnley?" William threw in somewhat dangerously.

Without a pause. Max smoothly replied, "Sure, there's Boff Whalley."

"Bloody 'ell, but that's impressive," said Glen, as William and Cee looked on, clearly unsure if they were part of the same conversational universe.

"Boff Wha....," Cee started to say questioningly, before Max cut in with "Boff Whalley from Chubawumba!" grinning from ear to ear.

"*I get knocked down, but I get up again, you are never gonna keep me down,*" chanted Glen and Max noisily, while fully respecting the tone of the original.

"'Tubthumping,'" Glen said.

"I don't understand anything!" wailed Cee. "Do you know what they're talking about?" she directed at William.

"I'm sure it was *I get knocked out, but I get up again,*" said William insistently, ignoring her.

"No, mate, I slept with Boff`s aunt's sister's cousin, not that that has anything to do with it, and she told me the story behind the song," Glen insisted.

"He's right," added Max. "It is *knocked down*. Do you fancy a wager? I bet you twenty quid we're right."

"I'll come in halves," Glen chipped in.

"You're on!"

"Ooh, this is exciting," said Cee, clapping her hands with anticipation.

William checked about four Google results before finally conceding defeat, even though he was still sure that Chubawumba had got it wrong themselves. But, to give him his due, he magnanimously handed over a twenty-pound note to Max before excusing himself and saying that he'd see everyone tomorrow.

Max changed the note for two tens at the till and handed one over to Glen.

"A nice day's work that," said Glen. "Friend of yours?"

"Met him for the first time today. Tells me he's a painter, abstract scenery with the occasional portrait."

"I'd love to have my portrait painted," Cee announced.

"Careful what you wish for Cee, and on no account mention that to William if you see him again," Max said, smiling but deadly serious.

"Young lady! Can I please have some tea!" bristled a very short, puce-faced old man with a classic comb-over and a broad Glaswegian accent, who had been waiting for service throughout the tubthumping conversation.

"Oh, I am so sorry, I didn't see you down there," said Cee, instantly regretting her choice of words.

The puce-faced man now turned such an amazing deep purple colour that the band would have been proud to have him as a mascot.

"You're just bloody rude! When I was a boy, waitresses knew all about manners and good service."

"Keep your hair on, er sorry, no pun intended," said Glen. "She's apologised, and to be quite honest, it really isn't very easy to see you. You thought of buying some of those Elton John shoes from the 70s? No, well I'll tell you what, why don't I give you a cup of tea and some of our special chili beef on the house?"

True to stereotype, the Scotsman`s skin quickly lightened by several shades on hearing he would receive something free.

"Aye, well, I accept your offer. I like my chili hot, mind. It's cold up where I come from," he added in a limp attempt at a joke.

"Don't you worry about that, sir," Glen answered, smiling maniacally. "Hot it shall be."

Max was dying to relieve himself and was torn between two imminent explosions. He opted to avoid his personal one and hurried off up the slope to the public conveniences.

Fortunately, he returned just in time to see the old man tuck into his free meal. He watched him get about five forkfuls in, chatting animatedly to an old coat and hat, before there was sudden and absolute silence. Then, peacefully, and even gracefully, he slipped sideways off his chair and onto a sleeping greyhound. The greyhound scarcely moved, but the coat and hat suddenly sprung into life, like an unsuspecting glove puppet who has had a cold hand inserted up it.

"Ooohh, my God, Billy!!" it said.

Two men who had seen what happened rushed over and attempted to revive the man.

"I think he may have a urinary infection, or been hit by lightning," said the first man, a British doctor. "If you make an appointment, the practice cleaning lady can see him in three weeks' time."

"He's fainted, probably through some kind of heat-induced shock," said the second, an unemployed former drug addict. "He'll be up and about in a moment."

"Too bloody right he will," Glen said out of the side of his mouth to Cee and Max. "If you think there's a load of chili in there, that's nothing to the laxatives I put in...."

"And they're going to burn their way out like volcano on speed," added Max helpfully.

"You two are really awful," said Cee.

"But we like you!" shot back Max and Glen without hesitation.

"Stop it, stop it! I don't know what's happening."

"Dick Emery!" Max and Glen said at the same time.

"Was he in Black Sabbath?"

"No, too hard-core," said Max, "although the same era. Look, guys, I need to head off. See you tomorrow. Maybe then you can tell me about the international Rick Wakeman party I saw advertised for next month?"

"Will do," Glen responded. "It's going to put Mead Bay on the map that will!"

***

Max started to climb another 151 steps up to his house and wondered why they never seemed to get any easier. As he reached the car park, he saw a 1960s VW camper van with its bonnet and doors wide open, parked halfway into a turn. Clouds of smoke poured out of every open space, and the inhabitants were completely obscured. Max was about to continue up the steps when a sixth sense drew him back. His hunch was rewarded when what looked for all the world like a retired roadie-come-down-and-out Father Christmas staggered out of the van, steaming with smoke.

"I need a wazz," said Father Christmas to someone in the depths of the van. "And then a nice cup of tea will help refill the space perfectly. You might give the engine some tea as well."

He barrelled off to find some suitable spot singing merrily, "*Yo, ho, ho, and bottle of rum, drink it all and stick it up yer bum!*"

Max followed him. There was something about the tone of voice, the rolling gait and the long straggly, grey-blond hair that touched a memory chord.

"Mr. Wakeman?"

The man was caught at something of a disadvantage, seeing that his knees were locked hard against a low wall to maintain balance, while his hands were engaged elsewhere. He half turned in response to Max's call, gave an enquiring smile and then somersaulted over the precipice. Max could hear his descent down the steep bank, accompanied by the kind of groans that might not have been out of place at an expensive S&M club. Fortunately, the bank was largely made up of bushes and shrubs, all held in place at the bottom by a retaining wall that ran along the pavement of the road leading down to the sea.

A small, slim, blondish creature joined Max from behind, smoke curling around her head. She reminded Max strongly of a character he had seen in a 1990s TV sitcom.

"I knew it'd only be a matter of time before he bloody killed himself," said the woman in a surprisingly low, flat Yorkshire accent. "I told him we shouldn't have come here in the first place. I mean, bloody Mead Bay for God's sake! In that bloody death-trap of a van. The man's as rich as bloody Croesus, but he says he feels nostalgic for the early days! So, no chauffeured limo for him. No, just a piece of junk that a scrap yard wouldn't even dare sell you. And for what? Because some bloody chef from bloody Burnley suggests an international bloody Rick Wakeman Day!! I mean you'd have thought that he was famous enough not to do this. Every kid and his stalker knows him from *Grumpy Old Men*, but that's the bloody problem. He feels that his worth as a grand keyboard virtuoso has been overlooked. Throws stuff at the telly if he as much sees Elton or Jools Holland appear. I mean, the man's got an ego the size of a planet and now the body to go with it. He witters on about how artistic differences drove him out of Yes, but the truth is that the others were pissed off with having to reinforce the bloody stage! And he keeps wanting to wear his bloody capes. I tell him all the bloody time that the Demis Roussos look is not coming back, but he's that stubborn he insists. Of course, the local parachute maker worships the bloody ground he sinks into."

Her flow was stopped suddenly by the re-appearance of Mr. Wakeman's head popping up over the wall.

"I must apologise," said Max. "Wrong time to call out."

"No problem at all, these things happen," the man replied jovially. "No harm done. In fact, it reminds me of the kind of things that used to happen back in the early 70s when I was in the Strawbs."

"The bloody who?!" the woman screeched.

"Ah, you've already met my lovely manager, Squiggle. And, for your education, Squiggs, it's the bloody Strawbs, not the bloody Who."

"I'm not called bloody Squiggle!!" she exploded. "My name's Marguerite, and any bloody way, that bloody woman in that bloody TV series who I'm not bloody like at all was bloody called Bubble."

Marguerite stormed off towards the van, and Rick extended a meaty, ring-encrusted paw. "Rick."

"Max."

"You may be wondering why I employ such a charming young person as my manager, but she's honestly not all bad. I always get paid, in fact sometimes more than agreed because the promoters are absolutely terrified of her. She also makes a great cup of tea and..." at this point, Rick leaned over confidentially, "...I think she may actually be my daughter, although for God's sake don't say anything."

As a lover of music, Max was delighted to meet Rick Wakeman, the man who played mellotron on "Space Oddity" and keyboards on both "Life on Mars" and "Get It On," as well as composing the peerless epic *Journey to the Centre of the Earth*, based on Jules Verne's famous novel. Admittedly, there was that alarmingly long period with prog rockers Yes, but Max realised that even talented musicians needed to pay the bills. What might Wings have been if Paul McCartney had had the readies in the fallow post-Beatles period to engage Rick on keyboards instead of Linda? He even looked a bit like Linda in those days. Mind you, Linda's playing improved by leaps and bounds over the years. A worrying thought suddenly crept into Max's head and was equally quickly banished.

"Down here on holiday?" Max asked conversationally.

"Well, er, no, not, er, exactly. It turns out that there's this huge, er, fan of mine who is planning a day of my music, and I thought it might be fun to show up unannounced and make the chap's evening."

"You bloody liar, Rick Wakeman!" exclaimed Marguerite, returning from the van with a tray full of mugs of tea. "You almost wet yourself with excitement when he contacted you, admit it. And now you've dragged me down here in that stinking pile of rust a month ahead of time just so you can check out the arrangements. You're only playing a bloody café!"

At this point Rick, drew himself up, smiled beatifically, and said, "Well, there, my little ball of fire, you are wrong. It so happens that I have contacts down in this part of the world dating from the time I provided highly tasteful and much appreciated musical support one summer to top 60s comedian Johnny 'Ferret Face' Jones. Johnny's grandson is now a big local cheese and has the council in his pocket. You see that rock out there (he pointed about 400 metres offshore to Shark Rock), well, that is where I shall be performing to an audience of thousands on the beach." He stepped back, beaming.

An intense whistling noise, like that of a missile leaving its firing tube, emanated from Marguerite. Max braced himself for impact.

"You bloody what!!"

In an instant, her eyes became as hungry and malevolent as those of a cobra who has not eaten for two years because it was banned from the jungle supermarket thanks to a snowflake rabbit complaining to the manager that the cobra's stare was unfairly undermining her confidence, and now that rabbit has just by chance knocked on its door asking for donations to the 'Snowflakes Say Everyone Should Love Each Other Campaign.'

"Yooouuu blooooddddy whaaat!!!"

Rick flinched as spittle venom was machine-gunned in his direction and a tray and two mugs of tea whizzed past his left ear.

Fortunately, Marguerite was so angry that at this point, she lost her voice. All that came out after this were violent rattling noises accompanied by stormy exhalations, as if she had swallowed a jar full of wasps and washed it down with a handful of Carolina Reaper chillies.

Rick took the opportunity to grab Max by the arm and direct him away quickly from the Marguerite. "She took that well," he said. "I was worried that she might have been more upset." And with that, he reached into the front of his trousers and pulled out a cricket box. "Damned uncomfortable, but you can't be too careful."

"Do you want to grab a cup of tea at my place? It's about a minute from here," Max asked. "You can also clean off a bit."

"You are a scholar and a gentleman. Done," said Rick.

They proceeded up the steps, stopping briefly while Rick felt around his back and peeled off a sadly flattened squirrel.

At the top of the steps, there was a public bench overlooking the sea, on which was seated a fresh-faced woman with sparkly eyes and a shock of pale, intensely frizzy hair. She was sucking thoughtfully on a pen, with an open notebook on her lap and a black daysack by her side, on which there was printed the picture of a tiny kitten with the accompanying slogan "Tiger in waiting."

She looked up as Rick and Max passed by. "Ah, kind sirs," she said in clear but slightly accented English. "I was looking for the Mead View Hotel but seem to have got lost somehow. Would you happen to know where I can find it? I checked in this morning and then stupidly went for a long walk without taking my phone with me."

"It's just up the hill," said Max, pointing over the tops of several houses to where the back of a large, yellow building of impressive size was just visible.

"Are those by any chance lyrics you're writing?" he added, pointing to the open notebook.

"Yes, I'm always putting down ideas, and this was a nice place to sit and get inspired."

Max glanced down and recited the lines,

"*I plunged my knife deep into his heart,*
Was this murder, or was it art?

I plunged my knife deep into his head,
He didn't like my singing, and now he's dead.

Er, yes, good, strong visual imagery. Why are you here in Mead Bay? Escaping from something?"

"I'm attending a residential songwriting course which starts tomorrow. I'm a bit nervous, as I'm very much of an amateur, and I'm sure that everyone else will be very professional. I can only play basic chords on the piano, just enough to write songs."

"That never stopped Elton," chipped in Rick feelingly. Turning to Max, he added, "Did you know that it's actually me on his early hits? I mean, credit where credit's due. He's managed to learn a bit over the years, but back in the late 60s he struggled even to play chopsticks."

"But wasn't he at the Royal College of Music?"

"Yes, he was AT the Royal College of Music, but as a piano shifter in the works department, not a piano player."

Max turned back to the woman. "I write songs, too. My name's Max by the way."

"Fizz," replied the woman. "From Amsterdam," she added.

"And this is Rick. He's a famous..."

"Yes!" she exclaimed. "You're a Grumpy Old Man. I've seen you on the BBC."

"Rick also played keyboards with Yes."

"Are they a band?"

"Quite a well-known one," interjected Rick in a slightly hurt tone. "In the 1970s."

"Like The Bay City Rollers? Sorry, I'm not very good on 1970s music, but I'm sure my mum would know about you, although she's more of a James Blunt fan."

Rick was completely silenced by this and resorted to kicking pebbles across the road.

"But you're great in *Grumpy Old Men*," Fizz came back, sensitive to the fact that her answer might not have gone down that well. "My granny loves the show and..."

"Right, how about that tea!" Rick said, cutting in decisively.

"This is my house just here," Max said, pointing over the wall at an attractive modern property with a large, first floor sun deck. "The main entrance is along the road, but there's a side gate here on the path which I share with the hotel. Do you want to join us, Fizz? I'm interested to hear all about the course."

"That's really kind. Thanks a lot."

***

They kicked open the long disused, wooden gate behind the public bench, entering a kind of no man's land, and then immediately turned and kicked open another one into Max's garden. It was a long garden, laid to lawn, with a small, rail track running down each side and, in the distance, just showing a hint of maroon colour from under a dirty grey tarpaulin, was a scale-model train of the size that would comfortably seat a small child.

"That's a Hornby Gamma-Delta Mini!" exclaimed Rick excitedly.

"Yes. My late aunt, who left me this place, was a huge Rod Stewart fan and put this in as a kind of tribute to him. The track goes right around the house and back. When I was a kid, I used to spend hours on it."

"Me and Rod go back a long way," gleamed Rick. "In fact, I helped him build his first attic-sized model railway set-up. We used to sit at either end and send miniatures to each other on the goods vans. We progressed to filling the open wagons with liquid refreshments and armed ourselves with straws. It was all in the timing. You needed to wait until the wagon was parallel to your head before quickly dunking in your straw and taking on board as much as possible. It could take ages to get really drunk, but it was great fun! Of course, I gave up when Ronnie started coming around, and the wagons were filling up with the finest Peruvian. I like a drink, but I'm not a powder merchant."

They reached the house, and Max unlocked the downstairs patio doors and took them straight up to the first-floor terrace with its untrammelled views over Mead Bay. "Ordinary breakfast tea do? Milk, sugar?"

"No milk or sugar thanks," said Fizz.

"Three sugars, and please let it stew," Rick said.

"How about some Jaffa cakes?" Max asked on returning with the tea. "They're sort of soft biscuits with an orange jelly centre and chocolate topping," he added helpfully for Fizz's sake. "Very British."

"Oooh, then well, yes, I'll try one."

"Rick?"

Rick looked around himself furtively. "Yes, that would be perfect. Squiggs won't let me eat anything with more carbs than organic cardboard," he moaned. "Er, leave the packet, there's a good chap," he said, wrestling the packet from Max's hands.

"Look, it's great to have both of you guys here," said Max genuinely. "A really unexpected pleasure." He sat down beaming contentedly. "Now Fizz, tell me all about this course you're going on. Sounds great, but Mead Bay is not exactly the location you'd expect to find an international songwriting course. South of France, yes, but this place?"

Fizz smiled. "It looks a wonderful area to me. The sea and hills around here are fantastic. The air is great. Even the sound of the seagulls is amazing. In Amsterdam the canals are nice, but the views are nothing like this. And the biggest hills are the humps on the bridges."

"Or a hooker's boobs," interjected Rick animatedly, then added very quickly, "Oo, er, um, just joking of course," and turned very pink.

"That's ok, I'm not a Millennial," Fizz said smilingly. "And you're quite right of course." Relief flooded Rick's face as she continued, "I saw this online advertisement and thought it sounded fun. I also managed to convince my company that the Mead Bay area would be the perfect place to trial our new product out. I am the marketing director for an electric bike company, and if our fantastic new bike can cope with the conditions around here, then I'll will be on to a winner. Ten bikes are being shipped out here and should arrive in the next couple of days."

"Do you drive at all?"

Fizz's brow darkened slightly. "I can drive, of course, but I am not really approving of cars, and I don't have one anymore. Electric bikes are the future. Zero emissions and so quiet."

At this moment, Fizz was interrupted by an explosive belching sound and the guttural rumble and roar of what might best be described as a very old tractor engine plugged into a Marshall amplifier. It was deafening.

"My God, what was that!" exclaimed Fizz, clasping her hands tight over her ears and crouching forwards.

"Sounds like a 1965 VW Camper Van to me," Max proffered.

"Oh, that wreck in the car park? I thought that was something that had been abandoned. I saw an old tramp and a crazy witch get out of it and figured maybe they were using it as a home."

"You are quite correct about the crazy witch. However, that wreck, as you call it, is a genuine 1965 VW Super S Camper Van, with added tape deck and milk rack. And, although I may have seen finer days, I have not been called a tramp for at least two weeks," Rick said in a mock-imperious tone, waving his mug of tea and Jaffa cake packet in the air.

Fizz looked completely mortified. "Oh, no! Look, I'm really, really sorry!! I'm just a crazy, car-hating, totally mad, Dutch woman, so just please ignore anything I say. In fact, I should be bowing down before you as a genuine proper musician when I'm just a sad wannabe."

There was a moment's silence before mirthful chortles hiccupped out of Rick's reclining frame. These escalated and spread to the group, until drowned out by Marguerite's less than dulcet tones screaming, "Rick! Rick! Where are you, you fat bastard!!" She emerged panting on the road outside Max's house and clearly visible to the three of them on the terrace.

"Ooh, heck," said Rick, shooting out of his chair and dashing into the house, at the same time brushing biscuit crumbs from his shabby floral chemise. "Can't let her see me eating Jaffa cakes."

After a further brush down, he re-emerged on the terrace and waved in Marguerite`s direction. "This gentleman was very kindly offering up some tea and the chance to clean up."

"I need to bloody clean up as well! Your heap of trash has just poured oil all over my trainers, and if it doesn't come off, then I'll have your bloody guts for garters. These are my special edition P.J. Harvey's."

"Come on in," called out Max. "I've got some good cleaning stuff you can use. I often have the same problem with my train leaking."

"Your what? Hear that, Rick, he's got a bloody train. Even you don't own one of them."

"It's only a scale model I'm afraid, but it works."

"Oh, you mean a bloody toy train, like what Rick and his geriatric mates play with?"

"Something like that. Anyway, come in. It's just up the next drive on your left." Turning quickly to Rick, he asked, "So, you're really planning to play on Shark Rock? You know, it's shaped like a shark's fin, stinks of thousands of years of bird shit and isn't exactly attached to the mains. I mean, it's a great idea but, seriously?"

"If Pink Floyd could play to hundreds of thousands from a barge in Venice, then I'm sure it won't be too difficult to arrange. Anyway, I'm an optimist by nature. We just need a boat with a generator, another one with lights and fireworks, that kind of thing, plus a good supply of chilled Chablis. Yes," he pictured in his mind's eye, "I'll blow them away."

"That's precisely my concern, Rick, your being blown away. Mead Bay isn't exactly Venice."

Rick waved his hand dismissively. "Once she's got over the shock and is on board, no pun intended, Squiggs will make sure I'm ok."

Again, Max hid his concerns, now not only unsure about the suitability of the venue but also about Marguerite's coming around to the idea. It occurred to him that Rick might suffer more damage from her than from the elements.

Marguerite appeared, blinking in the sunlight. "Nice place this, really."

"Give me your shoes and I'll sort them out," Max said. "Rick, if you fancy a shower, I'll bung your clothes in the washing machine." He took Marguerite's shoes and directed Rick to a large all-white bathroom at the end of the corridor. "You'll find a spare dressing gown behind the door," he said as Rick waddled in.

Back on the terrace, Marguerite settled down in a comfortable chair. She stretched her surprisingly dainty feet out on the tiled surface, sighed and smiled, her face taking on an almost human aspect. In a certain light, or perhaps shade, she was almost attractive.

"Do you fancy something a bit stronger than tea? I've got a decent bottle of Merlot that's just been opened."

"Please, that would be brilliant."

Max walked off but was stopped in his tracks by a "Yes, please!" hallooed in his direction by Fizz. "It's not just drugs that the Dutch like," she winked at him. "Although, of course, we don't like introductions..."

"Sorry, sorry. Fizz, this is Squig, er, Marguerite, Rick Wakeman's manager. Marguerite, this is Fizz, a mad Dutch woman who hangs around on public benches and who claims to be attending a songwriting course at the hotel up the hill. OK?" And with that, he disappeared off to the kitchen, leaving the two women to get on with it.

There are some days that started out stranger and just got stranger, thought Max to himself as he clinked around in the fridge, grabbing two bottles of Merlot, as well as some olives and mini sausages that were at least still within shouting distance of their 'sell by' date.

He reached into the top cupboard for wine glasses, grabbed some, and then exchanged them for ones with a much larger capacity. He tried to think of a Yes song to play on his old Wharfdale speakers using Spotify. Something under 30 minutes perhaps. He struggled, finally selecting a heavily edited version of "Close to the Edge." Armed with tray, Max took the steps carefully back up to the living room and out onto the terrace.

Using a drop stop, Max poured out generous measures of wine and handed out some paper plates with olives and sausages.

"Are the sausages supposed to be the same colour as the olives?" asked Marguerite, holding one up suspiciously.

"They're herb based," lied Max easily.

"Nice song," said Fizz. "Who's the girl singing?"

Marguerite choked on her wine with amusement. "That's Jon Anderson, lead singer in His Nibs's old band."

"His Nibs, was that before Yes?"

Marguerite collapsed into a fit of the giggles. "Sorry, love, I was referring to Rick."

"And that is some kind of title, like Earl?"

Marguerite fell off her chair while Max explained some English terms to Fizz and added on a very quick potted history of Rick Wakeman's career.

Fizz was amazed. "He played on 'Space Oddity' and 'Life on Mars,' and wrote 'Candle in the Wind?' That's just brilliant!!"

"Well, I think you might take 'Candle in the Wind' with a pinch of salt. I'm pretty sure that Elton contributed a little bit to that one," Marguerite interjected, winking.

"Still, that's incredibly impressive. Do you think he would play something for us?"

"Your problem will be bloody stopping him," Marguerite said, wiping her eyes. "Ever since he saw Elton play at St. Pancras Station, I have to keep him away from railway stations altogether, or we'd never make the bloody train. That's when he started telling people he wrote 'Candle in the Wind.' The truth is that he did write a song for Yes called '(She Put a) Candle in my Winch,' but the lyrics were too daft even for Jon to sing them."

"Doesn't Rick sing himself?"

"God no! Have you ever heard Keith Richards sing during The Stones toilet breaks? Right, well, he sounds like bloody Freddie Mercury compared to Rick!"

There was a noise of the bathroom door opening, and Max caught sight of a large semi-naked man tiptoeing quickly down the stairs. A few seconds later, Rick appeared wearing a bright red and yellow tartan rug.

"Um, the dressing gown in the bathroom was a touch on the small side, so I hope you don't mind my helping myself to this. I found it folded on the floor outside the kitchen."

"I don't mind," said Max, "but I'm not sure how Scabies will take it."

Rick looked concerned. "Poor old Rat, who'd have thought it. One of the most influential drummers of his generation reduced to sleeping on the floor. Well, well, it's a lesson to all of us, I suppose, never to take life for granted."

"I'm confused," said Fizz. "You keep a rat in your living room?"

"No," Max responded, "and Scabies is not a rat, he's a big, slobbery, old dog."

"I say, steady on," said Rick. "Have a bit of respect for the man. We've all seen better days, although (he sniffs the rug) I must say that old Rat does whiff a bit."

"Stop! Scabies is an old, black Labrador, not an old drummer, although admittedly, he does whiff a bit."

The sound of something heavy and canine could be heard coming up the stairs.

"Did you open any doors downstairs, Rick?"

"I might have."

"Well, it's worth advising you that Scabies is a randy old thing, his eyesight is not that great and you're wearing his bed."

"Oo-er cripes!" cried Rick, grabbing Marguerite from her seat and attempting to use her as a human shield.

Scabies lolloped in, moaned and made straight for Rick.

"Get your bloody hands off me!" shouted Marguerite, tearing herself away.

Rick ran behind a chair, picked it up and waved it about, adopting a hopeful lion tamer position.

"Good boy, there's a really good boy, you just stay there, eh?"

"You seem to be turning him on," observed Fizz, and indeed, the moans emanating from Scabies and the increasing drool pouring from his lips tended to support her comment.

"Bugger this!" exclaimed Rick and made a dash indoors. He had a few seconds on the dog, who wrong-footed for an instant, spun on the tiled floor of the patio. The musician's heavy steps could then be heard thundering down the stairs, followed seconds later by the windmilling of dog nails. The downstairs door opened, and a flash of tartan shot out into the garden. In a straight race between an old prog rocker and a bed-deprived dog, there was only going to be one winner. Rick had made it about twenty feet when the Labrador grabbed hold of the rug, causing them both to tumble.

"Get off me, you horrible, old mutt. I've known some pretty rough groupies in my time, but even I've got me standards! You're too ruff even for me!" he shouted, looking up at the terrace and bowing in mock majesty.

"Always trying to play to the bloody audience," said Marguerite to the others disgustedly.

The bow was a mistake, however, as it momentarily loosened Rick's grip on the rug. Within an instant, Scabies had snatched it away, leaving Rick to clamp his hands in front of his black and white notes.

"No need to do that," shouted Marguerite. "Your belly'll more than cover up all that."

Rick was working out a pithy reply when he was caught off guard by a voice shouting from the other side of the wall, which was just low enough to allow a tall person to see over. In this case, two heads belonging to two heavy-set, middle-aged men with beards and Iron Maiden T-shirts could be made out clearly.

"Don't let us stop your show, mate!" cried out one of the men with a strong London accent.

"You hoping to be on *Britain's Got Talent*?" said the other. "Not sure Simon Cowell's going to go for the naked dog act, but you never know. Better than collecting your pension, eh?"

There was a slight pause as Rick switched from thinking of something suitably slick to fire back at Marguerite to countering the London brigade.

"I...," he started, but was interrupted by one of the Maidens who said:

"Hang on a sec, I recognise you, don't I? Dave, do you recognise this bloke? He's from one of those 70s bands, you remember? Poor old bloke, look at him now."

"Eh, mate, do you mind if we have an autograph? I could swear I know you. Ri... Rog... begins with an R doesn't it?"

A momentary look of panic crept into Rick's eyes but was then swept away. He dropped his hands and marched confidently over to the wall, reaching out to shake hands. The men, seeing where his hands had been, stepped back a pace but recovered swiftly to hand over a pen and a piece of paper. Rick signed with a flourish and handed the paper back.

"Very nice to meet old fans," he said. "And glad you liked the naked dog act. Any time you want a show, just give me a call."

The first man looked at the paper. "Rat Scabies, I knew it began with an R! You was in The Damned, right?" He turned to other man, "Rat Scabies, The Damned. First punk band in Britain! Legend! What was that song? 'Nude Rose,' that's it! Really great to see you, um, looking so well and in the pink, as it were." He laughed, and the two moved off.

"Poor, old f****r," said the second man loud enough to be overheard. "I don't think he even knows what time of day it is. Poster boy for don't do drugs."

***

The afternoon drifted by in a leisurely manner, with the sun moving further on its arc, and with the unusual May weather continuing. Max, Rick, Marguerite and Fizz were buried deep in armchairs, with the open terrace door providing the perfect ambient temperature. A number of empty bottles of wine covered surfaces of the room, and empty crisp packets rustled in the light breeze.

"These green sausages are nice," Rick said thoughtfully.

"What are you going to do about accommodation?" asked Max.

"Yes, I'm afraid that the old van needs a bit of TLC, but that place just above the beach looks ok."

"Marguerite, do you want to use the phone to call them up? It's out there on the landing," Max offered.

"Ta." A few moments later she called out. "Is it the Noddy Holder figure?"

"Yes, that's it, and watch out for the noise when you pick it u..." He hadn't finished before a piercing *Baby, baby, baby!!* rent the air, followed by a shriek and the sound of Noddy being dropped on his head.

"Jesus H. Christ!!" yelled Marguerite. "Is your whole bloody house booby-trapped like that?"

"A little bit. I'm a dedicated music lover, and I love to pick up knick-knacks, gadgets and other useless mementoes whenever I can."

Marguerite managed to get Rick and herself two rooms at the hotel and returned Noddy's head to the rest of his body.

Gudbuy to you, Gudbuy to you, I said, Gudbuy Gudbuy to you, intoned the phone.

"That's not the actual words to the song," observed Rick astutely.

"No, but if you pay an extra twenty quid for the phone, Noddy records a special lyric for you. Pretty neat, eh?"

"That's wonderful," said Fizz. "Is there a James Blunt phone? I could buy one with 'You're Beautiful' on it for my Mum."

"I think you'll find that James has nabbed that one for himself," Max said, to sage nods from the others.

"Right, I think we should toddle off," Rick said. "We need to get the van towed somewhere safe and install ourselves for the night. It has been a real pleasure meeting you, Max, and you, er Fridge?"

"Fizz."

"Fizz. And you must be guests of mine at the show next month if you're around. I'm going to drop in on the chef chap tomorrow as well as Johnny's grandson to check on all the arrangements, then take in a few of the sights before heading off to Castle Wakeman to put in a bit of practice before the great event."

Max rustled about in a drawer and handed Rick a card. "Volksbay Motors. They specialise in VWs, and the owner is also a bit 70s music fan. Admittedly, he's more into Kraftwerk and Tangerine Dream type stuff, but I think he'll do you a good price."

Rick and Marguerite left by the main front door and headed off into the dying light.

***

"What a nice man," said Fizz. "Not what you expect at all. So normal, well, for a rock star at least. But we never got him to play piano for us," she added a touch mournfully. "Still, I'm so looking forward to the concert. I've never been backstage before."

"The concert should certainly be an experience. Backstage at Shark Rock is something I can only imagine. Are you in a rush, or do you fancy a bite to eat?"

"Oh, I might be persuaded," she said, shaking an empty wine glass.

"Great. The only thing is that I'm not exactly the world's finest chef. You have a choice between Uncle Ben's Rice and spaghetti."

"And which do you recommend?"

"Well, I know how to microwave the rice, but the spaghetti requires some more complicated cooking procedures."

"Rice it is, then. Do you have any salad or sauces?"

"By pure chance, there's an unopened and in-date packet of baby lettuce leaves and a few organic tomatoes. As for sauce, there's olive oil and, um,

Reggae Reggae sauce. Oh, and a few green sausages that Rick didn't get through. That's it, I think. Oh no, there's also some salted caramel ice cream, chocolate biscuits and a bottle of 18-year-old Glenlivet."

"Wow. You're spoiling me. Do all the girls you bring back get such a wide choice?"

"No, you're particularly privileged. Often, I don't have any spaghetti, or indeed, salad."

They stood in comfortable silence in the kitchen while Max supervised his guest preparing the food. He popped out into the utility room to find another bottle of red. "Malbec suit you this time?" he inquired.

"Anything that's liquid will suit me fine."

"Ok, Scabies, you can come out now." A crestfallen Scabies slunk into the kitchen but cheered up immediately on seeing Fizz there. "Don't worry about him. I was only joking when I said he was a randy old thing. But it was a bit of a shock to the system to find a substantial quantity of vintage prog rocker wrapped up in his bed. Do you have a dog?"

"No, I keep bats."

"Bats? Seriously!"

"It's true. I find the big ones so cute, like overgrown furry squirrels. They hang from the rail above my bed and like to snuggle up to me first thing in the morning."

"Ahh, um, do you have a boyfriend?"

"Yes, but he lives in Turkmenistan."

"Yes, I can see that," said Max nodding. "And you're not just a mad stalker who waits outside houses to catch single, middle-aged men in her web?"

"No, not just that. I also write songs about the experience."

Max, slightly concerned, took a step back towards the utility room and fell straight over Scabies. Fizz rushed over to help.

"I'm fine, I'm fine. Put that bag of rice down!" he said in mock horror, scrambling to his feet.

"I was only joking. And in any event, after a few glasses of wine, I usually don't kill my host. That would not be polite."

Max felt slightly reassured.

"Why do you call the dog Scabies?"

"I'm a big fan of all kinds of music, but I have a particular penchant for bands and musicians that are below the radar, like The Damned, The Pretty Things, Kevin Ayers, The Wurzels, that sort of thing. Anyway, Rat Scabies used to be the drummer in The Damned, Britain's first punk band. He was a wild, edgy, crazy guy, so I thought what better name for a Labrador? I must admit that I was also influenced by the fact that Keith Richards once had a dog called Anthrax, and Scabies has a similarly unpleasant ring. It's always fun yelling out his name in the meadows when I take him out for a walk."

"My bats have names, too. There's Genghis, Caligula and Alice. They were all blood-thirsty men, and I thought it would be fun, even though my bats are not vampire types. Keeps unwanted guests away beautifully."

They both sat down at the kitchen table, with Max eventually forcing himself up to prepare the rice. "How do you like your rice done? Are you a one-minute-45-seconds or two-minutes kind of girl?"

"Oh, a two-minute girl, I think."

Max waited for the microwave to ping and then served up the repast.

"These plates look really expensive," said Fizz, admiring the gold inlay.

"I do like decent plates and glasses," admitted Max. "And the less money I spend on food, the more quality plates and glasses I can buy."

"Very sound strategy."

"Thanks, I like to think so."

The conversation tailed off as they munched companionably in silence. The occasional glug of wine being poured and the odd clink of a wine glass against teeth, no longer protected by entirely sober lips, were the only interruptions.

Fizz eventually broke the silence by asking Max what he did for a living. He wearily explained that he had been an architect but had been made redundant and couldn't get another job.

"But it's not like I have screwed up in interviews or anything. I just haven't had any! Only one in over two years despite writing nearly 1000 letters, talking to every head-hunter in the world and spending £25,000 employing a company of charlatans in London to help 'market' me, with not one effing interview to show for it."

"So, what do you do with yourself all day? Do you write songs?"

"No, I'm completely uninspired, besides which, I'm also totally burned-out enthusiasm and confidence-wise and possess all the concentration abilities of a goldfish. All that would change instantly if I got a job, but at the moment, all I'm really good at is anger. I read books all day, listen to music on Spotify and plan, at least in my head, the death and destruction of all those people who got me into this f***ing mess. I mean, it's not as if those kind of vermin should be allowed to live, is it?"

Fizz, sensing that this was perhaps not a topic to pursue, attempted to steer him in another direction. "I know, why don't you join me on the songwriting course? I feel very uncomfortable with the idea of being with all those what I'm sure will be fantastic professionals. You would be doing me a favour, really."

"To be honest, that sounds like my worst nightmare. My songs are bad enough without being critiqued by some washed-up, has-been musician. Who is leading the course by the way?"

"I've got the brochure here somewhere." Diving into the daysack, Fizz rooted about for a bit, then pulled out a slightly dog-eared, green plastic folder. "His name is Steve 'Stevo' Roberts, and it says here that he attended the Chipping Sodbury School of Music in the early 80s and went on to play reserve keyboards and back-up guitar in the touring bands of top 80s artists like Haircut 100, Kajagoogoo, Nick Kershaw, and Black Lace, before launching his own unique solo career."

"Unique means totally uncommercial and probably self-released," observed Max. "Out of interest, when did he last actually release anything?"

"It says here that his last album, called *Dalwhinnie Platform & Other Love Songs,* was released in 2010 on Dodo records and that he has since concentrated on running his highly successful songwriting course while also composing pre-school musicals and creating ambient music for property storage units."

"Well up to what I expected," said Max. "Look, the course is not my kind of scene at all, but I'm very happy to go with you tomorrow to the registration, or whatever it's called. Also, if you need somewhere to write away from the hotel, then please feel free to drop by. I'll leave the back gate open and put a spare key under the train."

Fizz smiled warmly. "That's very nice of you. Registration is at 9:30 tomorrow morning." She looked at her watch. "Ooh, um, it's already 11:00, I'd better go." They walked out and along the garden to the gate at the end. Going through it, Max pointed to an adjacent internal gate which led to a path running up the long sloping hotel gardens.

Having waved goodbye, Max let himself out onto the public pathway, minded just to drop down the steps to check if the VW van was still there. It was dark, with the only light coming from a half-moon sea. He started to walk down the steps when a ghostly image appeared out of nowhere and said, "Hello?"

The fact that it was said as a question meant that Max, in the course of leaping several metres into the air, was able to name the ghost as Jessica.

"Jesus, you scared me," said Max breathlessly. "What are you doing out here?"

"Oh, I like walking at night. It's so peaceful, and I can get my exercise done."

"But aren't you worried about safety? It's very dark out here."

"No, that never concerns me. I'm used to walking around at night."

Several explanations for this behaviour bounced into Max's head, and he sought, not with total success, to put them away.

Max could see that he also owed Jessica an explanation as to what he was doing out at this time of night dressed only in a T-shirt and flip-flops. "I was just checking to see if the clapped-out van that was in the car park had been removed."

"And you needed to do that now?"

"No, er, well, I met the owner earlier, and he's a famous musician from the 70s, travelling incognito with his manager. I invited them to my place for a drink. I think they're staying at your hotel."

Jessica looked at him somewhat cynically. "Have you just come back from a party?"

Max was knocked back by the implication that he was drunk. Tipsy, perhaps, but nowhere near the full Mark E. Smith.

"No, seriously, it's all true." He struggled to come up with the killer punch. "You know Rick Wakeman from Yes?"

"Oh, my God, you're kidding me!! You are kidding me, aren't you??" The impact was immediate. Jessica shouted and moaned at the same time, impressing Max by her multi-tasking. He was also aware of being gripped very powerfully by both arms and of a pair of wild green eyes boring through his skull with astonishing intensity. "Rick Wakeman, Rick Wakemaaan!!" Jessica's voice tailed off into a kind of banshee howl. "I had such a crush on him when I was younger, such a CRUSH!?" and she tailed off again and shook her head. "And he's staying at my hotel?? You're sure?? You're not kidding me, because I'll hurt you if you are."

As it was, Max was losing sensation in his upper arms. *How could such a small woman have such strength? What do they feed them on in New Zealand? A diet of whale meat and Crowded House?*

Max extricated his arms and calmly recounted the events of the evening, carefully editing out any parts that might lead to embarrassment for any involved. He was aware that this robbed his tale of much of its interest but felt it advisable in the circumstances.

While telling his heavily truncated tale, in which Marguerite had made no appearance, he could see Jessica start to buzz. He felt sure that with very little practice she might take off like a human hover craft. As he finished, Jessica distractedly said good night and shot off towards the hotel.

Max called after her, "By the way, there's a guy called William I met who's also staying at your hotel and who I think may be part of his entourage. Claims to be an artist but looks more like an accountant."

Max let his words drift down the steps and then, turning and rubbing his hands together at the same time in a wickedly, gleeful manner, retraced his steps back up the road to his house.

Installed back in his favourite armchair, with bare feet parked on the coffee table partially covering up Alex Turner's face on the cover of *Q* magazine, Max gulped down a contented swig of Glenlivet, sighed and addressed Scabies, who was sitting up opposite him and wistfully eyeing up a plate of green sausages.

"Perhaps Mead Bay won't be as boring as usual, eh, Scayb?"

Scabies half wagged his tail and rotated slightly in a sausage-facing direction.

"No, there are distinct possibilities that things might look up for a while." He reflected a bit, then leaned forward and poured himself a top up. "Green sausage?"

There was nothing in the world that Scabies wanted in the world more at this moment than a green sausage. As a true canine connoisseur, he knew a rancid piece of meat masquerading as an herb sausage when he saw one. He lunged at the plate, causing it to tip its contents onto the wooden floor, along with a nearly full glass of Glenlivet.

"Oi, you miserable old scrote! That's about five quid's worth of whisky you've cost me."

Scabies's plan had worked. He was also a connoisseur of fine whisky.

Max re-filled his glass. Scabies burped, glanced in a studiedly meek fashion at his benefactor, then settled down peacefully to sleep. Max scrolled through his Spotify playlists, then glanced at his Release Radar. As usual, this gave him an opportunity to complain volubly to the room.

"Harry Nilsson: *Almost Live at Cleethorpes 74*, Phil Collins: *The Oliver Years*, Eagles: *Early Beagles Demos*. Doesn't bloody Spotify understand that this section's supposed to be for new music based on your likes? Not re-packaged, re-hashed, dug up from the grave, cremated, water-added and partially reconstituted rubbish!"

He said this out loud every week and still, Spotify didn't seem to listen. At last, Max found some new songs from Fatoumata Diawara, Souad Maasi and Gaby Moreno, played them halfway through and added them to his Rolling Mix playlist. That playlist was now some 400 songs and 24 hours long, and Max scrolled around for a few to trim. That proving difficult, he compromised by adding one from Anthony Joseph.

It was only recently he had figured out why his Spotify-provided year-end best of list never seemed to change. The so-called Shuffle button had a major preference for only shuffling songs it had already played many times before, with the result that every play reinforced its lazy internal view that those were your favourite songs. So now, Max deliberately played new songs in order for a few weeks to bed them down in the system. "Lazy frigging technology!"

Scabies half-opened an eye and closed it again. He'd heard all this before.

After about half an hour, and with the clock approaching 1:00 a.m., Max reluctantly dragged himself from the armchair, deposited Scabies in the utility room on his reclaimed blanket, which Max had washed after its prog elder encounter, and lumbered back upstairs to his bedroom.

Across his large bed lay an equally large but innocuous looking dark blue duvet, with matching dark blue pillows. There now being no risk of anyone stumbling across his room by accident, Max turned over the pillows and duvet to reveal, on the other side, an eye-catching "Yellow Submarine" themed display.

It had taken quite an effort to get the duvet right. For a start, the Beatles merchandise folks seemed to think that only the owners of a small, single bed might want a Yellow Submarine and assorted Blue Meanies as bedfellows. Max had had to buy two duvets and take them to a local clothing alteration shop to be sewn together. The owner of the shop had arched her eyebrows a little too high for Max's liking when he explained what he wanted, and he had resorted to telling her that it was for an American godchild in order to allay any suspicions. The ruse worked perfectly, and the owner even joked about possibly needing three duvets sewn together for an American child.

Slipping under his duvet and switching off the light was accomplished at the speed of a media troll forwarding to the world a condemnatory article that they hadn't read. But sleep would not come, no matter how many Blue Meanies Max counted. This was a constant problem, caused and then continuously exacerbated, by being out of work.

It was possible during the day to distract himself from the collapse of his life, but at night it was like his head exploded with rampaging negative thoughts. After half an hour of turning this way and that, Max gave up and switched the lights back on. He reached for a book.

Amongst the pile of reading always by his bed was something by P.G. Wodehouse. Tonight it was *Carry on, Jeeves* that came to Max's rescue. It was almost impossible to remain depressed when immersed in the world of Jeeves and Wooster; a world that never existed but which you wish had, provided, of course, you had Bertie Wooster's cash and Jeeves's sagacity to steer you through life. The book had the desired effect, and within a short hour, Max had drifted off peacefully to a better place.

***

Max woke ridiculously early due to a combination of the lights being on and a persistent banging on his front door. *Eight-thirty, what pre-dawn hour is that to be disturbing anyone?* Max said to himself as he staggered out of bed and down the stairs wearing, well, not very much. He peered around the front door and was faced with a ridiculously chirpy Fizz.

"Hi there, and good morning. I just wanted to make sure you hadn't forgotten about coming to the registration with me? I'm relying on you."

"No, no, not at all. Um, you'd better come in, but, er, just give me ten seconds to get upstairs first, as I don't want to shock you, you being a nice, clean, Puritan type, Dutch girl."

"You've not been to Amsterdam, then?"

"Yes, I have actually. The sex museum was dreadful. Even I knew most of the things on display there, and that's saying something. Most of my knowledge comes from David Attenborough."

"I think I've read his guidebook. Filthy old man."

Max shot up the stairs and could hear Fizz cackling as she walked in and shut the door. "Have you had breakfast?"

"Yes, thanks. I got up early as it was so beautiful and went for a short walk. There's a great little café down by the beach, and the staff are so nice!"

"It's been my saviour," Max said. "Since I was exiled to Mead Bay, I have been down to the café almost every day. It gives me something to do, and the sea is always fascinating whatever the weather. It's also the only time I get to talk to anyone apart from Scabies. Did you meet Glen and Cee?"

"Jolly chef and amusingly gloomy, tall girl?"

"Yes, that's them."

"I got chatting to them, and Glen was very interested in hearing about the course. It seems that he is a big music fan and has the same name as one of the Sex Pistols, Glen Matlock."

"Yes, he's rightly proud of that. Surprised you're old enough to remember the Pistols."

"I'm not, but I'm a wizard on Google, and I managed to impress him, I think, with my very newly acquired knowledge."

"What did Cee have to say for herself?"

"She asked if Glen Matlock was in Black Sabbath, or in something called Dick Emery. Is that another metal band?"

"Quite possibly early death metal."

"She's a funny girl. Kept on asking me about the meaning of life. When I told her it was '42,' it quite cheered her up, as she said it gave her something to look forward to. I like her and could see her as a singer."

"What, a kind of female Lemmy?"

"I'm not sure, but there's some hidden talent there."

A few minutes later, Max descended, having quickly shaved and showered. The old blue jeans were a no brainer, but he had spent a bit of time deciding on the right T-shirt. There were a lot to choose from, but what set the right tone? Nothing too obvious, so no Stones or Who stuff. Florence, Franz Ferdinand, Seasick Steve? In the end, he had plumped for a well-worn and faded, blue-green Drive-By-Truckers *English Oceans* shirt he'd bought at an inspirational gig at The Roundhouse. The blue Warren & Parker jacket with old, but still bright blue, New Balance running shoes completed the look.

"You're looking very smart."

"Don't want to let the side down," said Max, and then wished he hadn't, seeing that Fizz was wearing beige trousers with a kind of orange and brown floral smock, and grey trainers. The look might have been, he supposed charitably, described as eclectic, Granny's old clothes, extra reserve, junk trunk chic.

"You just have time for your rice," Fizz smirked.

"I don't want to spoil my appetite for dinner," Max served back, "so I'm afraid it'll just have to be gruel and water, failing which there might just be some cereal."

"Let's go up the public path to the hotel," she said. "The grass gets very wet with the dew. The hotel manager asked if I'd enjoyed myself in the garden last night, and I had no idea what he was talking about until I saw that there were footprints from the garden door to the lift, and then from the lift to my room. He looked at me as though I was some kind of, how do you say it, riff raff?"

"In true Rocky Horror fashion, perfectly put. Ignore him. It's the job of hotel managers to look down on customers. It's part of the training. They weed out the ones that like people. I hear that there's a lot of former human resources people who move into hotel management, or become cereal killers."

"Serial killers?"

"No, they're not that smart."

The path was quite steep, and, although Max sometimes jogged up it, he found walking up it far more tiring as it took longer. Fizz, on the other hand, was full of energy. If she wasn't rushing off to sniff flowers, she was commenting on the birds.

"What kind of bird is that one?" she asked, making a generic tweeting sound and pointing to something small, brown and singularly undistinguished looking bothering the grass. Like most people, Max was aware of birds. He liked the obviously pretty ones and was a fan of those that sang nicely. But as to the names of these creatures, who really gave a damn?

"It's a Lesser-Spotted Brown Drudge, I think."

"Lesser-Spotted?"

"Not often seen."

"But I saw lots of them yesterday on my walk."

"That's because of the unusual Mead Bay climate. The interaction of the Gulf Stream with the limbic ionosphere creates conditions where even the rarest of creatures can survive. There were cave bears here until recently."

"Wow, that sounds so amazing," she gushed, before a more steely note crept into her voice. "You are not pulling my legs?"

"My hands are nowhere near your legs, although it can, of course, be arranged. In fact, I was only just observing them, from a purely architectural point of view only, of course, in the context of the whole being, and conclude that perhaps some leg pulling might not go amiss. You are, how can I say this delicately, somewhat less of a ceiling scraper than the average Dutch person."

"I have no clue about most of what you are saying, but I think you're telling me that I am short by Dutch standards?"

"Indeed."

"While you are very lengthy by anyone's standards."

"Well, I must say, I am a bit hurt by that. I was merely speaking in a gentlemanly manner, while you are somewhat blunt."

"As a Dutch midget, what do you expect! Here I am escaping to a country where I can look people in the eye rather than their trouser buttons, and yet you drag me back to the horror of my everyday existence as Holland's smallest person!"

"On the contrary, I would have thought that as Holland's smallest person, you would be a celebrity and invited to loads of parties, as well as having a lucrative side-line in advertising dog kennels, cat flaps and the like."

"Yes, yes, but it all becomes a drag after a while. I mean the money's nice, and the parties can be fun at times when people don't mistake me for a cushion, but not all the dogs are that friendly, and as for the cats! Rough, hairy beasts!"

"I thought that was men, at least according to Jack Lemmon," Max added with levity.

"Jack Lemmon?"

"*Some Like It Hot!* Only the most famous comedy film of all time. Marilyn Monroe, Jack Lemmon and Tony Curtis?"

"Not famous in Holland. Our most famous comedy is *Being Hugh Grant.*" Seeing Max's blank stare, she added, "Surely you must know it? It's got Colin Firth in the lead role. He's so much better than Hugh Grant. In the film, Hugh Grant appears and tries to audition for his own role. No chance! I mean the director and producer had seen his other films, actually."

They arrived at the hotel, a huge, sprawling affair that had been built by some Russian prince back in the 1800s as a place where he could commune with nature in a temperature some 50 degrees warmer than back in Mother Russia. Like most hotels in Mead Bay, it had seen better times. Even a Mr. Magoo without his glasses on would have noticed the cracks in the façade, the peeling window paint and the faint smell of someone keeping a pond indoors. Back in the middle of the last century, the hotel was in its heyday, with bright young things whizzing gaily down from London in their open-topped sports cars for a weekend of partying and romance.

The problem was that the clientele mostly remained the same and looked generally in far worse shape than the hotel. The hotel now abounded with lifts, not only for going upstairs, but also for maintaining guests in an upright position.

In recent years, the hotel owners, the sixth generation of the same family and now firmly American, had tried to think up new ways to raise some cash. The family accountants had suggested that they simply extend the services to their main clientele by advertising the place as both a hotel and final resting place, giving over the sizeable gardens to that end.

This was a very good idea given that a considerable number of guests had already checked out of the hotel without leaving. In the end, the owners had gone instead for trying to bring in corporate events and residential courses. Time would tell if they were right to do so.

The longstanding, senior gardener had his own point of view and was quietly flattening out areas of lawn and cutting back trees, while fencing and planting flowers in such a manner that it would be a simple matter to add the headstones for final completeness.

The hotel manager intercepted Max and Fizz as they entered the reception lobby. Tall and angular, with short, slicked-back hair and a preternaturally disapproving eye, he addressed Fizz while eyeing up her shoes. "Did Madam enjoy another walk this morning around the grounds?"

He spoke with a textbook, hotel manager, Italian accent, his voice carrying sufficient disdain to remind any addressee that it was a mere 2000 years since the Romans ruled the world and that he was only occupying this lowly position out of the goodness of his heart until the matter was duly rectified. "I have placed some slippers by the back door, so your feet do not get cold if your shoes pick up some damp."

Max took an instant dislike to the man and addressed him with, "The toilets?" while casually flicking a practiced hand at him.

For a moment the manager froze, not quite believing what he had heard. The tone of Max's voice suggested a person in authority, but the dress suggested otherwise. He weighed things up in his mind and decided on a course of action. "If you would like to ask the concierge, she can direct you about the toilets."

A mistake that Max had been hoping for. "So, you don't know where the toilets are?" As Max spoke, he saw Fizz distracted by someone calling to her. It was therefore the work of an instant to add, "The countess is very particular about the toilets being clean, and it worries me that you appear not to know where they are. The countess was also not happy about the levels of damp on the grass last night and the fact that the gate was very hard to open. She is far too polite to complain but..."

"Countess?!" said the manager in a shocked voice.

"She always travels incognito posing as an ordinary person, but she is the eighth Countess of Arnhem, and her family are extremely wealthy hotel owners. I am her lawyer, Max Ahrenbee. I cannot tell you the real reason for her visit, but in complete confidence, I can say that the family is interested in acquiring properties. They are a very generous and loyal family to good employees but are ruthless towards anyone who crosses them. Such a person is unlikely to work again in the industry even if, er, physically still able."

The effect of this little speech from Max was instantaneous, and it was as if the manager had just received a surprise enema delivered by an unearthed electric guitar. His face grimaced alarmingly, and his hands twisted in a manner that suggested he might be double or triple jointed. As sweat materialised and fell from his brow, a ghastly smile of epic proportions engulfed his face, leaving his ears in danger of being entirely consumed. He emitted a laugh like a jackal being shaken vigorously by an insulted lion and danced a strange kind of involuntary jig.

"Ha, ha, ha, ha, ha!" he cadenced beautifully. "You misunderstand my little joke. So sorry, I am always trying to amuse the guests with a bit of the banter. We do not have a concierge, and that was my little joke, ha, ha, ha, ha! The toilets here are a joy to behold, and I am always in there checking the comfort of guests. But for the countess, I will personally polish the wood seats."

Max gave just the slightest nod of his head in recognition.

"And I will go and see personally to the damp garden. You know the gardener here, he is being very old and does not understand about the importance of dry grass. The gate will be replaced instantly. It was on the list of things to do next, but very regrettably, it slipped my mind. Not many of our guests are, um, capable of walking that far."

Fizz returned, having been handed a letter by the receptionist. She was amazed at the transformation of the hotel manager. She looked around for the source of the leak, as he was completely wet.

"As I was saying to your law, er friend, Count, er, Madam, I was making a little joke to amuse you. Ha, ha, ha, ha! I will now accompany you to the toilet."

He gave a small bow, reached across and slipped his arm firmly under Fizz's arm. As he steered her away, she glanced over her shoulder in bafflement at Max, whispering, "But I don't want to go the toilet!"

Max put up his hands in a 'keep calm' manner. "You'd better go with him, you know. He has a bit of a thing about the toilets, and it doesn't do to upset him so early in your stay." Max whispered a parting warning. "He's Neapolitan, you know," and made a sign that he hoped conveyed the message.

Fizz looked even more baffled as she was dragged away.

Reckoning that Fizz might be away for a while, Max cast around looking for signs of her course mates. He had in his mind's eye what the eleven other attendees would look like. But try as he might, no one sprang out at him. There didn't seem to be a person under 70 in the lobby area, and as Max well knew, any musician of that age worth his salt would be on a world stadium tour, not attending a songwriting course.

He walked over to Reception and targeted a young woman with black eyebrows, platinum blonde hair shaved up the sides and a small piece of metal, resembling a double bogey, hanging out of her nose. "Is there a songwriting course being held here?" Max asked. "It's just that I don't see anyone who, um, looks like that's their kind of thing."

The receptionist smiled, and in a sultry, Polish accent, replied, "You are right. Both times. The course is being held in the annexe, and breakfast and all meals are there." She leaned over and added, confidingly, "The manager think it best not to mix the two types of guest. Maybe drugs and orgy?" She spoke as if suggesting that such behaviour might well meet with her approval. "It is boring in Mead Bay, so I like having younger people like you around."

Max reckoned that she must be well beyond bored if she thought he was a younger person, given that he was touching fifty. But, of course, this was Mead Bay, so she was probably right.

"Go out of hotel and take first right. There is modern building with green roof. That is where the course is."

Max started to follow her instructions and was leaving through the entry doors of the hotel when a sharp call made him pause.

"Hey, Max! Where are you going? First you leave me with a crazy Italian guy, and then you abandon me altogether." Fizz rushed up to him.

"Sorry about that, I was just checking out where the course is being held. The receptionist told me that it is actually around the side of the hotel, in another building."

"Ah, good. But wow, that manager is really strange. He insisted on going into the toilet ahead of me and polishing the seat. That's pretty scary. And then he goes on about how fantastic it is to have me in the hotel and that my family and I are welcome any time. First thing this morning it looked as if he wanted to kick me out, and suddenly I am his favourite guest!"

"Excitable type and a bit eccentric, but it's good that he likes you. Just don't tell him about going to the toilet next time."

"But it was you who mentioned toilets, I'm sure. I didn't even want to go!"

They followed the receptionist's instructions and found themselves on a path of crazy paving. *Or not crazy paving,* Max thought on reflection as he stumbled on the broken, uneven paving. The annexe was in a far corner of the hotel property and was a wooden structure with a green, corrugated, iron roof. A small, covered entry porch was attached to the front, and there was a table, a chair, some forms and what must be Steve 'Stevo' Roberts.

The course organiser was unmistakeable to Max in his undistinguishedness. He was in his fifties, with light brown, fringed hair, showing a grey streak here and there. Round, tortoiseshell glasses adorned his youthful looking, but earnest, supply teacher-like face. He wore a faded, grey jacket over a black T-shirt with "Support the Musicians Union" in small letters on the breast, and thin, brown corduroy trousers finished off with cheap, round-toed, brown, faux leather shoes.

"Fizz," said Fizz approaching the desk.

"Er, no, Stevo," he replied.

"No, Fizz. You're Stevo," she smiled.

Stevo gave off that kind of smile that is meant to show amusement but actually conceals irritation. Not a man with a natural air of authority, he struggled whenever he perceived that he was not being taken seriously, which was most of the time.

He laughed thinly, and in a neutral accent with a dull tone said, "But of course, Fizz, our Dutch person." He looked at his notes. "'Very amateur, clunky piano playing and not confident about your singing voice,' it says on your entry form. Don't worry, we get some excellent pupils on this course, and you can observe them and join in when you feel like it."

Fizz's face dropped. Although she was an amateur, she had written lots of songs. However, her lack of confidence had led her to deliberately downplay any skill she might have on the entry form, by employing a humorous and very English type of understatement. She had been expecting the full support of her course leader and was dismayed at being so quickly dismissed. Max felt that Stevo knew exactly what he was doing and vowed to help reverse the balance of power when he could. In the meantime, Fizz masked her disappointment with a flat laugh, picked up some materials and entered the hall.

Max introduced himself to Stevo as someone who might be interested in attending the course in future. He spoke knowledgeably about concerts he had attended in the past, of which there were many, and without in any way being misleading, may have left Stevo to form his own impression that Max might be a music journalist.

Deep down, Stevo hated music journalists, but at the same time, he was awed by their power and influence. For the most part, they had ignored his career entirely, but when NME had given him his one and only review in 1992 for his debut solo album *Endless Rivers of Grey,* it had consigned him to the dumper with: *A startlingly average piece of work. Noodly and formless guitar laid over melodies so slight they would blow away in the slightest breeze, and all set to lyrics so dull they would put the most inveterate insomniac to sleep.*

"By all means, come along and experience how the course runs," gushed Stevo. "The interest in the course has taken me by surprise in recent years, and since 2016, I've had to offer it twice a year. Originally, I used to hold it up in Pennan in Northwest Scotland. I'm a big fan of Mark Knopfler's score for the film *Local Hero*, and it seemed like an appropriate tribute to him. The fisherman's hut that the town council assigned us there was great, too, although some concerns were raised by students about damp causing their guitar strings to turn black. That's when I looked around for a more central location and lucked out with this place."

Stevo started to talk in a markedly raised voice at this point as a rain squall came across the bay and dumped itself in a cacophony of sound on the corrugated iron roof of the hall. "Nothing like a bit of nature to inspire songwriting," he bellowed at Max as they moved into the main hall.

Inside the hall was a motley assortment of humanity ranging in age from their early 20s to late 50s. Six men and six women in a circle on plastic chairs. Stevo opened his introduction by stressing his commitment to gender equality, although Max was pretty sure that those present were the only people who had applied for the course and that Stevo would have been equally happy with twelve paying chimpanzees and a speech about supporting simian rights.

"It's so cool to see you all here from all over Europe. I apologise for being British, of course, given the recent, er, events." He had been expecting laughter at this point, but instead his students silently nodded in agreement. "Personally, I recognise the huge benefits of all Europeans living and working together, and," he added out of necessity, "I am not a racist."

He droned on for what seemed like an age, and Max tuned in and out, turning his attention for the most part to a beetle that was battling its way up Stevo's leg. He heard enough to know that Stevo fervently hoped and expected that everyone present would get something valuable and life changing from the course. Stevo wanted others to taste the success he had had, but even if that were not possible, he wanted them to feel vindicated as individuals.

Eventually, and with a somewhat self-satisfied smile, he asked all the students to introduce themselves. "Shall we start from left to right?" he suggested, not unreasonably.

An early 20s, kohl-eyed, blond and green, chubby-faced person of deliberately indeterminate nature, with a ring through the left side of its lip, kitted out in baggy, formless, battle fatigue clothes, yellow Doc Marten boots and pink socks, immediately intoned, "Much too old fashioned and orderist. You're discriminating against people sitting further along the line who may have their ideas pre-spoken by others and are therefore disadvantaged as a result of sitting where they are sitting. It plays into the hands of people who want to dominate with their opinions and so always sit on the left. I'll start. My name's Usan, and I create future reality fusion sounds using keyboards as a development existentialist medium. I don't believe in structure or categorisation and reject as fundamentally wrong all attitudes before 2015."

Stevo was about to ask Usan about the significance of 2015 and what Usan was hoping to get out of the course but decided that this might risk his losing any semblance of authority.

"Thank you, Usan, and you?" He pointed to a tall, bearded man with long, tied back, greying, dark hair and John Lennon glasses.

The man bowed his head slightly, and with mellow tones coming from somewhere in the north of England said, "Name's Jeff, but everyone calls me The Yeti. I live in the mountains in Switzerland and play the alp horn. I believe that the greatest British philosopher was John Laurie, and I'm on the course so I can communicate better with the other survivors of Armageddon."

Stevo started to melt visibly at this point, wondering what had happened to his life. He subsequently paid only intermittent attention to the course members, most of whom were semi-professional musicians, including Magnus, the Icelandic plumber-turned-blues guitarist, and Neil, the Welsh sheep farmer, bass player and Manic Street Preachers fanatic.

Max meanwhile smirked while Fizz gulped when they all presented their credentials, although both of them eventually settled their eyes on Sapphire, or Saff, as she liked to be called. Saff was, frankly, arresting. In her mid-twenties with long auburn hair, magnetic green eyes, perfect features and the kind of body that not even the most ill-fitting clothes can hide, and hers were not ill-fitting at all.

Having lost concentration, Stevo was now in the zone completely. Saff's smooth RP vowels washed over him, cleansing his thoughts of anything, or indeed, anyone else. This was the reason, he told himself, why he plugged away at his dismal career, just for moments like this, the chance to meet a stunning musical princess who he, Steve 'Stevo' Roberts, could personally assist to attain goddess-like status.

Saff explained that she was a guitarist-singer-songwriter who mostly played small venues around the countryside when not modelling. "Stately homes, garden parties, that sort of thing." She hugely admired Joni Mitchell and Carole King and was on the course to improve her performance skills and to gain ideas for lyric structure and cadence.

It turned out, would you credit it, that Stevo was also an enormous fan of Joni and Carole and was quite blown away by the opportunity to sing some of their songs together at communal sessions.

"Right," he said after dragging himself momentarily out of Saff's thrall, "I'd like you to get together in pairs and try to write a song about the 1980s. You can use your guitars, keyboards, anything you like. I see most of you have brought instruments, but I also have some spares if you need them. No rights or wrongs here, just an ice-breaker session. You can either write together or do alternate verses, or (looking at Usan) anything that fits in with your approach to songwriting. You can write here or go outside, but I'd ask you come back by 12:00 for lunch. This afternoon, we'll run through the songs and the motivation behind them."

Stevo walked over to Max. "You are welcome to join in any time you like. I think you will find the structure of the course, er, interesting and the way that the students develop. I try to work with all of them individually, although some need more support and encouragement than others."

Max felt sure that he knew exactly who was going to require Stevo's individual support and encouragement. "Thanks, I may take you up on that. You never know where it may lead," he dangled, adding as an aside, "You must have a broad musical taste. Joni Mitchell and Carole King are brilliant songwriters, but not everyone today knows their songs. Just love 'Bring on the Clowns,' and 'Coat of Many Colours' is great, too."

"Absolutely," said Stevo, but added, "Wasn't it 'Bring on the Night?'"

"'Because the Night,'" said Max, making a mental note that attending a few communal sessions might be well worth it.

Max took his leave of Stevo and went to seek out Fizz, who was talking to Jeff. "Fizz, I'm off. Looks like you'll have fun with your course mates," he said, raising his eyebrows quizzically. "Keep me posted about how things go. Stevo has basically given me carte blanche to roll up whenever I like. He seems to have this strange idea that I might be a music journalist."

"I wonder how he got that idea," Fizz said, winking. "I've known you for all of a day, but I'm already beginning to suspect that beneath that angelic exterior lies a full time subversive."

"Nah, I'm as dull as Stevo's shoes, and about as talented. Still, thanks for cheering me up. It's been a boring couple of lifetimes since I was stopped from working. Only the deaths of former colleagues to plan. But the last day has started to show up distinct possibilities if only I could concentrate long enough to work out what they are. It's a bit like being in a murder mystery thriller but not quite getting why no one has died. Does that make sense? No? Well, it's as good as you're going to get right now. Feel free to drop by later for a drink, and even some rice. Here's my WhatsApp details in case anything really exciting happens in the meantime."

***

Max sidled through the hotel gardens and out through the side gate. Only there was no gate, just a vexed looking gardener complaining to the empty space where the gate used to be.

He spotted Max and posited, "You the gennelman what lives 'ere below the 'otel?"

"Yes, that's me," Max breezed back cheerfully.

"Well, I'm sorry that yer goin' ter be disturbed today, sir, 'cause the manager 'as just 'ad a fit and wants me t'replace the gate. Tha' gate's been there for a 'undred an fifty years an ain't never done nobody no 'arm. In fact, nobody ever uses the dang thing. And then this mornin' that crazy Italian manager shouts at me like I've jus' murdered 'is family an tells me I've not been doin' me job proper 'cause the gate don' work perfect like. Tells me the countess is not 'appy, and if I don' replace the gate t'day then I'm fer t'chop. And I says t'myself, What damn countess? The only person what I seen usin' this gate recently was some daft lookin' frizzy 'aired woman what walked mud and wet grass though t' hotel last night. I dunno, sir, whas the world cummin to?"

"I think that the manager is suffering from stress. Maybe some kind of breakdown. Might be worth keeping an eye on him. I heard that he wouldn't let one of the female guests use the toilets this morning until he had personally polished the seat for her. A bit strange, eh?"

"Sowns like 'e's proper off 'is rocker. Excitable, them Italians, 'specially the ones from the South. Too many bloody pizzas if you ask me, with that there chili sauce on 'em. Not nat'tral is it? Tha's why I voted out of Europe. We need proper English food like curry an' chips."

Max walked up his garden and entered the house by the back door, straight into the utility room, and Scabies.

The dog was happily curled up in the gap beside the wall and the washing machine and emerged blinking into the daylight offered by the back door opening. His tail adopted a hopeful food-beckoning wag. Max unscrewed the top off a jar on the counter above the washing machine and chucked Scabies a handful of Doggy Chocs in the shape of Eddie, the Iron Maiden mascot. The side of the jar showed a photo of singer Bruce Dickinson in full WWI pilot regalia saying, "Eddie's Doggie Chocs will give your dog the edge in any dog fight." The dog sucked them down almost without chewing, burping in a satisfied manner and then licked his lips. Max wondered what there was to lick given that the chocs had scarcely touched them on the way down.

He picked up a dart and launched it at the bloated figure of his former boss, or rather the photo of his former boss that he had had turned into a darts board, and which hung on the utility room side of the kitchen door. *Straight in the bollocks again,* thought Max with deep satisfaction. *Getting better every day,* he hummed to himself as he went into the kitchen and flicked on the switch for the kettle.

"Drat it, Scabies, there's no Breakfast Tea left. How is that possible when the box says it contains 200 bags? I mean nobody drinks that much tea, do they! You haven't been sniffing the stuff, have you?"

Scabies had learned to ignore the frequent strange rantings of his owner and chose not to communicate a reply.

"There must be something to drink," Max mumbled as he removed antique packets of one kind or another from the unexplored world of his upper shelf. "Georgian Gun Powder Tea? Where on earth did I get that from?" He examined the use-by date and found that it had yellowed to an unrecognisable extent, and in any case, seemed to be written in Russian. "Well, it's tea, isn't? Provided it's not got wet, it should last forever like salt or sugar, shouldn't it?" He nodded to himself, and Scabies, who might have had some useful input, chose instead to lick something brown, sticky and interesting off of the floor by the sink.

Max took down the packet and opened it. It smelled vaguely historic, and a scene from Woody Allen's *Love and Death* conjured its way into his consciousness. A pot would be required for this kind of tea, as it was annoyingly loose leaf. Max looked in vain for a teapot in the cupboard but then, with a flash of inspiration, remembered one that sat on top of his bookshelf on the upstairs landing. Brown and white, ah, yes, there it was. OK, blue and white after Max had run it under the sink tap for a while. How many teaspoonfuls? He ruminated and decided that six should do. After all, the tea had probably lost some of its flavour over the years.

"F***ing hell!!" gasped Max as he spat the tea out faster than a politician tells lies. So fast, in fact, that he missed the sink and evil dark liquid sprayed down the cupboard door below.

Scabies eagerly advanced and lapped up the liquid.

"F***ing hell!!" said Scabies, momentarily blowing the cover of the whole canine world.

Max heard nothing, however, as he noisily alternated between gulping, gargling and spitting water sucked up direct from the tap. The intense, burning, acrid taste would, however, not so easily give up its grip, and Max was forced to take a swig of neat Plymouth Gin to drown it out. Still dripping water from his chin, Max sought out some chocolate to complete the recovery process.

Five minutes and a couple of squares of Chocolat Madagascar's 100% bar later, Max's equilibrium was back to merely out of kilter, which was the best he ever achieved nowadays.

It was by now late morning, and Max wondered what to do. In general. With his life. Having no ready answers at hand, he climbed the stairs and distractedly looked through his bookshelves for one of the many books he had bought and then failed to read. Max knew the importance of reading the right book at the right time.

Python in My Pants: The Sex Life of Michael Palin sounded moderately stimulating, as did *Twat: The Complete David Cameron Story* by Danny 'Prince' Dyer. In the end, though, Max plumped for *Vineyards I Have Drunk* by Gerard Depardieu, his favourite French actor and industrial-level wine consumer. Equipped with the Depardieu tucked under his arm, Max called to Scabies and attached his lead. The earlier squall had vanished without a trace, leaving another beautiful spring day.

The sloping woods that looked down on Mead Bay were an ideal place for exercising a dog without having to outlay much effort on the owner's part. This was due to there being a series of parallel paths cut at different levels into the hillside. Dogs were soon reduced to panting wrecks by racing up and down the steep slopes in between in search of attractive bottoms to sniff and disgusting food to eat and/or roll in.

Scabies, unleashed, rocketed off into the depths of the endless greenery, giving the occasional bark to signify a conquest or a banquet. Max knew that he could safely leave the dog to its own devices while he ambled along towards his secret reading spot.

Behind a massive, old, oak tree deep in the wood, there was a scarcely perceptible track, like a fox run, which angled steeply up the slope into what looked like impenetrable bushes. In fact, if you crept up behind the bushes, a small opening appeared and gave onto a flattened enclosed area. Nobody apart for Max ever went, there. Nobody at all, ever.

"Woah, you scared me!" cried Max as he squeezed through the gap and found himself staring at the ghostly features of Jessica sitting on a log.

Jessica did not so much as twitch at Max's sudden appearance, but smiled an ethereal smile and said, "Hello, I hope I'm not disturbing you. I can go."

"No, not at all, good to see you. How on earth did you manage to find this place? Even Google Earth couldn't track a person down here."

"I like to investigate places, you know?" she responded. "The regular paths can get a bit boring and crowded, and it's peaceful here, right?"

"And you don't get worried about it being so secluded on your own?"

"Oh no, I feel perfectly safe, I mean, who's going to attack *me*?"

Max saw she had a point. Attractive though she undeniably was, there was a disconcerting element to her that might well freak out any would-be assailant.

Today Jessica was reading *Without Leaving a Trace* by Amanda Historica-Novella and seemed to be on the last page.

"Good book?"

"I haven't started it yet. I don't like to read a book unless I know the ending. Otherwise, how do I know if it's worth reading?"

"Ha, well, I'm the opposite. If I know the story, then I don't want to read the book."

"But what if the book isn't any good?"

"I stop it and read another."

"Oh, I can't stop a book once I start. It's not fair to the author."

"But the author has no clue you're reading their book unless you're maybe sleeping with them."

"I guess, but it still doesn't feel right, so I like to know I'm going to like the book before starting. It's comforting to know the end to make sure it's the right one. And you know, books take up so much time to read, so I don't want to waste it."

"Errands get in the way?"

"Yes. People think that I don't do stuff, but I'm always busy." Jessica's voice went up, down and up again for emphasis.

"Travelling?"

"Yes, no," she giggled and punched Max with the force of a George Foreman jab on the shoulder. "Are you making fun of me?"

"Absolutely not." He moved the topic on. "This is a cool spot, isn't it? Great view through that gap in the trees."

"Yes, and it's more fun because no one knows you're here."

"I'm with you on that one."

Further conversation was interrupted at this point by an explosion of black fur propelling itself through the thickest part of the bushes.

"Scabies, get down! Get off her! Sorry about that. He's harmless, as every pit bull owner with 'Kill' tattooed on his forehead no doubt says."

"Oh, that's fine, I love dogs."

With that, she grabbed Scabies and proceeded to half stroke, half strangle him in a professional way that Scabies might well get to like. *What did Jessica get up to at night?* Max pondered again.

"How's the hotel? It doesn't exactly look very modern, but I guess at least you must have a great view with all that money you're paying?"

"The room is fine. Nice and quiet. It's got high ceilings, although it's probably higher than it is wide and looks out over the kitchens. The hotel needs the front rooms for guests who have booked for a few weeks. That make sense?"

"You must be their perfect guest. So accommodating. Washing your own sheets, too?"

"I use a sleeping bag. You know, it's easier to just get up and go that way. No?"

These conversations with Jessica, fun though they were, left Max slightly uneasy, as though playing with a tiger cub.

"Seen anything of Rick Wakeman?" Max asked.

Jessica suddenly turned almost human colour and increased noticeably in volume. "He was at the bar last night, and I wanted to say hi to him, but he's got this crazy woman that hangs around him all the time? Whenever I tried to walk towards him, she kept dragging him to another part of the bar. I mean, I only wanted to say hello, you know? She must be some kind of a groupie. I kept on trying for a while but no luck."

"So, what time did you get to bed?"

"Around four o'clock."

"And you were in the bar all that time? Wasn't it shut?"

"They kept it open for him, so I just hung around."

"And you never got to speak to him?"

"Yes, I followed him to the toilet this morning after breakfast and managed to introduce myself. He said he'd speak to me later, but he never came back out of the toilet, and I waited for an hour."

"Poor you," said Max with an air of amazement. Surely it wasn't going to be another strange day like yesterday?

"I was kind of disappointed, and that's why I came out here for a walk to figure things out."

Scabies was almost unconscious by this point, and Max felt that he could do with a break, so suggested that they continue to walk together. "I'm just going as far as the castle, then down to the meadow and back along the sea front."

"There's a castle?" said Jessica animatedly.

"Not a castle as such, but it looks like a fortified place with a draw bridge and everything. Actually, it was built as a formal walled garden with a folly, but about thirty years ago someone, in a fit of madness, extended the folly so that it looks like a real castle keep. Great views across Mead Bay because it sits just above the tree line.

Max and Jessica extricated themselves from the hidey hole, and Scabies began to breathe again.

"Is there a cinema near here?" enquired Jessica.

"Yes, it's tucked away off the main charity shop street in town."

"Where's that?"

"It's still officially called the High Street but only by the druggies that hang out there. The town centre was killed off years ago when they pedestrianised it and at the same time turned every space that could conceivably take a car into a parking meter zone. All the main shops are now a couple of miles out of town at the Leylandii Centre."

"That seems such a shame, as I think the place is beautiful. I love those old buildings and all the boats in the harbour."

"I agree entirely with you," Max said, launching into his patented potted history of the place. "Mead Bay has a beautiful core of buildings dating back to Georgian times and then really came into its own under the Victorians. The place was originally a winter resort, and wealthy people came down here for its mild climate and the waters. Eventually, a significant number stayed on full-time, and all those villas you see that are now split into 500 crappy apartments were single family homes. The steep pathways that you see interconnecting roads around here were built so that servants could get to and fro easily. Wealthy people meant that the town had a fully functioning economy. If you don't have people with money to spend, a place dies. Unfortunately, after the Second World War, the type of tourists changed to summer-only tourists, and it was all coaches coming down from the north of England with factory workers on their annual holidays. Now, there's nothing wrong with that except that it meant that the only money coming into Mead Bay was during a two-month season. Over time, that was not enough to keep the place going. Also, the huge increase in numbers of ordinary tourists gradually drove out the wealthy brigade. But the start of affordable overseas holidays in the early 1970s was the death knell for Mead Bay, as even working-class holiday makers started heading to places like Spain where there was more sun, and even the fried eggs and bacon were better."

"That's really sad, but why didn't the town just adapt and change?"

"Ah, you've nailed the problem. That might well have happened, but the government of the day tragically passed a secret law stipulating that only people with an IQ below that of a stegosaurus could stand for the local council. This has resulted in them trying to do everything possible to not only not make Mead Bay better, but to make it worse. For example, what should you do when your hotels are in terminal decline and half empty, why build more, of course! And when you want to create wealth, what better way than to encourage more and more old people's homes? Ok, that's not all bad because it at least does create one wealthy person per old person's home, namely the owner. The harbour is a great asset as you noticed, but no one dares go there at night now because it was thought a brilliant idea to move all the clubs to the harbour end of town. I mean, they're a great draw, don't get me wrong. They manage to pull in punters from as far away as Plymouth who find the violence in the famously rough Union Street area just too pre-school for them."

"I walked down by the harbour at night," Jessica said. "Just kids having a good time and drinking too much."

"You didn't feel scared at all?"

"No, I just sort of float by, and nobody notices me."

That didn't tie in with what Max knew of the lairy, drunken, vomiting, and usually semi-naked club clientele, but he let it lie. Instead, he said a propos of nothing, "Do you like skipping? When the pathway is clear, I sometimes indulge myself at this spot where the path dips."

"I'm up for it," smiled Jessica, as if this was something she did every day.

With that she grabbed Max's arm, and they took off together singing, *We're off to see the wizard,* at a volume that threatened the local bird population's monopoly on woodland sound. After about fifty metres, they reached the bottom of the dip and stopped, slightly out of breath and laughing like two naughty school children.

"It's good to act in a way that's out of the norm from time to time. It's fun," Max said breathlessly.

"Oh, I'm very normal," Jessica said honestly, and difficult to believeably.

As they walked on, Max tried to open up the conversation and found out that Jessica liked films, but mostly underground French Classics such as *Regarder la peinture sècher*, and *Toujours rien ne se passe*. Max couldn't swear to it, but he felt pretty sure that he had seen them both, as well as a number of sequels.

"What about *Boudu Saved from Drowning* and *La Grande Illusion*?"

"Oh, yes! That tramp's so cute in *Boudu*, isn't he?"

Max realised that he hadn't watched the film in quite the same way, but half nodded as if to signify that anything was possible.

Before long the path descended to the meadow, and Max got to the most enjoyable part of his daily stroll, the bit where he got to get up really close to pensioners and shout "Scabies!" very loudly.

It never failed to amuse him the often-shocked reactions that came from people thinking that he was addressing them directly. Jessica was reduced to a fit of questioning giggles by the performance, and Scabies gave plenty of opportunity to keep the game going by his persistent refusal to return when called. But why should he? Scabies knew perfectly well that until Max arrived within about twenty feet of the beach road, he was free to do exactly what he liked. Then, and only then, would he look up, surprised, and quickly bound to Max's side.

"We were going to meet for coffee this afternoon, but do you fancy a bite to eat at the café now, since we're passing?"

Jessica coughed for the first time that day when faced with making a time-related decision. "I can join you for a quick coffee, but then I've got some things to, er, do."

The seagulls would be happy, Max told himself.

Arriving at the café, the couple was greeted by a beaming Glen. "D`you know who was here a few minutes ago?!"

"Yes, or at least a former part of it."

"Ha, ha, you're right! Rick himself dropped by to ask about the arrangements for the concert. Nobody recognised him apart from me, though, did they, Cee?"

"Who are we talking about? The old fat man in the gold cape?" she asked.

"That's him."

"Why didn't you tell me he was famous?" moaned Cee. "What band was he in?"

"Yes?" replied Jessica with her usual intonation.

"What band was he in?" repeated Cee.

"Yes," said Max.

Cee looked around despairingly at Glen.

"What's going on? Why doesn't anybody answer me?"

"Yes," said Glen.

"Nooo, this isn't fair, you're all just trying to confuse me!"

"No, 'Yes' is the name of the band the bloke was in," Glen finally said. "Come on, Cee, you should know that. You helped me get the posters printed for the concert."

"I didn't know he was in a band!" she wailed. "The draft poster says 'Rick Wakeman, famous for his Journey to the Centre of the Earth.' I thought that he was a famous explorer like, um, Ralph Fiennes."

"It's Ranulph," said Max quickly, "and I think that's a trip too far even for a crazed old loon like him. Besides, it's six thousand degrees Celsius at the centre of the Earth, and that's at least six thousand and fifty degrees hotter than the Ranster likes it."

"I didn't know that," said Cee with a degree of awe. "How do you all know so much stuff?"

"Common knowledge."

"Not for me. I knew I should have read more widely and not just focused on Glue Theory at university."

"Ah, that's the theory where adhesion occurs by the penetration of adhesives into pores, cavities and other surface irregularities on the surface of the substrate isn't it? The adhesive displaces the trapped air at the interface." This was lobbed in by William, who was settling himself down at a table of four behind them and spreading his things out carefully.

The others looked over quizzically, assuming the answer was a joke.

"Well?" he said, looking directly at Cee.

Cee was momentarily stunned but recovered admirably.

"Absolutely correct. And now you can see why I don't know anything. That glue just clogs up your brain cells if you study it too much."

Max was confused. "Wasn't it String Theory you studied?"

"Oh, damn it!" extorted a severely rattled Cee. "So that's why the others on my course looked like they slept rough! I knew I shouldn't have tried saving money by going to Princeton University."

"But that's a great uni," said Max forcefully.

"Not the one in Devon."

"There's a Princeton in Devon?" asked Jessica.

"Famous for its granite prison housing top murderers and the like," intoned William.

"So, it is similar to an American college then?" asked Jessica.

"Completely the opposite," said Max. "Princeton, Devon is for people who have already committed murder, while in the US, students GO to school or college to shoot each other. It's a sort of rite of passage. I'm not even sure it's illegal, as otherwise they would have introduced laws to prevent it from happening."

The group nodded collectively in agreement, and Max ordered his favourite lunch, a variation on a sausage sandwich except with the sausages on their own with white toast and butter on the side. It somehow seemed so much healthier that way.

Jessica passed on lunch but had a latte to go with Max's tea. They found themselves some space at the end of the terrace, and Jessica put on her sunglasses and wrapped herself in a voluminous scarf.

"That guy who talked about Glue Theory, he's Rick Wakeman's manager, right?"

Max tried to use words that threw some doubt on this promotion while his eyes were trying to convey the opposite message. "He looks a bit like a manager I guess, but more of a backroom guy, don't you think? Not a rock star manager?" he said.

"Oh, no, there are plenty like him. Not all the managers look like gangsters, you know?"

"Is that right? How do you figure that out? I thought that they were all like Peter Grant and Don Arden?"

"I used to come across them in the 90s when I did some stuff for bands. There's plenty that are backroom types that don't hang anyone out of the window."

"Did some stuff?"

"Yes, you know, services kind of thing."

Max let that sink in but didn't follow up, as it was a lot more fun not to. "Apart from late night walks, do you have any other plans over the coming months, if you happen to hang around?" he questioned.

"I'd like to do some painting maybe. I used to paint a bit, but, you know, life got so busy."

"You could have a word with William about that. I mentioned last night that he told me he was a painter. That would give you the chance to suss him out and find out if he is who you think he is."

Jessica beamed. "Hey, maybe you're right about that."

"William!"

William looked up and avoided, with practiced skill, engaging eye contact with a fragile, old couple who were eyeing up the other chairs at his table. He beckoned Max over, standing up and asking the old couple if they minded moving back. Max brought Jessica over.

"William, this is Jessica. Jessica is from New Zealand but lives in Vienna. She's a sort of publicity writer-type person with an interest in the night. Jessica, this is William. He's a commissioned painter who's British but lives in Paris and also dabbles in financial stuff. I thought I'd introduce you because Jessica is interested in doing some painting while she is here in Mead Bay."

William's ego blossomed at the description of his artistic profile, and he adopted his expert persona in a flash. "Very nice to meet you, Jessica. Do I detect an Australian accent?" he asked, using his best attempt and coming across like a slowed down London cabby.

"New Zealand."

"Ah, forgive me, I always get them mixed up. The good old colonies, not that I see you as a criminal, ha, ha," this time spoken in something that approximated to a South African accent by way of a Cardiff pub.

Jessica looked bemused more than offended as William steam-rollered on. "I have held a few art courses in Paris, and they went down, er, um, surprisingly." He pulled over the chair with his art bag on and extracted a few choice examples for Jessica to admire.

"Bar Codes?"

"Abstract. This one here is Mead Bay. Note the seagulls..."

Max left William to dazzle Jessica and caught up with Glen at the counter. "So, what did you make about Rick wanting to perform out there on Shark Rock rather than here at the café?"

"It's brilliant. I couldn't believe it. He told me that his technical team reckoned it was a piece of cake, and we could have up to 5000 people here on the beach. He's going to send down his manager to talk to me later on about the details. I'll have to re-print all the posters."

"And take out medical insurance."

"I'm sure Rick's got that."

"I was thinking about you. Have you met his manager?"

"No, but I've seen a picture. Nice little thing, eh?"

"Can I suggest that you keep the counter between you and her when you meet?"

"Passionate, is she? Don't worry, I'm a married man."

Max looked back at the table and could see that Jessica was now deeply engaged in conversation with William and was exerting an impressive influence over him judging by the more than usually flushed look on his face. Max decided to quietly slip away and leave them to it, signalling silently through use of dog biscuit semaphore for Scabies to join him.

***

So much had happened since this time yesterday that Max was feeling in a reflective mood. He had met more people in one day than in all the previous nine months put together and yet, despite having only just met, he felt somehow like he had known them for years. How was that possible when there are many people you have known for decades and never get beyond a nod of the head, a polite enquiry about their health or, more likely, a rhetorical statement about the weather? That Jessica, William, Fizz, Rick and Marguerite should end up in Mead Bay ever, let alone at the same time, must have odds as long as for winning the lottery, or of finding a lead singer who aspires to be a bass player and just stand quietly at the back.

"Interesting. Interesting and intriguing," he addressed collectively to Scabies, a large cypress tree and the blue-tiled street sign that was cemented to his outside wall.

Still in a pensive mood, Max went into the house, climbed the stairs and slid into a room off the living room on the view-facing side of the house. Designed as a single bedroom, this was where Max kept his musical possessions. Two acoustic guitars, one an old, light wood Yamaha, the other a newer, black Washburn, a grey Hagstrom electric, a turquoise Fender bass, a mid-range set of Sony keyboards, a scattering of Shure microphones, an old Bolt valve amplifier, various things to hit, shake and blow and a Tascam four track recorder. The room had a dusty smell despite the fact that Max often left the door open. He liked to see all the instruments; they were like beautiful sculptures to him and frankly served much the same purpose. "*Inspiration, have I none*," he sang as he picked up and dusted down the Washburn. Once a keen songwriter, unemployment had killed all his musical creativity and transferred it lock, stock and smoking machine gun barrels into thinking up creative ways to dispose of his former bosses.

He strummed an A chord, then a D, then a G. They sounded clunky. "Bloody chords. You don't have much do, and you can't even sound right!" he snarled.

He tried again, more successfully this time, and hummed a snatch of melody that vaguely pleased him. It was upbeat.

Doo, doo, doo
Put a gun to my boss's head and blew his brains out
Doo, Doo, Doo
There wasn't enough there to even cover a spoon
Dah, dah, dah
So, I took out my knife and tried to cut his heart out
Dee, dee, dee
But it blunted my knife, so I left him and went to bed
And in the morning, I saw that he'd fled
Should have shot him through both of his heels instead.

This was very promising stuff, and Max put down his guitar and walked around the living room five times trying to nail down the tune in his head. That done, he reached out instinctively to switch on the kettle and, with a shudder, realised that only the Gunpowder tea was available. Tea was even more essential than rice and alcohol to Max, and so, with a despondent sigh, he grabbed his car keys, shoved Scabies into the utility room, banged shut the back door and went out.

Come to think of it, there wasn't much in the house to eat, so perhaps a bit of general shopping wouldn't go amiss. Usually, Max settled on the local convenience store up the hill from the meadow where he could shop blindfold in two minutes. But, bearing in mind that he might have more than the postman (who counted as a visitor in Max's eyes) dropping by, he instead turned his comfortable but weary, old Jaguar towards the Leylandii Shopping Centre.

This was normally something he avoided at all costs. Parking there was always a nightmare, the supermarkets deliberately hid anything you wanted, and all the while there was the stress of encountering the great unwashed on their own territory. Today was well up to par.

Two people took car parking spaces from under Max's nose by driving the wrong way up the lanes, and in the end, he was forced to squeeze into a space reduced in size by a white van which had its wheels well over the line. Fortunately, as Max was pretty lean and flexible, with some interesting flexing and contortions, he managed to extricate himself from the car, body part by body part. The satisfaction in this came from knowing that the van driver would not even be able to think about opening his door to get in.

There were no trolleys available, and it took a while before Max spotted a lone specimen abandoned inside the entrance. And with good reason. It was the cart from hell, wanting only to go left, and requiring a superhuman effort to steer anywhere else.

A plan sprung up in Max's get-out-of-here-fast mind, and, after some intense observation, he honed in on another trolley, temporarily abandoned at the end of an aisle and with only a few items in it. In a mere five seconds Max had neatly swapped the items over and was able to set off without leaning to the left. Slightly regrettably, an officious and right-minded female of advanced years spotted the switch and pursued him.

"You got no right to do tha'," it said.

Max kept on going on the grounds that not enough correct English was being used to merit stopping.

"Oi, you bugger, you got no manners or what!?" it then said in raised tones.

Max stopped, turned around and in a musically cheerful and enquiring voice said, "Pyth yw dhe hanow, koth sagh?" Continuing on with a smile but in a more serious tone, "An jynn-ebbrenn yw yn privedyhow benenes." And then ending with a stern, "An amanyn du nyns yw melyn."

"Bloody Polish! Bloody EU!" said the old crone feelingly and then turned on her heel snorting violently.

In the belief that he had best depart before encountering other irate local wildlife, and before his rudimentary Cornish ran out, Max concentrated on loading his cart with whatever he thought people who didn't live on Uncle Ben's Rice might like, topped off with a good swim's worth of alcohol.

"Planning a party?" enquired the rubicund, bald, male sixty-plus, surplus to life, teller.

"An orgy," confided Max.

"Some people have all the luck. I'd like a nice orgy myself."

Even served up as the main course and with an apple stuffed in his mouth, Max thought that highly unlikely.

On leaving the supermarket, Max could see the trapped, white van driver prowling around waiting to vent. He paused, waiting until the man had walked about twenty metres away in the opposite direction before squeezing quickly into his car and zipping out of the space at lightning speed. Another car zipped seamlessly, and at the same speed, straight into the gap after him, perplexing the van driver who, incensed at missing his target, took out his frustration on the new occupier of the space. Seeing that the driver was a Millennial in her early 30s with a granite jaw and black laser eyes, the van driver would have been far better placed in booking himself an immediate ride in a hearse.

Taking a short cut through one of Mead Bay's many red-light industrial estates on his way home, Max spotted a figure he recognised talking animatedly into her mobile. She turned and stared at him, initially unseeingly, then suddenly stopped the call and rushed towards his car. Max stopped and wound down the window. A perfect agitation of blonde stood before him.

"That bloody van is going to take another bloody week to bloody fix. Can you bloody believe it!"

Max uttered something inane and soothing and opened the passenger door, and the agitation stepped in.

"Nice old car, this. Proper leather and wood, not like that rusty, bloody old heap in there," Marguerite said pointing back at the garage. She settled, sniffed the air, sighed and pressed the CD button.

"*Hex Induction Hour*! Bloody amazing!" she exclaimed and turned towards Max with a look of curiously heightened interest. "Have you got a decent printer? The one in that dump of a hotel is steam bloody driven and keeps packing up after a couple of pages."

Max said that he possessed a top-quality machine on which he had printed nearly 1000 wasted letters looking for work. In fact, he had often felt like contacting Greta Thunderberg to get her to hunt down all the companies that had not responded to his approaches and accuse them of perpetuating the destruction of the Amazon rainforest.

"We've got to re-print thousands of posters for that stupid, bloody concert that Rick has agreed to do now that he's finally gone totally, bloody bananas and wants to play on that shitty rock out in the bay."

"You're not wrong about the 'shitty rock' bit. For the past 100,000 years, the shags have sat on that rock heroically crapping themselves, probably with this very concert in mind. About twenty years ago, during a very hot summer, I kitted myself out in polar gear and swam out there. Apart from nearly bleeding to death because the rock surface below the waterline is as sharp as a school of well-honed steel razor blades, the smell on the rock when I climbed up was completely overpowering, worse even than a rail carriage full of Inter Railing students."

"Ooh, you've cheered me up," Marguerite chuckled. "He deserves all that and more, silly old fool."

"What about the stage? I can't quite see how that's going to work given the angle of the rock."

"Our so-called fixer promoter idiot, who's some relative of some forgotten bloody comedian from the last bloody century, tells us that it's all fine because at low tide the rock is only about eight foot out of the water and the stage can be built from the seabed upwards."

"And he's done this kind of thing before, has he?"

"Apparently he knows a bloke who built a stage over a pool once in Marbella. Well, his daughter now lives down here..."

"No worries about Rick's safety then?" Max asked.

"No, it's the crowd I'm worried about, if anyone bloody turns up, that is. If Rick falls into the sea, they'll all be drowned."

"Look, if you need any help, just ask. No idea what I can do apart from help you out with the printing, but like, whatever."

"You know I might just take you up on that. You're saner than anyone I've met so far on this trip, although that chef chappie's ok. I shouldn't have hit him, really."

"You hit him?!"

"I can't hit Rick, at least not while he's looking, and I sort of needed to blame someone for this farce, and he was the bloke who started it all. Then he went and called me Margie and that was it. How was I to know that he's deaf in one ear? Anyway, I apologised straight away and bought him a steak."

"That was nice."

"Yes, it was for his eye. He told me once he'd used it, he was going to cook it and serve it to the next customer that annoyed him. I liked him a lot after that."

The Jaguar ambled along the main town sea front, past beds of retired flowers and the odd, reluctant palm tree, all planted in long, flaking, concrete-edged beds. Sorry-looking strings of poorly coloured lights were hung between the lampposts along the sea side of the road, and in places, an obesity of tourists gathered. Occasionally, this turned into a graffiti of tourists and, more often than not, a combination of both. Still, nothing could quite take away from the natural underlying charm of the place.

Further along, the car passed by the theatre, another jarring monstrosity from the sixties. Naturally, local planners never wanted to knock this place down, preferring instead to search for buildings of quality where there was a much better chance of annoying the hell out of the locals.

Back in the day, the theatre had hosted the cream of British comedic talent, real stars. Nowadays, those slinking on and off the stage under the entertainment banner would probably have settled for being regarded as small, black holes. Certainly, most of the punters would have liked them to disappear down one.

***

On past the harbour, right the way round, and up a steep hill, past a seemingly empty bird attraction. The whole sky above the place was covered in thin mesh wire, presumably at the demand of the birds to keep them protected from the tourists. Further on up the road, another ghostly form emerged. Once a magnificent five-star hotel, this huge building of majestic stone had been cleverly disguised with concrete cladding in the 1960s and now had all the charm and appearance of a down-at-heel car park in a nuclear fall-out zone.

At last, the car spun a sharp left and right and emerged blinking into the remnants of Mead Bay's glorious past, now mostly confined to the Kentswood area of town. A few hardy souls had even talked about declaring UDI from Mead Bay and twinning Kentswood with Cannes, St. Tropez or Portofino. Sweet dreams are made of this.

"Scabies, here's Marguerite again, come to see you."

Scabies slunk away quickly, there being something about her he didn't entirely trust.

"Funny that, animals always seem to run away from me, just like men. It's not fair, is it?"

"You don't look that frightening," said Max politely.

"Keep telling me that, will you? There are days when my confidence is so low, I just want to punch people to remind myself I still exist."

"I'm very similar except I usually do the running away, and I just want to punch people period."

"You're nice," she said.

"I'm glad you recognise that," he smiled back.

At this point, Max busied himself getting the tea ready, feeling that he had crossed his emotional game-line. No point in unnecessarily encouraging the girl to think he was normal.

"Why don't you make yourself comfortable on the terrace while I'm doing this? Then I can show you the printer."

Marguerite went upstairs, followed at a safe distance by Scabies, who, whilst still cautious, was instinctively curious to observe the creature some more.

"Do you write songs?" called down Marguerite. "'Cause there's loads of instruments up here."

"Terrible amateur I'm afraid. Haven't written anything for years, although funnily enough, I did jot a few ideas down this morning. Must have been meeting Rick and, you know, Fizz being on that songwriting course."

"Play it for me, will you? Promise I won't be too sarcastic."

Max doubted that very much but indicated that he might think about it after tea. He ascended a few minutes later with two large mugs, handing Marguerite the Iggy and the Stooges "Raw Power" one, and keeping the "I Love Kryptos" one for himself.

"Always wanted to see Iggy," she mused.

"I saw him at the Hammersmith Apollo in 2010, hence the mug. Fantastic concert. I was expecting a seriously burnt-out case just going through the motions for a bit of pension money, but it was so not like that. Literally, within five minutes, he'd stripped down so much that he was walking with his knees turned in to stop his assets dropping out. Then, five minutes later, he was hurling himself into the crowd despite having promised two weeks before that he'd never do it again. I've never seen someone over sixty with such explosive energy and with a full vocal range from cat-strangled and shredded high notes to Leonard Cohen-is-a-woose low notes. He really needed it, too, with that bunch of songs. The best bit was that a mate of mine, who's a huge Iggy fan, and only found out about the concert at the very last minute thanks to me, turned up as the concert started. He texted me, but I couldn't see him until Iggy invited the crowd onto the stage. All these cool as f**k characters were doing their moves and there, bang, right behind Iggy is this great big, lardy, middle-aged bloke in a f***ing black suit and tie pogoing like it's 1976. I think even Iggy was impressed by his sheer balls."

Marguerite laughed, a genuine laugh of amusement, and her nose crinkled as she did so. Max observed her for a moment. She might be slight, but everything was nicely in proportion, and when her face was relaxed and her mouth not engaged in pouring vitriol on all around her, it was actually rather nice to look at. He made a mental note to be extra vigilant around her.

"Do you go to a lot of concerts, then?"

"Used to go to loads when I lived in Paris and London. There's nothing better than live music, and I always make it my business to get right to the front of smaller venues. You can't beat watching the band interact, particularly when they really hate each other. I can't understand why some people insist on standing right at the back where you can't see a thing. I mean, I'm average height, and I struggle, so some short arse, um, smaller person has no chance at all."

"Tell me about it! I spent enough time when I was younger looking at blokes' sweaty backs and arses to last a bloody lifetime. It was only when I started working for Rick that I realised it was possible to see the artist."

"I suppose that's because he's both a big bloke and not many people come to see him?" suggested Max.

"Ha, ha, there is that! But no, it's just that now I get to sit on the side of the stage or in the front row if it's a seated concert."

"Well, I hate to tell you this, "but although I've got a really broad taste in music, I've never seen Rick or any of the Prog rock brigade in concert."

"Don't worry," she laughed, "I'll not hold that against you. I'm only doing this because..." and then she suddenly paused, and a thoughtful look came into her eyes, before continuing with a lowered voice, and in a slow and deliberate manner, "I'm only doing this because Rick's my dad."

"Wow!" Max said, his eyebrows raising in a way that would have had Roger Moore reaching for his golden gun with jealousy.

"For Christ's sake, don't mention it to anyone! Especially not Rick!" Marguerite exclaimed.

"You mean he doesn't know!?"

This was definitely an Oscar winning performance. Admittedly, probably Best Costume Design in an Animated Feature rather than Best

Actor, *but an Oscar's an Oscar,* thought Max, and better than old Roger managed anyway.

"No, not a clue. My mum went to a Yes concert and got very drunk," Marguerite explained. "She thought she had slept with the guitar player, but then, when I came along with blonde hair, she had her doubts. It was dark in that cupboard. Now my dad, that is, my mum's husband, never suspected a thing, and it was only when he died a couple of years back that she came out with it. I mean I was so shocked you wouldn't believe it. A Prog rocker for a father, and me a Fall fan! I thought prog was some kind of prostate condition. So, I went to one of his solo gigs and found a few hairs on the floor after the show and sent them off for DNA testing."

"Then why haven't you told him about it, and how come you're working for him?"

"Well, the results aren't 100% certain and, anyway, I wanted to know more about him. I didn't want to make a connection with some real saddo, sleaze ball, not that you can afford to set the bar too high in the music world."

"So?" Max asked.

"So, I did some research on him, and that's when I found out he was looking for a manager. Now, my background's more in PR and event management, but I blagged my way into the interview and said I could get him a lot more money than he'd been getting. It was actually quite easy to persuade him after he had checked out my CV a bit."

"And are you ever going to tell him?"

"Yes, but the problem is that, as time goes by, it gets more difficult to find the right moment. I mean, I don't want him to drop dead on me with shock."

"But surely, and I don't want to seem mercenary here, surely you want him to recognise you from a financial point of view?"

"I'm not daft, of course I bloody do. But if it gets out in the wrong way that he has an illegitimate child, then the bloody flood gates will open and every bloody kid who's mum ever slept with a blond bloke or their dog will claim to be related to him."

"Do you think he has any other, um, spare children out there?"

"Bloody loads!! I mean, I know he was only a keyboard player with a weird cape and a face like an overcooked cabbage, but back in the 70s, if you were in a well-known band, that was enough to get you laid ten times over! Of course, it doesn't happen anymore now 'cause all the blokes in bands are terrified of sleeping with a girl if she could pass for under 40. Forty is the new 14 for rock stars."

"So, you're guessing about the kids, or you have something more than that?"

Marguerite was quick to answer, "I've had at least a dozen claims come through, and frankly, they could all be valid from what I know of Rick's past activities. But being his manager gives me the upper hand since I'm the one that has to reply to everything. Mostly I just send out denials. You know, like Rick was never at the place at the time claimed, or that he's impotent, or gay or all three. There have been a couple of tough ones, though, where the greedy little bastards have demanded DNA samples. I got round that by passing off samples from my old school mate Kunle."

"Who's Nigerian?"

"Yeah, great bloke."

"And African."

"Well, we're all bloody out of Africa, Max!" She paused. "But anyway, just to make sure there's no questions asked, I have the stage crew vacuum up every bloody hair from the stage and wipe down all surfaces Rick has touched. He thinks I've got some kind of bloody OCD, but that's fine by me."

"I was just thinking," Max said, "Rick's got a shed load of legitimate kids as well, hasn't he?"

"Too bloody right he has, so I've got to make sure absolutely no one else apart from me gets added to the list. I'm making him loads of money at the moment, and it's in my interests to keep on doing it. He's amazingly lucky to have me."

At this point, Max was congratulating himself for having steered Marguerite away from the topic of him playing anything, but alas, she was made of sterner stuff. A few minutes later, he found himself, guitar in hand, successively denying all responsibility for bringing the musical world into disrepute, laughing in a shrill, high voice, coughing revoltingly and shifting his position as though sitting on a bed of red-hot ball bearings.

"Put a gun to my boss's head...." He finished and clunked the guitar heavily down on its stand and glared petulantly at Marguerite.

"That was great. Really. Amazing lyrics, and I can so relate to them."

Max was speechless.

Marguerite slid over and kissed him.

Max was legless.

Literally.

The shock of such an unexpected move made him lurch backwards, lose his balance and crash into the keyboards, causing them to fall off the stand and take out, one by one, domino style, all the guitars. The noise of grinding strings and wood was spectacular, and unexpectedly reduced Marguerite to tears of laughter.

"You are a one!" she cried. "Anyone would think I'd been trying to poison you. I should be deeply insulted, but you're just too funny for, for, reality," and she tailed off in paroxysms of mirth.

Max smiled like a dog that has just eaten a small child's birthday cake, and burbled incomprehensibly, trying to brush the whole thing off as an accident, the sort of thing that could happen to anyone caught unawares like that.

"Not your type, am I?" Marguerite fired back.

"Ha, ha, ha, ha, yes, of course, no, yes, lovely, such a surprise, and all the guitars, couldn't have been expecting, really, glad you liked the song, must practice more. Scabies!"

Scabies peered around the door frame with a "this-is-going-to-cost-you-a-lot" look on his face, to which Max responded with an "and-you'll-get-it-but-if-you-don't-step-up-it's-the-dog's-home-for-you-my-lad" look.

Terms duly accepted, Scabies arrowed towards Marguerite and started licking her bare legs.

"Oo-er, gerroff me! You're like some daft schoolboy."

"He likes you," said Max encouragingly, wondering what kind of schoolboys Marguerite had encountered.

"So, you think you can give me the cold shoulder and then palm me off with a bloody Labrador, do you?!"

"Well, I was rather hoping. He is a pedigree."

"And you're saying I should be grateful for that. I'm the daughter of a bona fide bloody 70s rock star!"

"I hate to point it out, but, according to you, so is half the UK, so it's hardly game set and match to you on the exclusivity front, is it?"

At this point, Marguerite swung a playful fist at Max, missed and knocked down a signed Ronnie Wood print of Charlie Watts that was hanging, lugubriously, on the wall. Freed from his nail, Charlie plunged floorwards, surviving intact only thanks to the cushioning effect of Scabies's tail. The dog emitted a howl like Joe Strummer in "London Calling" and took off faster than a Van Halen solo.

"You've blown your chances. Should've taken them while you could."

Max reached over, picked up Charlie and hung him back on the wall. Charlie gazed back, Mona Lisa-like.

Disentangling the guitars took a bit longer. It's a strange law of nature that whenever metal makes contact with anything else metal it somehow takes on the properties of string, with the same propensity to get irretrievably tangled up. Marguerite tried to help matters by picking up the keyboards and yet couldn't quite reach over Max to put them back on the stand. Max, not seeing her, started to crawl backwards with a freed guitar in hand, causing her to lose both her grip and her footing. The keyboard dropped on Max's head an instant before Marguerite herself was launched into mid-air as if she had placed her feet on a strategically placed banana skin, coming down with a whoomph on Max's back. The force left both of them winded.

"You don't give up easily do you?" he wheezed like a veteran smoker crawling up the side of a step. "Harassment that might be called in these sensitive times."

"What do you mean? You did that deliberately! You moved back so I would fall over on top of you. That's pre-meditated harassment that you've tried to pass off on me."

"That's libel on top. First, you sexually assault me, causing me physical and emotional trauma as well as material damage to goods, then you commit a second assault with a deadly weapon in addition to using physical force, doubling the emotional and physical scarring, and on top of that, try to frame me for your actions, threatening my reputation and career. The damages are going to be colossal. I would say they'll amount to at least what you'll fleece, er, inherit, from Rick."

"Which is precisely bloody nothing at the moment, so you'd better help me out!" She rolled off Max, compounding her crimes by grabbing another quick kiss, grinned into his face at close quarters like a Cheshire cat, yawned and stood up, shaking her hair back into position.

Max was feeling discombobulated but with distinctly bobulated overtones. He felt out of his depth but at the same time, was sure that by maintaining a high gag count he could maintain Marguerite at lip's length, if not the full arm's.

A message buzzed on his phone, breaking up the moment, and Max scrambled relievedly to his feet and hurried into the living room. The message was from Fizz, reporting in that she wouldn't have time to hook up until later that night as she needed to do some homework. Stevo had apparently set them all the task of writing a song about underprivileged children, to be sung to the melody of "Happy Talk."

"Can't repeat what Usan said about that!" she had written with suitable use of emojis.

"Thank God I'm not on that course. The pretentious bloke running it would wind me up in five seconds flat," Max said.

He showed the message to Marguerite who sniffed dismissively and said that if he thought Stevo was pretentious, he should try listening to *Tales from Topographical Oceans*.

"That's not fair!" he complained. "We're not comparing like and like here. I've told you the equivalent of my niece having a cold, and you've responded by telling me your whole family died from an overdose of Sting's lute music. Anyway, 'Revenons à nos moutons,' as my dear sheep-shagging, old French teacher used to say. What else can I do to help other than with the printing? I've pencilled in my funeral for 2068, but the diary's pretty free until then."

"Let me think about it," she answered. "There's going to be loads to sort out between now and the concert. Apart from all the permit rubbish, we'll need a support act I suppose, though I dunno who's bloody mad enough to want to play on that rock, and then there's also security. Actually, talking about security, there's some obsessed old groupie hanging around the hotel. Really creepy, she is. Blonde and looks like a ghost. Tried cornering Rick in the bar, and I had to keep fending her off half the night! Then, this morning she traps him in the toilet. Says she just wants to talk to him, but that's a load of bollocks. Who wants to talk to a frigging musician? They're only good for songs and shagging, and most of them are not even good for that. Anyway, it took us an hour to free Rick from the toilet window. Had to grease him down to do it, and that's not a pretty sight I can tell you. The hotel didn't have any Vaseline, so they used duck fat. All it needs now is a few chips, and you could serve him up as a bloody main course. Would feed 5000 and all."

"How did the groupie know he was here? It's not exactly groupie territory except for a gaga of Elvis and Cliff Richard fans."

"You wouldn't believe the lengths some of these women go to stalk Rick. It doesn't matter to them that he's over 70, shaves an area of chin each day the size of a small allotment, and probably hasn't even seen his todger since 1990. No, to them he's some kind of blond Adonis who can send them to heaven and back with a single touch. The one in the hotel is a hardened stalker, I can tell. Sounds like she's come all the way from bloody Australia after him. I had a word with the management and tried to have her kicked out, but it seems that she's paying them so much money that they won't hear of it. You wouldn't want to help distract her a bit, would you?"

"You mean groupie bait? I'm hardly in the Wakeman league, am I?" protested Max lightly. "I'm literally half the man he is and couldn't tinkle an ivory even if my life depended on it."

"I don't think you need be worried about that," Marguerite replied. "This girl could probably tinkle the tusks off an elephant."

Max looked suitably thoughtful and assumed what he hoped was a reluctant but valiant stance. "Look, I don't mind sounding her out for you, but you'll probably find that she's really nice. A teacher or something."

"If she's a teacher, then I'm bloody Elvis Presley."

"Ok, Elvis, have it your own way. I'll start observing the target as soon as possible if you'll kindly point her out."

"Come to the hotel in a couple of hours, around six, for a drink. I'm sure she'll be there." And with that, Marguerite headed for the door, stopping just to call back, "And don't forget, Poirot, not a bloody word to Rick about anything, or I'll hurt you." She winked prophetically and left.

Max exhaled deeply and sank into his sofa for a minute or two, momentarily spent, before finding the energy to knock back a restorative shot of Louis Roque's finest Vieille Prune. He gasped as the burning liquid seared his throat and lungs and then plunged straight into his beckoning bloodstream. Scabies sneezed as Max deliberately sought him out and blew the fumes down his nose. "Come on now, don't look at me like that. I promised you something nice, didn't I? Try a bit, there's a good boy."

Max poured the tiniest amount into Scabies's bowl. Enough for Scabies to bolt for cover.

***

Two hours to kill before going to the hotel. Hardly enough time to do anything except read. In the old days, a newspaper would have filled the gap, but Max had long given up reading them. Their columns betrayed scarcely any sign of intelligent life and were mostly full of views that were either patently untrue, laughably sensationalist, utterly fantastical, or in the case of the right-wing press, straight out racist but presented as patriotic.

Maybe time to start the Andy Fletcher autobiography Me and Two Other Blokes, he thought. But no, that would have to wait until he had a month or two, given its one thousand page-plus length. The first two hundred pages alone were given over to discussing dance moves.

Out of the corner of his eye, Max spotted *Death Ray*, the Dave Davies story, tucked under an old CD audiobook of Montaigne's writings, narrated by Nick Cave. The Davies book looked perfect, and Max went out onto the terrace, dragged a chair into position and stuck his feet up on the railing.

Once upon a time, many years ago, there was a very beautiful and very talented young singer-songwriter-guitarist. He lived in a house with his vicious, evil, scene-stealing elder brother who wanted nothing better than to destroy his innocent young brother's life. "Let's form a band," said the elder brother....

This looked very promising, and Max settled down contentedly to enjoy the tale.

"Ahoy there!"

Max ignored the voice and kept on reading.

"Hello, Skipper, can I come aboard?"

A touch irritated, Max looked down and saw William standing in the middle of the road waving at him. A car, coming along the road from the opposite direction, started to honk its horn as it encountered this oblivious obstruction.

"Nice place you've got there. Good for checking out the local talent, eh?"

The car horn became more persistent.

"The Brummie chap from the café told me you lived somewhere up here, and I thought it would be worth coming up here anyway to scout some new locations for my painting. Devil's View is just up the top of the hill, isn't it?"

The car horn became continuous.

"Yes, it is," Max answered. "There's a gate just around the corner if you want to come in. Open it, then open the gate just inside on the right."

"Right ho, sir. Will do."

William turned and began to walk along to the gate, staying firmly in the middle of the road. A shout emanated from the car driver as he revved his engine and shot forward, clearly with the intention of swerving around William close enough to put the fear of God into him. Unfortunately, and as often happens when anger dictates, the driver applied rather more power to his accelerator than intended, with the result that he failed to carry out the seamless left/right swerve he had intended. The right just never happened and instead the left claimed a stunning victory as the car ploughed effortlessly into the only car parked on the road.

Seconds later, William materialised at the end of the garden, to be greeted by a four-legged bounce of Scabies.

"Just ignore him, and he'll calm down in a moment. He verges on the pansexual at times."

"All dogs are actually gay," stated William. "I read it in the *Daily Patriot*, so it must be true." He waved a tabloid paper at Max and removed Scabies from his leg.

"Tea? Got some lovely Georgian loose leaf if you prefer it to breakfast."

"Why not, I'll have some of the Jimmy Carter, please." William put the paper down on the kitchen table. Today's edition focused on "Pope grants special dispensation to non-paedophile priest," and "Making Brexit work: could Britain become a province of Canada?"

Max walked back out into the garden, thinking it the safest place to combine William and Georgian tea. He handed the mug over, stood back and tensed his body, waiting for the inevitable chemical reaction.

"Very full and spicy. Is that cardamom I can detect, with maybe a hint of peanut?"

"You're feeling ok?"

"Never better. And nothing like a good cup of tea to keep you feeling that way. You not joining me?"

Er, no, I'm cardamom intolerant."

William cheerfully continued imbibing. "Yes, I read that all dogs are essentially gay and fancy their owners."

"Some of whom may be female..."

"Lesbians, of course, and who wouldn't fancy a bit of that!" he guffawed.

The logic and probity of this statement didn't bear further enquiry, so Max just stood back and told himself to remember William's words of wisdom in case he ever wrote a book. "So, I am guessing that dogs may just die out then eventually?"

"Yes, life's a bitch," William guffawed again.

"Tres amusant mon brave."

"Ah, si! J`avez oubliez que vous parles la belle Francaise."

"Yes, but not as well as some. You haven't thought about giving some

French lessons while you're staying here? Maybe you could even combine French and painting."

"Thanks so much for that idea. I could ask that Australian girl you introduced me to earlier. That was a great introduction by the way. She's very attractive and was very interested in my painting. I think I could be in there, and I've offered to teach her all I know." He paused a moment before continuing, "What do you know about Rick Wakeman, the chap from Status Quo?"

"A tolerable amount, why?"

"Jessica seemed very keen on him, and it's part of my seduction technique to learn about the lady's interests and impress them a bit." With that, William started to hum an unrecognisable tune, then came in with a chorus of, "*Pictures of matchstalk men and dogs.*"

"You might just find that it's *Pictures of matchstick men and you,* although I know that the Quo and Brian and Michael are almost indistinguishable except to the most avid fan," Max observed, sagely.

"Ah, yes, could be."

"You know that Jessica's staying at the same hotel as you?"

"No, I didn't. That's excellent news, although I did ask her, and she wasn't very forthcoming. She mentioned something about not wanting to be tied down to a particular hotel."

"That's just her sense of humour. I can tell you that she's staying at The Darwin for three months, so you've plenty of time to work your magic. My prediction is that Rick Wakeman is the key to her heart. If you're really knowledgeable about him, then the sky's the limit. Give her the impression that you really know Rick inside out."

William's eyes positively glowed with enthusiasm, matching his permanently glowing complexion. "Very kind of you. That's really very helpful. I'm not normally a huge music fan, although I like James Last and Ed Sheeran as much as the next man, but I see this as a project. You don't happen to have any CDs, do you?"

"Masses, but the Rick Wakeman section is sadly lacking. You could try Amazon, or maybe a charity shop. The town centre's maxed out with them."

William polished off his tea and announced that he must be going.

"Keep following the path up the hill. You'll pass the big yellow hotel you see up there, and Devil's View Plain is a bit further up on the left. You like golf, I seem to remember? Well, I used to watch people practice their golf shots up there when I was a kid. It's banned now, but you still get the odd person who creeps up there when it's quiet. There's a large impenetrable patch of what look like triffids on one side of the plain that I reckon must be absolutely full of free golf balls. Mind you, you'd need to be crazy to risk going in there."

Max waved William off and returned to Dave Davies.

Another message buzzed through on his phone.

"Would 8:30 be too late?" WhatsApped Fizz.

"No, that's perfect for me as out for early evening drink with Marguerite," he WhatsApped back.

"Oh, yes! Your new girlfriend?"

"Sorry, that list already full. Just doing this to be charitable."

"So kind of you, what a gentleman!"

"Comes naturally, although I'm too modest to mention it to anyone unless I've known them for at least 24 hours. By the way, spotted potential boyfriend for you – will mention later on in case travelling to Armenia gets too much."

"Kurdistan."

"Oh, yes, my mistake."

"Will need big drink later. Course stressful, crazy colleagues, and teacher never talks to me!"

"No problem! But last comment a positive I would have thought?"

"Good point! See ya later."

Back to Dave Davies, but only for a few seconds before a series of muffled oaths attracted Max's attention away from the page. Looking up, he could see the old gardener and a younger looking version, struggling down the hotel garden with a gate that wouldn't have looked out of place at a Scottish castle.

"Do you need a hand?" Max shouted.

The younger man, distracted, let the gate drop onto the ground at his end. This upset the delicate balance of the older man, who was lower down the slope. He pulled when the gate dropped and, rather like a person who has jumped into bed and pulled the duvet over them, the old gardener slid neatly under the gate leaving only his head showing.

"Get this thing offer me you dozy scallop. It weighs a bloody ton!"

The younger man looked over to Max for help and tripped, falling spreadeagled onto the gate.

"You wuzzocking swordfish," or words to that effect, emanated from the old man. "Oh, me ribs are crushed. Can't breathe!"

Max, though enjoying the show, and believing that the death of a gardener or two was probably not the end of the world, nevertheless made haste out of the house and up into the hotel grounds to assist.

The old man was extricated with care, as neither Max nor the younger gardener wanted to damage the gate, and he sat moaning to himself on a stone seat.

Max fetched some tea. "Here, this should get you up on your feet."

There were a few seconds silence with just the sound of tea being gulped gratefully. "Thank you, sir, that was graaaaaaaaagh!!!" and in a flash, the gardener was up on his feet as if he had been plugged straight into a generator. For a moment or two, he sort of hovered on the spot with the kind of horror in his eyes of a veteran actor meeting Ronan Farrow for the first time in a lift, but then, gradually, the horror subsided and was replaced by a kind of Zen- like trance.

"Cor! What was that you gave me, sir? That were no ordinary tea I'll be bound. I can't even feel me ribs now." He gave them a thump and then danced a mercifully short jig.

"Georgian Gunpowder Tea."

"God Bless Jimmy Carter! God Bless America! That's what I always say. Not like them thieving Europeans!"

Max helped the men carry the massive oak slab down to the bottom of the garden, where it was quite obvious there was not the remotest chance of it fitting the existing space.

"And whas more," said Old Bill, "we'll need to fix completely different hinges. Those ones there wouldn't be any more use than a doctor in a surgery. Boris, you and me'll have to open up that wall a bit. Go and get the sledgehammer from the shed."

"Boris?"

"Yeah, bloody foreign name. Can't trust anyone with a name like that now, can you? Sounds like a Russian spy, don't it? His mother thought it sounded sophisticated. Daft cow. As if!"

Max nodded in agreement and asked him if he wouldn't mind trying to unstick his own gate while they were doing the hotel one.

"Be a pleasure, sir."

"And who owns the gate onto the public footpath?" Max enquired.

"You know, I think that's lost in the mists of time, sir, but I'll have a look at it anyway since there's no point in us putting up a new one here if no one can't get through t'other bugger."

***

Max retreated back to his terrace but couldn't find the energy to read. *Exercise is the key,* he thought, remembering that today was one of his three running days a week. He kitted himself out in a black Kasabian T-shirt, black shorts and red New Balance running shoes. He had wanted the blue, but Amazon had disagreed, and who was he to take on the mighty Jeff Bozo?

Scabies was disappointed at being left behind, but Max had learned that his idea of a run and Scabies's were wildly different. While Max liked to run constantly on a set route, at even pace, for a measured five miles, Scabies looked for 15 miles of detours, sudden stops, rapid starts, with as much added pissing and shagging as could be fitted in.

The problem with Mead Bay was that finding anywhere remotely flat was virtually impossible, and the skill was in navigating away small percentages of incline while maximising down slopes. Max was pretty good at it, but right at the end of his circuit was a one kilometre hill that led up from the beach road and looped around to his house. He saw it as a way to avoid total cheating, but even here he had a secret weapon.

He didn't know her by name but by her general loveliness. She worked in the village delicatessen and ran her own circuit, including Max's hill, as regular as clockwork. If Max got his timing right, he could arrive at the junction where her run crossed his, just up from the bottom of the hill, about ten seconds behind her. When this happened, all the pain of the climb was instantly forgotten in the glow of following in her perfect posterior's slipstream.

Today was not one of Max's good running days. His legs felt tired even leaving his drive, and his lungs were in sympathy with his legs. As he struggled along, an odious pre-teen specimen in school uniform called out, "Hello, Rudolph!" Max despaired of modern youth. Surely, they taught them at school that Rudolph had a red nose and not a pair of red New Balance running shoes? He felt sorry for the parents. A kid that stupid couldn't even be sold for medical experiments.

And on past the first of the nursing homes where old Mrs. Shevansky sat outside in her usual orange chair. "Going for a run?" she called out, as she did three times a week. Max wondered what juicy phrases she had for other passers-by. He liked to imagine her saying things like "Going to talk to God?" to the local vicar, or "Going home to play with your conkers?" to small boys. The reality was probably more mundane and `going for a run` and `going for a walk` were probably as good as it got.

As usual, he replied with a cheerful, "Going to shoot some doctors!" knowing that she was as deaf as a post.

She replied as always with a wave and "Keep it up," which Max always felt showed deep insight.

Sometimes Max felt like he should wear headphones and listen to music when he ran. His main objection was that he hated other people doing it, given that they usually demonstrated an Olympian lack of awareness of the existence of trams, buses, cars and pedestrians the moment their headphones went on. Besides this, Max liked to see what his in-built Spotify came up with. It was surprising what the subconscious could drag up when under the influence of exercise, and it was not unusual to find himself pushing up a steep hill to the unconscionably cheery ring of "Dancing Queen," sweltering in the summer heat to "Singin'in the Rain" or squelching across grassy meadows to "Top Hat, White Tie and Tails."

Today, it was Spandau Ballet's "Musclebound" that inconsiderately slipped into his head for the first part of the run, morphing into "Light My Fire" by the time he entered the woods and segueing into Blur's "Ong Ong" along the sea front.

Instead of meeting his favourite jogger on the way up the hill from the beach, he encountered the much more substantial and significantly less gratifying sight of Glen, labouring on his way home from work, laden with two trays of uneaten brioches. Fearing he was about to be mowed down by an errant steam train, Glen glanced over his shoulder and pulled into the inside of the path.

"Hoi, Max!" he called out, "I thought that you were supposed to be fit?"

"And so were you, just not in the same way. You're a poor substitute for my usual hill climbing motivation."

Glen started to question what on earth Max was talking about when Glorious Girl materialised just ahead of them.

"Ah, I get it, mate! She's really something, isn't she? What's she called?"

"Not the faintest. I can never catch her up. Thankfully, she's faster than me."

Turning his attention to the trays of brioches, Max enquired between gulps of air whether Glen was feeling a bit peckish.

"No, mate. The bakery insisted that we replace all our normal buns with these damn things. Thing is, they're too foreign sounding for our locals down here, so I can't shift them."

"Going to feed them to the gulls then?"

"No, the foreign language students."

"Same principle, I guess?"

"Yeah, just chuck them on the ground around the harbour and the students fight over them. For them it's proper food, see? Believe me, the gulls don't stand a chance against them froggie kids."

"Do you get many of them down at the café?"

"In season the place is thick with them. Boys in posey shades and girls with about a bikini's worth of material between the lot of them. They all line up and buy a Coke each, but never anything else, despite the fact that most of them have got loads of money. It's not only that they don't like our food, I think that Coke is the only English word they know. I've a good mind to double the prices for anyone just buying Coke."

"Sound commercial idea. Go for it."

By now Max had stopped his train impression and was merely looking like something that had emerged from a swamp. The hill was going to be too easy now, so he might have to put in a short extra loop to make up for it. He made signs to leave, but Glen grabbed him by a sweaty shoulder.

"Before you go, I wanted to mention that we're going to have a fancy dress party at the café this weekend. The weather's set to be great, and we thought it might get people geared up a bit about next month's concert."

"Brilliant plan. Count me in. Any particular theme? Leather?"

"No, but you must wear a mask, and I don't mean dress like a gimp."

"No problem, the gimp outfit will remain in the cupboard."

"We're also going to have some live music. This Dutch girl with electro-shock hair came down to the café and said that there's a songwriter's course going on in Mead Bay. So, I've asked to meet the guy running it to sort something out. Apparently, he was big in the 80s."

Max smiled to himself and offered to help Glen and Cee set things up on the Saturday morning.

***

A shower and a couple of squares of Sheardown's Honduras Indio Rojo 72% chocolate later, Max was ready for his drink. He quickly emptied a tin of Osbourne's super nutritious Bark at the Moon dog food into Scabies's bowl and threw in some meal. "Lucky old you. Seems this stuff was personally developed by Ozzy in the 80s to wean himself off bats."

Leaving Scabies inhaling his food in satisfied gasps, Max closed the door and walked along the garden to inspect the work being done on the gates. His own gate and the gate onto the public path now swung open like a dream, and he found that the gardeners had even given them a coat of Duffy's jet black paint. The hotel gate area, by contrast, looked like an American had tried to walk through it. A massive hole now sat where there had once been an archway. Masonry was strewn about all over the grass, including several pieces of what must have once been a sledgehammer handle. The gate itself was propped up against a small tree that was listing heavily under the strain.

Reaching the top of the S-shape steps, Max, feeling in an unusually buoyant mood, sat on the rail and attempted to slide down in classic YouTuber style. The result was also the same, and about eight feet down, at the first turn, he rotated to an interesting angle and scattered a clutch of sparrows who were enjoying a late afternoon snooze in the depths of the hedgerow.

Extricating himself was not the work of a moment. Now that the hedgerow had got him, it was rather reluctant to let him go. Sparrows were small, rather dull and difficult to catch, but this creature, with its green Jethro Tull "Flutes of Fantasy Tour" shirt was a far more interesting prospect altogether. *The hedgerow might have distant links to Mirkwood,* thought Max, as he struggled to untether himself, or perhaps it had recently discovered embarrassing musical ties to The Hedge and was taking it out on him.

"What you doing in there, mate? Need a hand?" called out a wizened cloth cap with faded blue shorts and hand-me-down legs.

"Fine, thanks, just communing with nature. There's nothing quite like getting up close to a bush," Max answered.

"I'll take your word for it. Too old for it myself."

"Oh, I doubt that. And it does take years off you, you know. Something to do with the chlorophyll. I'm eighty-five."

"But that's amazing! I wouldn't put you at a day over sixty. Can you show me how to do it?"

"It would be a tremendous pleasure. Now, just get on the railings and let yourself slide down. It's all part of the process. No, I suggest that you start much higher up. That's it, off you go." *F***ing sixty!* thought Max indignantly as he descended the rest of the steps, leaving muffled cries behind him.

On the sea road, just above the café, was a pedestrian entry to the lower end of The Darwin's grounds. Max pushed open the gate and wended his way up the path past a swimming pool where thin, angular, but aesthetically pleasing shapes mixed with large amorphous masses. Occasionally, the masses would leave the angular shapes and jump into the pool.

Just above the pool lay the tennis courts, today stocked with vintage specimens who talked a magnificent game while actually seeming not to move at all.

"Oh, well done, Rosemary, old sausage, you very nearly hit that," followed by, "Splendid shot!" when a rare ball ventured over the net, connected with the back of her head and was spirited back on a seeming cushion of air to land bounce-free on the other side. This was in contrast to Rosemary's accompanying airless plunge and impressive bounce off the court.

Entering the reception area of the hotel, a genuine 1960s experience, Max turned right to the bar which, by contrast, was unashamedly 1970s. A long, dark stained, wood counter with a brass rail ran along one side of the room, while worn, brown leather chairs and banquettes were arranged around the other walls, and a scattering of non-matching tartan fabric seats were to be found in the empty spaces, surrounding round, grey, lino-topped tables. The ceiling was very high, and enormous thought had obviously been given to distracting attention away from its height by the introduction of a series of orange and yellow shard glass chandeliers. On the walls were prints of David Shepherd elephants, alongside signed, yellowed photos of the good and the great who had once stayed at the hotel. Darwin would have had a field day with some of the characters there, included amongst which was a splendid Dick Emery as `Bovver Boy.`

Propped up against the far end of the bar was Marguerite, in a white patterned shirt and short, white skirt, iPhone in hand. On the far corner wall, occupying a table for four and cataloguing CDs was William, all in brown, pen in hand, expectant. In the opposite corner, wraith-like in black, all but invisible with book in hand, sat Jessica.

The tension was sharp enough to cut through a diamond. From a door behind the bar, emerged the bartender, sensing trouble. "Drink?" he directed at Marguerite, playing it as cool as the response of an audience to the prospect of a James Blunt encore.

"Whisky," she shot back. "Better make it the bottle."

"Jack?"

"Shit! Make it the Macallan 25."

"Yes, ma'am, Macallan 25 coming up."

He placed the bottle and a shot glass on the worn and chipped counter. Marguerite looked up and stared into his grey-green eyes, fixing him with a cobalt gaze as she very slowly edged the glass away with the back of her free hand. The hand came back in equal slow motion, and she opened up her long, thin fingers, tipped with King Crimson varnish. Encircling the bottle hard by its waist, she lifted it up, wrist straight, to her gleaming lips. At the same time, her other hand shifted its grip infinitesimally on the iPhone 18. Two hard slugs of the scotch followed, and then she slammed the bottled down hard, causing the bottles behind the bar to tremble.

Her eyes lifted again, and she scanned Max thoughtfully. "You want to come over here and take a drink?"

It was a command. Max gave a fractional nod of the head and moved forward, Marguerite pursing her lips and smiling a quarter smile.

She held out the bottle. "Take it. Nothing on my lips that's gonna kill you."

Max drew his shoulders back, grabbed the bottle and sunk a third of it without blinking.

"I like a man who can take his liquor. You up for the job?"

"Reckon I am."

"See the trollope in the corner, the one that looks like she's had a blood by-pass?"

"Reckon I can."

"Well, she's the one that's been bothering my man. I'd take her out myself, but this thing needs re-charging."

"Is she dangerous?"

"Anyone who looks like that gotta be dangerous, it figures, but that ain't gonna scare a man like you, is it?"

"Reckon it won't. Who's the stooge in the corner? Is he connected to her?"

"That loser! He ain't like no pimp I've ever seen, but I guess you'd better make sure of him. I'll keep an eye on the vampire bitch while you suss him out."

"Hi, William, how's tricks?" Max asked cheerily.

"Oh, hello, Max. Just doing my homework on Rick Wakeman. That was a great tip about the charity shops by the way. The 49p Store had a huge selection of old 70s CDs including the Bay City Rollers, Alvin Stardust and Mr. Wakeman himself. They were so keen to clear the space that I picked up ten for three quid. I think some of them may be foreign editions."

Max picked up the first CD on the pile. It was true that the Arabic script was rather dominant, and Jeddah Records was probably not an official offshoot of EMI. However, the title of *The Mitts and Legs of King Arthur and His Nights on the Round Table* sounded distinctly appealing.

"I think you're in for a treat there."

"I plan to work my way through in chronological order. If I start this evening, I should be pretty much up to speed by the weekend. I just need to find a way to keep Jessica from talking about him too much in the meantime. Do you think she has sex much?"

Max paused. William's tendency to burn up the conventional means of progressing a conversation was still a bit new to him.

"I'm not sure. I'm just going to have a word with her, so I'll let you know."

"I'll come with you," were not the words Max was keen on hearing, as he wanted time with Jessica to find out her strategy vis-à-vis Rick.

He glanced at Marguerite, raised his eyebrows and ventured over to the dark corner Jessica was trying not to crowd. "Hi there, long time no see. Just popped in to tell you and William that there's a fancy dress party this weekend at the beach café. Not much happens around here normally, so it should be a laugh."

"Ok, that sounds fun. I may drop by for thirty minutes later in the evening."

"Hello there, Jessica. Coming to the party as the Invisible Woman?" William chortled. "No? When was the last time you had sex?"

Max pulled a face at Jessica that tried to convey outrage, amusement and sympathy at the same time.

"I'm not telling you that!"

"Come on, I'll bet it's not often. I'll sleep with you."

Her "No!" came out in an elongated up and down wave of noise, then, "As far as you know I may sleep around all the time."

Jessica, while seemingly outraged by William's outrageousness, was not in the slightest put out. She had his number down well and was storing it up for future use.

"Unlikely, I'd say, but of course, I don't mean to be rude. You're very attractive but a little odd."

"I'M odd!"

"You always dress in black, and Max tells me you walk around the town on your own in the dark. That's not likely to attract many men."

Jessica and Max locked eyes and shared a private moment of mirth at William's pricelessly unselfconscious trammelling of social norms and niceties.

"So, Jessica," interjected Max to shift the topic of conversation, "what do you make of that girl at the bar, the one that keeps eyeing up William?"

"The Rick Wakeman groupie?"

"So, she's the one! Not surprising that she's got her eyes on William then, eh?"

William saw Max's encouraging eye wink and, despite not having the faintest idea what was going on, he picked up the cue. "Yes, well you know, it's my natural charm."

"I was guessing that you and Rick went back a long way. I had heard some rumours that he was staying in the hotel, and with you here, too, that seems more than a coincidence," Max offered.

William looked wonderfully wrong-footed and as out of his depth as Bob Dylan being called upon to sing "Wuthering Heights" at a Kate Bush tribute show. "Can't really say much about that," he spluttered, which was true and a perfect response from Max's perspective, as Jessica pricked up her ears.

"I think more should be done to keep these kinds of people away, don't you?" she said. "You would think that management would look after their artists better, eh?"

Max nudged William. "I think that's right, don't you agree?"

"Yes, of course," William agreed. "No one wants unpredictable people about. I am a strong believer in social conventions." Max and Jessica exchanged another glance and fought to maintain their composure. "Shall I have a word with her?"

"Ooh, yes! Er, sorry, I mean, that sounds like a good plan. I suggest you play it a bit cool, though, in case she's slightly unhinged."

William stood up and walked over to the bar. The barman was cleaning glasses with his back to the counter, which enabled William to look over to Marguerite.

"Enjoying your ginger ale?"

"Whisky."

"Because I knew a girl once who only drank ginger ale, and she started developing migraines as a result. It's not wise to overdo it."

Marguerite looked at him as though he had been scooped out of the bottom of a bin. "Well, this is whisky. I don't like ginger ale at all."

With that conclusive conversation closer, she turned back to her iPhone and pretended to be looking for something.

"You're holding it upside down. These new phones can be complicated, though, can't they? My mother is always leaving hers in the kitchen."

Flecks of red started to break out on Marguerite's cheeks, but she resisted the temptation to say anything.

"Do you come here often?" joked William, snorting lightly at his own wit.

White spots started to intersperse with the red flecks, and, with teeth so clenched they were close to forming a vacuum, Marguerite replied, "No, I am just here on business," the esses being delivered in a manner so elongated as to create the perfect imitation of a talking snake.

"It's nice to travel for, um, work, isn't it? But it is important not to get too obsessed by your work."

"What are you on about?!" flashes of orange now mixing in with the white spots and red flecks.

"You know. You and Rick Wakeman. It's fine to be a fan, admirable even, but it is possible to take things too far and, um, things have changed. It's not the 60s anymore."

Marguerite looked at him uncomprehendingly for a moment; his kindly vicar-like look of beneficence filling her whole view. A moment cannot, however, last forever, and a sound like a whip crack suddenly rent the air. William disappeared from sight as fast as if a trap door had opened beneath him, and Marguerite stormed through the space where he had been but an instant before, vanishing in a vortex of anger. Max came over and helped William groggily back to his feet. On the side of his face was the prefect imprint of an iPhone.

"Hmm, I should say that's an 18, wouldn't you Jessica? See the way it curves round there?"

They sat William down and fetched him a drink. In fact, Max ordered three large Plymouth gin and tonics, reckoning that he could always drink Jessica's.

"That's nice," said Jessica, blowing his chances. "What kind of gin is this?"

Max briefly explained the history of Plymouth Gin and how it often won out against all-comers in blind tastings but was not produced in large quantities because it had to be made in Plymouth itself, or at least until a large multinational who didn't give a toss bought it.

William started to regain his senses and was clearly somewhat confused by his experience. "She's completely mad. I had no idea that obsession could do that to a person. No idea at all."

Jessica excused herself and disappeared to the bathroom.

"Sorry to drag you into all of this, William. I feel somehow guilty," Max said.

"Not your fault. Not your fault at all. You know, I think I will have to try to help that girl."

"If I were you, I'd leave extremely well alone. Next time, she might not just hit you with a phone."

"No, I think it's important I point out to her that her behaviour is unacceptable and that there is treatment available. I will spend some time looking into it. I will also warn Mr. Wakeman if I see him."

Right on cue, a large and slightly shambolic figure in stretch purple and green meandered into the bar humming "Nellie the Elephant."

"Look, William, I bet that's Rick Wakeman at the bar. I think I recognise him from your CD pile. He's the chap I spoke to a couple of days ago about his van blowing up. He must have checked in here afterwards."

Max was impressed how easily lying came to him. Perhaps he should consider politics after all.

"What, the old tramp?" William asked.

"Yes, yes, that's him. Let me have a quick word with him."

"Oh, hello, Max, what brings you to this mecca of the 1970s?" An overwhelming smell of duck fried in cologne hit Max like a planet colliding with an ant (or dec).

"I said to Marguerite that I would help out with printing your new posters and anything else that needed to be done. We agreed to meet here for a quick drink to discuss."

"That's very decent of you. Have you spoken to her already?"

"Yes, but she zoomed off a few minutes ago."

"Shame. I wanted to check up on my stalker."

"Marguerite told me all about it, and I've agreed to try to find out about her."

"That's incredibly decent of you. It was bloody uncomfortable getting stuck in that window, and I've spent an age de-canardising myself. Smells gone now, though, hasn't it?"

"Oh, yes, not even a trace left." Max checked his nose for growth. "I should tell you, though, that there's another person in the hotel who claims to be an artist but seems to be researching your life history. He's over there in the corner."

"Oh, God, that's all I need. A stalker and some crackpot journalist trying to dig the dirt. Never join a successful prog rock band, Max."

Max was able to assure Rick that he would strain every sinew to avoid such an occurrence. "But do you think he might be a private investigator, rather than a journalist? He doesn't look much like a journalist, does he? And you were telling me about er, Squiggs maybe being your daughter. You don't think this guy may be checking up on you?"

Rick turned pale and then took off vertically when a loud voice spoke from directly behind his left shoulder. "Mr. Wakeman, delighted to make your acquaintance. It's a pleasure meeting one of music's elder statesmen. My name is William. I'm an, er, um, artist staying at the hotel for a while. Very much looking forward to your concert. More of a James Last man myself, but I'm really planning to get to know your history."

Rick, out-blanching dubois, reeled and rocked. "Ah, hello, yes, Rick. You're an, er, um, artist, are you? Good place for painting is it, here?"

William assured him that it was and reached for his phone.

"See the seagulls..."

Rick looked haunted. The man was clearly a private investigator or ... maybe not. The dawning thought of having a crazed male stalker was absolutely terrifying. You couldn't even shag them before getting the restraining order.

"Yes, very nice. Very, very, very nice, er, what is that mark on your face?"

William had stepped into the light, and the iPhone imprint showed itself in stark relief.

"That was caused by one of your fans! A completely crazy woman with blonde hair. All I did was mention your name to her, and wham, she lashed out at me viciously with her phone. It was like I had got between a lioness and her prey."

A small blonde figure appeared in the bar doorway.

"Hi, guys."

Max had never supposed Rick to be much of an athlete, and the decades of good food and fine wine accumulating on his frame like a rock rolling down a mountain through particularly adhesive snow might, in any event, have been expected to have taken the edge off any remnants of sporting prowess. It was, therefore, with unbounded admiration that Max watched Rick vault clean over the bar from a standing start and vanish through the bar staff door without his feet seeming to have ever reconnected with the ground.

"Was that Rick?"

"Yes, you've just missed him," Max replied. "He's off to his fitness class. Talking of which, I also need to fly as I've got someone coming round for dinner, and the microwave needs some TLC."

"I'll walk with you," said William with a degree of urgency. He rushed over and packed up his booty.

Max meanwhile exchanged phone and WhatsApp details with Jessica and suggested that they catch up before the fancy dress party.

"There's so much to talk about," he smiled.

"Yes, I get the feeling I'm missing something here. I mean, that stalker was plum crazy, and Rick seems to be really jumpy. And I'm not sure what William is going to do about it. Maybe he needs my help?"

"He definitely needs help. It's just a question of narrowing the list down to a single page."

They gave each other a peck on the cheek combined with a warm hug, and then William re-joined, and they took their leave.

Just outside the hotel, William held out his hand. "I am going up to my room to think and study. I just wanted an excuse to leave so I didn't get caught up in any conversations with Jessica about Rick. Here's my full contact details by the way," and he handed over an expensively embossed card with William Rutherford Art & Wine printed on it.

***

It was still wonderfully light, and Max stood looking out to sea for a few minutes, watching a few of the remaining care home escapees splashing about near the shoreline. For Max, entering any water with a temperature below about 28 degrees was tantamount to having an ice bath and, as ice was only for accompanying spirits, naturally, any persons swimming in temperatures at least 10 degrees below that were certifiable. If it were up to him, the names and addresses of all such people would be taken upon exiting the water to ensure that they were removed from the voting register. There was a long list of people Max would like to see removed from the voting register, and he was constantly reflecting on and revising the content of his proposed UnReform Act.

Reluctantly breaking his reverie, Max started the climb back up the long and winding stairs. He found a crowd of onlookers had gathered in the carpark and were looking at the back of a jacket and cap buried deep in the undergrowth. The clothing kept up a constant ripple of movement and was accompanied by the kind of noises a pig might make if it had accidentally snootered some red-hot chili peppers by mistake.

"It's completely disgusting," said an upstanding matriarch with an orangey rinse. "I mean to say I'm as tolerant as the next man, but where will it end?"

"Bloody foreigner!" chipped in another paragon of tolerance.

"I am not a foreigner," puffed the matriarch. "I come from Stafford."

"I wasn't talking to you, love, but while we're on the subject, why don't you bugger off back to the North and leave England to the real English like me and my mate here."

"F**k off, mate!! I come from Padstow and that's not in England. Frigging colonists!"

This friendly banter between tolerant people threatened to get too amusing for words, and so the local policeman intervened. He checked his phrasebook.

"Now look here, ladies and gentleman. Ooh, sorry, that should be look here, persons of any sexual identification or non-sexual identification and/or any combinations in between and/or other identities that may have not yet been classified, what's all this about?"

"There's a bloke stuck in a bush," said Max helpfully.

"And is he a foreigner?"

"I believe not, but the bush itself originates from Spain, if my horticultural knowledge serves me well."

"Bloody foreign bush. It must have attacked him!!" pitched in another local.

"Now then, persons of whatever I already recited earlier, let's get our facts straight before we start accusing anyone of anything."

"We'd never have had a bloody empire if we'd hung around waiting to get our facts straight, would we! It's clear that this here foreign bush attacked a British citizen. It doesn't matter if he's a screaming sexual deviant or not, that's his business, but what's not alright is Señor Bush here giving him one, er, at least without being asked to."

This little outburst went down well with the local citizenry, folks who still insisted on calling a spade a spade.

"Can I suggest that it might be a good idea to help separate the two of them and then worry about who, if anyone, to arrest?" Max offered.

"Thank you, sir, er, person, er pardon, damn! Bollocks!"

"Nicely summed up, Constable. Can I be of assistance?"

Together they clambered into the undergrowth and, obtaining what meagre purchase they could, the man being so deeply entrenched, heaved for all they were worth. At first all that happened was that the moaning noise increased ten-fold as the bush redoubled its efforts to hold its prey fast by whatever means it could. But little by little, progress was made until, with a great cry of agony and the rending of material, something approaching a human form emerged. All that was left of the man's clothing was a torn undershirt and some threads of underwear, while his whole face and head were adorned with a wreath of twigs and leaves, leaving just a pair of bloodshot eyes peering out through the foliage.

"He's one of them Distinction Rebellion blokes, isn't he?" intoned a local worthy. "You know, like that Bonobo bloke that's always trying to save the world from overpopulation. He does a great job, I've got to say. Lectures most people to death and then finishes off any survivors by singing to them."

"Now then, what were you doing cosying up to that there bush?" asked the constable.

The man tried to speak but was greatly impeded by the amount of foliage in his mouth. In the manner of a conjuror, he kept pulling out leaves, one after the other. A veritable small forest's worth finally emerged, and it was all Max and the others could do to not applaud the feat.

"Man told me, nature, commune, feel younger," were the only words that came out of his mouth in the end, and you could see that the crowd was not nearly so impressed by the denouement as with the leaf trick itself. It lacked the killer punch somehow.

"Come again?"

"Slide rail, bush, nature, commune, guarantee younger feel, stuck!" the man yowled in an agonised wail.

"Alright, sir, I've got no choice but to take you in for questioning on the grounds of damaging public property, namely Bush One, possibly of

Spanish origin, as well as the possible performance of a lewd sexual act with said foreign bush, and finally, for incorrect and improbable sentence construction."

The man was led away, scattering unconnected words and leaves in equal number as Max hopped up the remaining steps to the road and popped through the gates to his garden.

***

There was still time to tidy up a bit and sort out some food options, so Max whizzed around with his Dyson, grabbed a duster and transferred several layers of dust off his kitchen and coffee tables back onto the floor and put some stuffed olives in an old Fortnum & Mason bowl. The cupboard under the stairs held the wine supplies, and Max picked out a couple of bottles of Julien de Savignac's Bruno red; he was a sucker for the basset hound on the front, and another two bottles of Pinot Grigio for the fridge. Thinking again, he replaced the Pinot Grigio and opted instead for Sharpham Valley Estates `Yellow` Sauvignon Blanc. The photo on the front was supposed to be Chris Martin, but actually bore a closer resemblance to Thom Yorke, which Max thought could only help with credibility and sales.

Satisfied with arrangements, Max sought out a few more stories from *Death Ray* while listening to the soothing voice of Sekou Kouyate over the speakers. So soothing that he may have dozed for some twenty winks before being propelled back to the present by the sound of the doorbell and Scabies's half-hearted bark.

"That's a wonderful bell," said Fizz, all bounce.

"I picked it up online. It plays whatever you like from your playlist. Today is 'Hippopotamus' by Sparks. Know them? They've been going for ever but just get better and better. Piano player has a Charlie Chaplin moustache but talks a lot less."

Fizz dropped her bag on the floor and out spilled notebooks and coloured pens.

Max pointed out, "I like the way that you name your lyric books with different themes. I'm not disciplined enough for that. It would take someone constantly holding a gun to my head to get me to do that, and you can't believe how expensive that is nowadays. Anyway, what can I get you to drink? How about some white? It's a local vineyard with an excellent reputation, and they've just done a hook-up with Coldplay."

"That's not bad at all, and my God, I needed that. Same again please! Er, isn't that Thom Yorke on the front of the bottle? Bit of a mistake, that, surely."

"No, I think that was their ploy to sell the stuff to more discerning customers. I enjoy seeking out the new ways old rock musicians find to make money. No one sells records any more unless they're the tattooed ginger bloke."

"Sheeran?"

"Sorry, no bland language in this house please!! Olive?"

They settled down with their drinks, and Fizz picked up an olive.

"No green sausages today?"

"No, they were a special treat for famous musicians. Of course, that could be you soon."

"Oh, my God, the course is a nightmare! I'm so out of my depth it's unbelievable."

"But you only started this morning. How is that possible when all you had to do was write something about the 80s? Wasn't The Yeti any help?"

"Not really. Most of what he experienced we couldn't use. He was in some kind of secret army unit, and as far as I could tell, it was all sex and drugs, and they weren't very particular about the sex. It turns out that he got given the name Yeti by his mates, not because of his appearance, but because that was the only animal he hadn't slept with."

"So, no bestiality then, but that doesn't leave much. What were you up to in the 80s?"

"At school, so it's mostly braces on my teeth and crushes on pop stars."

"Simon Le Bon, David Bowie, Jon Bon Jovi, that kind of thing?"

"Nick Cave, Jaz Coleman and Shaun Ryder were my pinups," Fizz answered.

"Hmm, you realise that you're doing a great job at making The Yeti's 80s sound quite appealing? Do you have what you wrote in the end?"

Fizz handed over a crumpled sheet of lined exercise book paper.

"Ok, so that's not bad at all. I don't know what you were worried about. It all scans well, and the rhyming is not bad. Not sure Astley with ghastly quite works, but it's well intentioned I'm sure. Did you have to sing it as well?"

"Thank goodness no because we hadn't got as far as writing a tune. There wouldn't have been time for us anyway, as Stevo spent most of the afternoon telling us how brilliant Saff's song was about the threat of nuclear war and the need for peace. I'm not impressed by her voice. She uses so much vibrato and singing around the note that it's difficult to tell if there's really a tune."

"But all this should give you confidence. What about Usan? Who worked with Usan?" Max asked her.

"No one dared. Usan also wrote about nuclear war but from the angle of what Usan would have targeted for extermination, which was pretty much everything."

"Look, just stick with it. Songwriting is all about what you want to express. There's no right or wrong, just stuff that sells and stuff that doesn't. And let's face it, most of the music that does sell you'd pay not to have written."

"Thanks, keep on with boosting my confidence. More wine will also help. Do you by any chance have anything to eat that's not rice? I know it's a long shot, but I just throw it out there for entertainment value."

"I'm truly shocked by your low expectations. I'll have you know that I paid my annual visit to the supermarket and have bought food so varied and so exotic some of it doesn't even have a name, or hopefully, a visible use-by date."

With a regal gesture, Max opened the fridge for Fizz to examine and approve his culinary delights.

"My goodness, this is full. This could feed a whole American family for breakfast. It must have cost you a fortune!"

"My pleasure. No expense spared. Consider yourself to be my American family."

"Ah, such a compliment. I really can't understand why you are single."

"It's a constant battle. I try to hide the politeness and charm, but frankly, it's a futile battle."

"This round spiky thing, is it a fruit or a vegetable?"

"I was assuming some kind of vegetable but, on second thought, it might be a small hedgehog. Do you like hedgehogs?"

"Not whole. And squid and marmite fritters, is this a local speciality?"

"Yes, or at least it takes a certain discerning kind of person to eat them. I thought that person could be you. If I'm honest, the squid sounds healthy but yucky. However, marinated in finest yeast extract and it could be quite unlike anything you've ever had before."

"That's what worries me. I think I'll pass on the squid, thanks."

She rummaged some more, picking up packets and then putting them back quickly. "I'm beginning to feel that rice might not be such a bad option," she sighed.

"I cleaned the microwave specially, just in case. And rice can be delicious with sauces and condiments, you know. Usually I stick with olive oil, but there's nothing like grinding a bit of pepper on top or spicing it up with a soupcon of tabasco."

"I don't know how you survive. Really, I don't. Ah, at last! Chicken fillets, potatoes, tomatoes and garlic bread. Walnut ice cream, too. You do have some things that an ordinary person would recognise!"

"Yes, but it's a mystery to me how they get from there to the plate."

"It's called cooking. You do have a stove, don't you?"

"Oh, you're not going to mess up my stove, are you?! It's the cleanest thing in the house."

A squid fritter connected with Max's back. "Ok, ok, careful, squid can be dangerous. Did you know that a Japanese woman ate raw squid and had her tongue fertilised with eggs? No? I thought that would interest you. Only joking, put the hedgehog down!"

Fizz somewhat reluctantly relented and went in search of cooking implements.

"There are some cooking pot things under the counter, and a frying pan, too. You'll need to just give them a quick dust."

Fizz pulled out a sorry looking frying pan.

"That's fine, a little steel wool will lift the rust. Rust acts as a protector, you know? Ow! I'm beginning to think that you're quite a violent person."

"That's so true. The Dutch are so nice that I've had to supress all these angry feelings for years and years. But just two days of knowing you has allowed me to release those pent-up feelings. Thank you so much. It just feels so natural to want to hit you."

"Glad to be of service. You wouldn't mind just finishing up the cooking, would you, while I look after the wine?"

Another squid fritter zinged past Max's right ear and caught Scabies right in the chops. Or would have if it hadn't been for some last-minute remedial action in the form of opening his mouth wide.

"You've made a friend for life there. Hey! I've thought of the perfect win-win situation solution for your anger issues. When you feel an irresistible urge to make public your scorched soul, you could focus your murderous thoughts on me but actually throw the food at Scabies. Then everyone's happy, and honour is fully satisfied."

Several hours later, suitably replenished, satisfactorily wined and having finished with attempting to put the world at rights, Max and Fizz turned their thoughts to current events in Mead Bay.

"I heard from Glen at the café that you volunteered your course to provide the entertainment at this weekend's fancy dress party. Given your current feelings about the course, isn't that tantamount to a death wish?" Max began.

"Oh, I'm not going to play at all. I was actually volunteering Stevo. Firstly, I thought that he might see me in a new and positive light, and secondly, my evil little mind thought that it might be fun to see him perform to a load of drunken holiday makers."

"Very good thinking, Moriarty. Let's just hope that he takes the bait."

"Oh, I think he will. I might just have mentioned that a famous rock star is down here and may come along. Plus, he thinks you are a music journalist, and he knows I know you. Do you think Rick will come along?"

"That I doubt. As soon as his beloved van is repaired, he's going to hot wheel it back to the castle to get some practice in. But Marguerite is likely to be down here and besides which, as this is a masked party, who knows what rock stars may turn up?"

"Fantastic, I hadn't thought of that. You're a genius! We could set him up wonderfully," Fizz said enthusiastically.

"Thanks for the praise, but the idea only came to me as I was speaking. But it could be fun, couldn't it?

"It's perfect!"

"A glass of Bruno while we discuss our plans? I also need to bring you up to speed on everything else that's been going on. Maybe two glasses?"

During the course of what turned out to be slightly more than two glasses of wine, Max, to her increased amusement and amazement, put Fizz firmly in the picture viz the various scenarios that were playing out in their end of the bay.

"Wow, this place is so much more exciting than I ever imagined possible," she said. "I must meet this William, as he seems to be great entertainment value. And I'm intrigued by Jessica and her mysterious late-night walks."

At this point, Fizz cast her eye out into the gloom as if half expecting to see Jessica floating by. "And Rick and Marguerite, that's just so funny! Maybe we should all pretend to be his children?"

"No need to pretend. I read that a high proportion of the world is related to Genghis Khan, and he wasn't even in a band."

"What would you do if you were related?"

"It's quite simple. There's a British comedy movie from the 1950s called *Kind Hearts and Coronets* in which the main character gradually bumps off all his rivals. I have memorised the plot and feel certain that my Alec Guinness disguise will work a treat."

"Alec Guinness?"

"Famous British actor, best known for being in the original *Star Wars* as Obi-Dobi. Not that I'm a science fiction fan apart from *Alien*, which I can at least relate to."

"What about *2001: A Space Odyssey*?"

"That's not science fiction, that's just genius! The music alone makes the film worth watching. But just imagine what classic films would be like with different music? In *2001*, for example, replace the Khachaturian with 'Space Trukkin' by Deep Purple, and the Strauss with Scott Joplin's 'The Entertainer,' and you get a whole different film! Also, think 'Jive Talkin' when Clint comes into town as the Man with No Name. And, what about taking that scary music out of *Psycho* and replacing it with 'Self-Preservation Society' from *The Italian Job*? You could turn horror movies into comedies and vice-versa. Come to think of it, if you put the *Psycho* music into *The Office* whenever Rocky Gervais appears, that would be much more realistic. Genuinely creepy bloke, isn't he, and it's not acting either. Did you know that Stephen Merchant actually started out as his psychiatric nurse?"

"Er, no, but can you help me with my homework at all?" Fizz asked.

"Underprivileged children to the tune of 'Happy Talk?' Should be a breeze."

Max retrieved his Washburn, sucked on his edible, Alex James, hard-cheese pick thoughtfully for a few seconds, then sang,

"Poor unhappy, happy, Yankee kids
Give them a gun and send them off to school
'Cause if they can't have a dream
To play keyboards in D:Ream
Then why shouldn't they shoot a kid or two?
Not too dark, you think?"

"No, excellent, very cheery. I think this may lay down a real challenge to Usan. Only, don't you think the kids would just shoot themselves if they had to be in D:Ream?"

"Maybe you're right. It's my Brian Cox fixation coming out again. Just imagine how different the world would have been if he'd just stayed put? Ok, how about if we replace the D: Ream line with *To become king or queen*?"

"And the gender non-aligned kids?"

"That's why the 'or' is there. But we're talking privileged Western kids, right? What about those in the rest of the world who don't get a choice?"

"Good point."

"It's easy to forget the rest of the world," said Max, continuing to proselytise tangentially, "and to mistakenly assume that your country is somehow inherently better, more cultured and civilised than all others just because it is doing well at the moment. Total bollocks of course. Just read some history. In my view, all exceptionalists should be strung up by their shortcomings. Of course, when I become prime minister, I reserve the right to completely change my mind and do whatever's best for me."

"Why stop at prime minister, what about becoming Supreme Being!"

"Already self-appointed. Don't like to publicise it too much, though, just in case I find myself put in a higher tax bracket by non-believers."

"Can I try out your keyboards?" said Fizz, changing the subject. "I have got a song about a wolf that needs finishing,"

"Be my guest. You'll find that the fourth C above middle C is sometimes reluctant to work due to its imbibing rather more brandy than was good for it."

"That's ok, the fourth C above middle C is totally uncharted territory for both wolves and me."

"It may be a coincidence, but I also wrote a song about a wolf at university. There were lots of them about in those days on campus. I was lucky to escape intact. Young love, eh?"

"I think you may be talking about what used to be called girls, while I am talking about a real male wolf. He was gorgeous," Fizz stated.

"I'll take your word on it. Out of my frame of reference a bit, that, but go for what you want in life. Now, put down those maracas! Ow, no, ow! If I was a wolf I'd make myself scarce if you were on the prowl, extremely alluring and attractive though you are."

"Did you just call me extremely alluring and attractive?"

"Ah, well yes, but you know context is everything, so don't get upset."

Fizz looked at Max in an extremely alluring and attractive manner. "But you did say it, and that's what counts. It's good to see you open up like that. Come over here and sit down beside me."

A man about town would have spotted the humour behind the statement. However, Max was not a man about town type but much more a man about a dog type.

"Ho! Ho! Yes, Ha! Ha! More wine? Or rather less because I guess, yes, you'll be off now to finish the song, both songs in fact, at the hotel, up the hill. Take the keyboards with you, and text me with the result, which I'm sure will be tremendous. Have your bikes arrived yet because it would be fun to try them out. Perhaps a ride around the bay? Feel free to come over for a spot of breakfast any time, or tomorrow, in fact."

And with this, Max spun around, picked up a coat and handed it to Fizz. Fizz handed it back, as it was Max's coat.

"Take it, take it, it's no problem."

"Am I to understand you are throwing me out?" she said in mock imperious tone.

"Not at all, not at all," said Max in a dramatically casual way, his swinging hands sending the hanging light crashing upwards against the ceiling and plunging the room into darkness.

"Ooh, that's nice," Fizz said. "So romantic. But get off your knees and, um perhaps less licking my legs."

"Scabies, get off her! Sorry about that. Let me find the other light switch a second."

Light returned to show Max deftly positioned by the stairs and Scabies gently being whacked on the nose by Fizz.

"Ah, well, more rejection," sighed Fizz. "But I can take it, and it will be good for my songwriting."

At the front door, Fizz turned to Max and said, "Actually, the bikes arrived late afternoon. I haven't had time to unpack them yet, but I'll bring one round tomorrow for you to trial. Do you think the others would like one, too?"

"I think William's a certainty if it's free, and Jessica if she can get one in a dark colour with no lights. As for Rick and Marguerite, I'm not sure. It's probably been four decades since Rick was on a bike, and his centre of gravity has shifted dangerously in that time. But if it has a drink holder and bottle of something good to put in it, you may win him over. Marguerite will probably blow the dynamo with her energy levels, but it could be a good test of the bike's endurance. By the way, I advise you to go up by the public path, as the hotel gate has vanished along with half the wall."

"Yes, I saw that. There's something strange going on at that place. I keep finding staff following me around."

"It's probably just your being so alluring and attractive that does it."

"Yes, but of course, you're so right. Goodnight."

Max pottered about, clearing up plates and liberating the rest of the wine from the bottle. He made a mental note to drop by the café in the morning to ask Glen if he wanted any additional posters for the fancy dress party mentioning the entertainment. After that he settled down, in a manner of speaking, with Dave Davies to see the latest horrors being inflicted on him. One of them seemed to be having his minute-long, proto-metal guitar solo stripped out of "Dedicated Follower of Fashion." Eventually, Max found his way to bed. The yellow submarine needed a wash, and he rifled through his wardrobe looking for a suitable replacement for the morrow. Settling on the *Who's Next* duvet cover, he extinguished the lights and prepared not to sleep.

***

Strangely, sleep after a fashion did creep up on Max, and he woke tired but refreshed after a dream in which his former bosses had all died in a freak, exploding ego accident. Unlike the previous morning, Max had time to get up in leisurely manner before he heard the unmistakeable sound of a bicycle bell ringing persistently outside the house. He opened the front door to see a bounce of Fizz with not one, but two bikes.

"Morning!" she chirruped. "I thought we could take the bikes and have breakfast at the beach café."

"What a clever idea, and you've managed to find the one mode of transport that will take us twice as long to get to the café as walking. Let's go!"

Max quickly grabbed his phone and locked up. The e-bike worked surprisingly well going down the hill he noted. Almost as well as an ordinary bike.

At the café, the e-bikes, with their bold "Endorsed by the Duke of Attenborough, and a damn sight faster" logo attracted attention. Some old tweed dress said, "I love that there duke, and I remember him when he was young. You remember, Fred," as she elbowed a crumpled red cardigan, "it were when the world was still black and white."

"Oh, yes, I remember that. But he wasn't young even then, mind. He started when it wasn't just black and white but silent, too. All those animal noises were added in by Attenborough later on, you know?"

"Now that's what I call talent. I reckon he probably invented some of those animals."

"What'll it be Max and, er, Fringe?" Glen asked.

"Fizz."

"Fizz. The old full English or the post-Brexit special?"

"What's the special?"

"Soup."

"Old English for me," said Max.

"Do you have a Dutch breakfast? It's the same as the English but with a side of grass," said Fizz, with a wink.

"We're out of grass aren't we, Cee?"

"I can get some if you like, but it may be a bit doggy."

"Doggy?"

"It's near the edge of the path."

"Ok, ok. Cee, why don't you just make the tea?"

"Why are you smiling at me like I'm crazy? It's not me who ordered grass for breakfast!"

Max and Fizz sipped their respective teas and contemplated the sea meandering gently in the soft morning light.

"It's going to take a lot of work to put a stage up around that rock," Fizz observed, shaking her head fizzily. "I don't understand how they will get health and safety clearance."

Max rubbed his fingers together. "Money talks in a place like this. Pay enough to the right people, and you can get anything done."

"Yes, but there could be consequences, surely? People could get badly injured."

"And you think that comes above money in the back pocket? Do you know nothing about how local government works, my poor child?"

A buzzer went off indicating that breakfast was ready.

Cee looked at Fizz and smiled. "Sorry about the grass, but I managed to find some spinach instead."

An enormous plate piled with spinach, looking unerringly like a fresh cow pat, complete with rising steam, was handed over with due ceremony.

"Oh, thank you so much," Fizz said. "You've made my day. Never have I seen so much spinach in one place before." Back in her seat, Fizz turned to Max and exhorted him to eat spinach. "That's taught me a lesson. Never make jokes in public."

"Don't be too hard on yourself. We are talking Cee here, and she's hardly the public."

"Hello, hello, mind if I join you?" asked William merrily. "And who is this lovely lady?"

"William, this is Fizz, and vice-versa."

"He's such a charmer, isn't he?" joked William.

"Not that I had noticed" replied Fizz, deadpan.

"Aha! I'll just order some breakfast."

Max and Fizz watched with anticipation as William approached the counter.

"Can I help you?" said Cee.

"I see you do spinach, but it's not on the menu. Can I have some with the old English breakfast?"

"I am sorry, but that was a one-off special. The lady ordered a side plate of grass, and we didn't have any, but I did manage to find a packet of spinach. I'm afraid I gave it all to her."

"Any cocaine or heroin then? I'm sure that Glen knows all about it, eh? Birrrmingham is full of the stuff!"

Cee looked confused.

"We don't sell drugs, do we, Glen?"

"Not yet, Cee, no, but we do serve idiots."

This sailed harmlessly over William's head in the manner of a delicate butterfly floating on a sweet, summer breeze.

"A side plate of idiots then, please," he beamed.

Cee looked worried.

"Glen, is this something new because no one ever explains anything to me, and why am I here doing this?"

"I'll tell you what I can do, sir. How about a lovely steak for breakfast? Just got one left, gift of the Wakeman establishment," Glen offered.

"Now that sounds perfect."

William re-joined at an awkward moment as Max and Fizz had just exchanged some whispered words and looked close to tears.

"Everything all right?"

"Never better," said Max, dabbing his eyes, while Fizz had her face buried in a handkerchief.

"It's probably that there's too much fresh air here and not enough grass for a Dutch person." William winked at Max.

"That's so true. However, Fizz is only an amateur admirer of the green stuff. Her parents on the other hand, whoa! They have to take their holidays in remote areas of the countryside so as to be kind to the environment, but you can always find where they are staying by the fact that the squirrels are lying under the trees reading Ginsberg, and the birds are singing free-form jazz."

"Have some grass substitute, William, and tell me all about your painting," Fizz said, looking guileless. "Max tells me you hold master classes in Paris."

"He's too kind. But it's true that I have held a number of classes for those interested in the abstract view of the world. Abstract minimalism requires a great deal of thought. I was originally inspired by Sippl's writings, then followed through with Reiter, before getting into Cheetham. I held an exhibition recently. Let me show you." William reached for his phone and scrolled to himself for a while. "Here you are."

"Most impressive. That's a very industrial kind of setting, too. Some kind of warehouse?"

"My bathroom. I felt that for a first exhibition it was a good idea to create an intimate atmosphere."

"Did you sell anything?"

"It was highly successful. I charged €5 to get in and €3 for a glass of wine. I made over €50. Here, let me show you some work in close-up."

Fizz was well prepared for this and looked over the photo with a practiced eye.

"It's shouting to me dark, sandy beach with, yes, unless I'm very much mistaken, seagulls everywhere. Really very good. Excellent, in fact."

"Um, well, yes, this ones's actually a portrait."

"Reeeally, uh huh. And the sand is then in fact earth?"

"Not quite. It's actually pube, pube, pube, er undergrowth."

"Very clever. I think you should do more portraits. There are a couple of people on my course, I'm doing a songwriting course, who would be really good subjects."

"I do believe that it is best to paint the subject au naturel in order to capture the true character of the sitter."

"Better and better, I mean, tremendous! I'll introduce you to some potential commissions on Saturday if that's ok."

"I do charge a fee, although, of course, for a friend of a friend I can offer a 2% discount."

Fizz was in a joyous reverie for a moment, and Max had to give her a nudge to remind her to eat her spinach.

A few seconds later, a juicy steak arrived for William.

"Steak à l`oeil, our speciality," said Glen, all brilliant, white teeth.

William tucked in as Max and Fizz watched from close up and Glen and Cee from a couple of feet farther back.

"This is so good. And that sauce is so creamy and rich, with nice, chunky, chewy bits. You two should have had the steak."

"We're enjoying you enjoying it."

A few minutes passed, but when nothing happened, Glen and Cee, slightly puzzled and disappointed, sloped off back to the kitchen.

"How's your research on Rick going?" Max asked.

"Very well, thanks. Although I must be missing some of his recordings, as there's no Status Quo here, just some pretty tortuous music with a band called Yes. The solo recordings are quite good, though. *Journey to the Centre of the Earth* and *The Mitts and Legs of King Arthur* are definitely worth hearing. By Saturday I should be able to impress Jessica enough for Stage Two."

"Don't ask, Fizz, and don't say, William," said Max intervening as a matter of urgency.

"What about the stalker?"

"Oh, yes," said Fizz gleefully, "tell us about her."

"I've decided to invite her for a quiet word this evening on the terrace. It's very important to help her understand that obsessive behaviour is destructive. I am going to suggest that she might like to have some art sessions with me as therapy."

"Oh, that's superb. Well beyond the bounds of what a normal, er, average person would do for someone like her. I'm sure she'll give you her full attention."

"I thought that I might ask Jessica, too, what do you think?"

"I think that you can have too much of a good thing. I recommend starting them off separately," Max said.

Fizz interrupted, "Look gentlemen, I need to head off to my course. William, how would you like to help trial an e-Bike?"

It was arranged that William would collect a bike from Fizz's hotel later on in the day. He was very enthusiastic about the thought of being able to venture further away to paint and was trying to work out how to carry his golf clubs with him.

Before leaving, Max picked up a draft poster for the fancy dress party from Glen and agreed to print up 250 copies. He noted that the evening would feature well-known singer-songwriter 'Stevo,' and it included a quote from the NME: *... startlingly... guitar laid over melodies... set to lyrics.*

"Good luck with today. Did you manage to finish off your homework?" he said to Fizz.

"With the aid of the mini-bar and God, yes," she answered. "A small bottle of Drambuie, followed by ten minutes with Gideon gave me all the inspiration I needed."

"Let me know how it goes. I might pop up if it gets interesting. Doesn't Stevo have any kind of agenda worked out?"

"He's giving it to us this morning. One of the things he wants us to do is get out into the countryside. He did mention holding a picnic somewhere called Dartmoor?"

"Yes, it's a huge national park about twenty miles from here. A great test for your e-bikes! Definitely count me in if you go there, although I may take the old Jag, just as back up of course."

"You're just lazy, you are!"

"That's very unfair. I haven't been called lazy in years. It's one of the reasons I don't talk to people much."

Max and Fizz parted ways, with Max deciding to trial the bike on nearby Murrain Drive, a steep hill with panoramic views at the end of the beach that wound along the cliffs before dipping down and re-joining the meadow at its far end.

Very expensive, flat-roofed, pre-fab houses, with that distinctive Soviet car park look now adorned its slopes, having replaced beautiful, but obviously not saleable enough, Victorian villas on the same sites. Most of the new homes were empty year-round, as their Russian owners presumably kept one step ahead of a sharp umbrella. Soon, no doubt, the Chinese would move in and reconstruct the area again. *At least that would add to the local cuisine somewhat,* thought Max. He hadn't noticed any Russian bars or restaurants popping up, only slightly more bodies than usual washing up on the shores.

***

The e-bike grumbled a bit, but it was nothing like the torture of cycling a normal bike up the hill, or worse still, running. On the crest of the hill, Max saw a thin, tallish man of Scandinavian appearance. He must have been in his mid-40s but looked well preserved. Not exactly handsome but with presence. As Max passed him, he was performing strange one-legged hops, as if trying to perfect his crane-mating skills.

"Hello," the man called out in perfect English with just a hint of the Bjorn and Benny's. "Have you seen any girls? I am missing some."

"Aren't we all?" Max replied somewhat waggishly.

The man cracked open a smile of white, uneven teeth.

"Aha, yes. I mean that I am missing three particular girls who were running with me and said they would catch me at the top of the hill."

"Maybe they decided not to catch you?"

"Ha, ha! That's never happened before, at least not with so few girls." He chuckled to himself and then reached over a surprisingly sweat free hand. "Sven," he said.

"Max," said Max.

With that came the noise of panting, and over the brow of the hill, came three of what Max could only describe as models, looking attractively dishevelled. They stopped in a heap by the two men.

"Oh, Svenny, you are in such good shape," said the first girl in an unmistakeable Russian purr. "How you do it?"

"My body is like, how you call it, a tentpole. During the day, I like to exercise it well so that it also remains strong and upright during the night."

"Ooh! Can I come camping with you?" said the second girl, with a French ring to her voice.

"Me, too. I just love communing with nature and all that," said the third girl, with a distinctive Texan twang.

"Are you guys at some kind of convention?" enquired Max.

"No," responded the Russian. "We are all down here for international beach volleyball competition, and we meet Svenny on the beach."

"You play beach volleyball, too, eh, Sven?"

"Ha, ha! No, I work for Kiruna Oil, and we are doing some surveying in the bay for the next few months. I happened to be on the beach doing my exercises when I bumped into the ladies. We decided to keep fit together."

"Where are you staying?" Max asked the Russian girl. "The Strand?"

"Yes, but it is not good. Since Brexit there are no proper staff, just poor people from North of England who don't speak English so good. What does 'Fancy a shag, loov' mean? Some kind of bread? If so, I don't want it. Bread here in England so white and limp."

"I'm afraid that you won't find many hotels down here that are habitable. Eighty years ago, yes, but not now. The best places to stay nowadays are the converted villas that have six to eight rooms. But, if you want a bigger place, then the Mead Bay View Hotel is close to here, and, while the clientele date from Roman times, it does have a fantastic view and a crazy Italian manager. There's also a songwriting course taking place there with some interesting characters on it."

"Ok, we check it out. Thanks."

"Sven, are you at the same place?"

No, I am stuck on the edge of town at the Corbyn's Rock Hotel. It's ok but too remote for a long stay, so I am also thinking about moving. Have you heard of the Sedgefield?"

"Yes, that's one of the small hotels I was mentioning. It's just on the street below where I live. Here, take a card with my details. If you fancy a drink later on, just give me a buzz. I can also introduce you to a few other strangers who are based here for a while, although it looks like you don't need many introductions."

"Oh, I am always interested in meeting new people. Thanks, I'll give you a call."

With that, Max left the group and continued on his way down the other side of the hill and then hung a right up to the village to buy a lottery ticket at the Post Office. Admittedly, he was getting somewhat disillusioned with buying lottery tickets. He had planned meticulously how to spend the money, and yet every time, some complete imbecile won instead. Now, Max knew that the odds against winning were long, but surely a lot of people were automatically disqualified from winning on the grounds of overwhelmingly self-evident stupidity? That should leave him with at least a one in four chance of the jackpot every week, but somehow, it hadn't happened.

As he was waiting for his ticket to be processed, Max glanced at the wood pulp pile, or newpapers, as some people still insisted on calling them. A partially hidden headline caught his eye, and, with not inconsiderable embarrassment, he found himself buying a copy of the *Daily Empire*.

Back home, with Scabies asleep on his crossed feet, and nursing a restorative cup of Yorkshire breakfast tea, Max opened up the paper.

"Rat Denies Naked Dog Dancing Act," was emblazoned across the front page.

Rat Scabies, 65, former drummer of legendary punk band The Damned, has denied claims of animal cruelty over an alleged new show involving him dancing naked with a black Labrador. Speaking from his private island home in the Caribbean, Scabies said, "I don't have a bloody clue what you're talking about, mate. I don't even have a bloody Labrador, and the only time you'll find me dancing naked is on Sensible's grave." When presented with the evidence of two fans who saw him performing the act in Mead Bay and who he signed autographs for, Scabies became upset and angrily accused our reporter of not being a terribly nice person, adding that all autograph signing was anyway done by his valet. On being asked how he could afford a Caribbean island in the absence of having a successful naked dog dancing act, Scabies, in between acute observations about our reporter's character, told the Daily Empire that The Damned "were huge" in places like the Faroe Islands, Siberia, and Bhutan. "We literally raked it in as we always got paid in goods. The Siberian salt alone made me a million, so let's stop all this naked dog dancing bollocks, shall we? Sensible's behind this, isn't he?" We contacted Captain (now Admiral) Sensible, 66, lead guitarist and band philosopher, who denied the claim but said that it sounded like a great idea for The Damned and would help keep lead singer Dave Vanian, 83, on his toes. We tried to contact Mr. Vanian, but he was uncontactable on holiday in Transylvania.

Max took a photo of the article and sent it to Marguerite and Fizz with a "LOL" message and hoped that Rat never found out who was really behind it. He then spent a frustrating couple of hours trying to sort out a printer problem. The printer kept saying that it was out of paper, and Max kept hitting it and telling it it was not. Eventually, mustering up all his technical skills, he picked the printer up and dropped it from the height of about a metre. The fascia cracked, the paper extension section snapped off, but the message disappeared. Result.

***

Feeling peckish at lunchtime, Max rifled around in the cupboard and found some biscuits to eat with a bit of Newport Blue Cheese. The biscuits did taste a bit of calcium, and were vaguely bone-shaped, but went down well enough. Scabies was disgusted, however, and went to chew on broken bits of printer as a consolation.

Having finished his snack, Max went out to inspect work on the hotel gate. Progress had been remarkable. The stonework had been re-built, and four massive hinges inserted to take the monstrous weight of the gate. The gate itself had been given a full protective undercoat and, by the look of the various pots of paint lying around, was about to be transformed into a work of art. The only thing that had not fared well was the tree against which the gate had been leaning. It was now at a gravity defying angle that even the Tower of Pisa would have been justifiably jealous of.

Max walked through the gap and up the garden path to the hotel. He could see that the songwriters were still having lunch and wandered over to talk to them. But before he could reach them, Fizz detached herself and rushed over. Max thought it was to discuss the Scabies story, but it became clear that she had not read his message yet.

"The manager has gone completely nuts! I went back to my room after breakfast to find that my bags had gone. So, I rushed down to reception and was informed that the manager had personally moved my stuff to the bridal suite. He must be a total pervert!"

"He hasn't tried anything on with you, has he?"

"No, but as I said, he and the whole staff seem to follow me around."

"And the service is bad?"

"No, no, actually, it is too good. Even the gardener came up to me this morning and asked my views on colours for the new gate and how he hoped that I would enjoy using it. It's all very weird."

"That's Mead Bay for you. Last bastion of eccentricity. I take it you haven't read my message yet?"

"No." Fizz scrolled though her messages. "Ha, ha! That's brilliant! Is Dave Vanian really eighty-three?"

"Older. It's those blood transfusions in Transylvania each year that keep him going. Any news about the picnic?"

"Oh, yes, it's planned for Thursday if the weather holds. Jeff is very excited because he can use his alpine horn for the first time. So far, he has had to make do with a kazoo, and it sort of spoils the effect. Mind you, with the amount he smokes, I would have thought that a kazoo is about all he can blow."

"How is he going to carry an alpine horn? Those things are massive!"

"The modern ones are collapsible, so actually, it's not too bad, but still, he might want to go with a lazy person in their car."

"You see, I do have a purpose in life after all!"

"Yes, but it's hardly what your parents would have planned for you."

"No, but when you combine it with bespoke former boss eradication services, it starts to look like a half-decent CV. What's on the agenda for this afternoon?"

"We're supposed to be learning about chord progressions and how they create different moods and soundscapes. I'm actually looking forward to it, although Stevo has become more obsessed by Saff than ever. She just needs to say something remotely intelligent, and he treats her like a guru. It's sickening."

"What do the others think?"

"That's just it. Somehow, they don't seem to notice how stupid he is. Maybe it's just me being jealous because I have no looks or talent."

Max was silent, distracted by one of the elderly residents keeling over on the lawn.

"Oi! You're supposed to disagree with me!" Fizz exclaimed.

"Sorry, I got distracted for a moment, what did you say?"

"That's even worse! Do I even exist?"

"Now don't be like that. You're sounding like Cee down at the café, and there's no room for two of you. Oh, look, she's not dead after all," said Max looking over at where the old lady had been helped to her feet and was now laughingly re-enacting her fall for the staff. "That's why I got distracted while you were having your existential crisis. Do you think the staff place bets on who's going to go next?"

"That could be me in forty years' time," reflected Fizz.

"Stop being so gloomy, it might be less than that. Ow!!"

Fizz overextended herself in whacking Max and found herself deposited on the grass at his feet.

"Just getting some practice in?"

Max leaped gracefully away from the dangerously low punch.

"Are there any evening activities for the group? Campfire singing?

Morris dancing? Ouija Board sessions with long dead musicians? Maybe Stevo could even get in touch with his career?"

"Stevo has in-depth Saff sessions lined up, and that's about it. But I'm going to suggest going out for a pizza tonight with anyone who's interested. Interested?"

"Definitely. I suggest the Da Vinci near the harbour. It's like a family-owned Pizza Express and can seat big groups easily. If you text me, I can make a booking. I might ask a guy I met after leaving the café if he wants to come. He's called Sven."

"Tall, thin guy who does crane-mating impressions, followed by girls?"

"That's him."

"I met him in Amsterdam. Nice guy, very, er, fit. Hates not being remembered."

"Small world. Right, I'm off to have a word with hotel reception. Sven's current girls talked about moving from The Strand Hotel to here, and I want to check if they called up or not."

Max left Fizz to go back to her course and strolled around to the main hotel. In the entry area, he felt a swoosh of air as the manager rushed up to him.

"It is so nice to see you again, Mr. Ahrenbee," he gushed. Max instinctively stood to one side having experienced managerial-level halitosis before. On this occasion, though, his fears were uncalled for as he sniffed nothing worse than a questionable aftershave, Canal No. 6 perhaps, peeking its head through the surface of a powerful wave of grappa.

"You see," continued the manager, "we are making a very nice gate which I will ask the countess to open, although, of course, I will not say anything officially about her status. But maybe you will come? I have also changed her to a much more suitable room, and listen, I have found some Dutch music to play in the hotel." He looked serious for a moment. "This was not easy to do, I will admit. The Dutch are maybe not so big on music, but Spotify help me a lot."

Max listened and could hear the strains of "Radar Love" by Golden Earring floating around in the ether. A slightly strange ether.

"The damp on the lawn is more of a problem, but I am working on a solution," the manager added.

"I am sure the countess will approve your efforts. I came to check whether some ladies that I mentioned the hotel to this morning have called? A Russian lady in particular?"

"You mean the sports lady? Yes, she is coming this afternoon to check the place for herself. Do you know much about her?"

"Only that she is one of about 100 beach volleyball players who are staying in Mead Bay for an international tournament. She is not very happy at The Strand."

The manager placed his hand on his head a moment to stop it erupting.

"You do know what beach volleyball is?"

"Yes, yes, all those healthy professional ladies. So talented. So..." Words failed him at this point, and he mopped his brow. "But the countess, will she approve this kind of guest? Most of our guests are quite old and very quiet. The only exercise they take is to breathe, and some of them, you know, are not very good at that."

"I think the countess will be delighted," Max assured him. "This hotel used to be famous for its, er, classy society, and what could be better to show how modern the Mead View is?"

"You are right! I will lay on the red carpet for this Russian lady, no?"

"I'm sure that will be a treat for her, although I'm not convinced you're her type."

Max left and walked up to Devil's View, at the far and of which sat a wooden voluntary Coast Watch Tower. Max could hear a heated argument coming from the far side and went to investigate. There he found William, with canvas, easel and a bag of paints engaged in conversation with a vexed looking old man with grey whiskers and a faded nautical cap.

"Ah, hello, Max," said William in a jovial manner. "Just trying to persuade Captain Birdseye here to let me use the tower to paint the bay."

"This is not an artists' colony," the old man interjected. "We do a serious job here preventing accidents at sea and can't have every Tom, Dick and...
"

"William."

"Every Tom, Dick and..."

"William."

"Will you stop that! I won't have you being disrespectful to the Royal family."

"So, saying Harry's ok, is it?"

"Perfectly fine. Not a recognised member of the Royal family."

"So, you're a royalist, are you?" Max asked.

"Yes, sir, and proud of it, too."

"You know that the Countess of Arnhem is staying at the Bay View? Relative of William of Orange. I'm sure she'd like to visit the tower."

The old man took off his cap smartly to reveal a polished dome. "That would be an honour, sir. Does she like Jaffa cakes?"

"Anything orange. In fact, she's quite insistent on things being orange, but that's hardly surprising, is it?"

"No, sir, not at all. Very correct. When might she be expected?"

"I will let you know. But sometime later this week. Now, I'll just be taking this gentleman with me."

Max smiled at William and gently turned him away. "I've got a better spot for you," he whispered.

Turning back to the old man, he leaned in conspiratorially and said, "Lucky for you I came along when I did. That's William Rutherford, one of the Rutherford twins. You know, Pennan gang kings? Only just got out of maximum security. Total psychopath. Very violent if crossed. Sees humans as mere strips of paint!"

The old man slammed the door of the tower shut faster than Chuck Berry pocketing cash, and Max could hear the lock being turned and what sounded like a piece of heavy furniture being dragged across it.

Satisfied, Max directed William towards the coastal footpath leading off the plain.

"If you go down there about 30 metres, you'll see a small promontory on the left which has a clear view across the bay, while also allowing you to look down on people walking on the path. It's a perfect observation spot."

Leaving him there, Max retraced his steps back to the road above the hotel. As he was passing it by, the unmistakeable figure of Marguerite could be seen coming around the side of the building wheeling two e-bikes. She was struggling somewhat and hallooed at Max.

"Hey, Max, lover boy! Give us a bloody hand will you! I got a text from Frizz asking if we'd like to try out these bikes, but they're a real bugger to push. She's quite amusing, that girl. I asked her if she wanted Rick's endorsement, and she told me, no, she didn't want to kill off the project at this early stage."

Max took one of the bikes from her. "Shall we ride them down to the harbour and have a tea there?"

"Ok, good thought, and it's better than hanging around that crazy hotel. Honestly, you come down to stay in a forgotten backwater of history, where you don't expect to find more than a few old ladies with blue rinses feeding the gulls, and it ends up being full of bloody lunatics. Did you see that nutter last night in the hotel accusing me of being a bloody stalker! And with the stalker sitting bloody opposite me! I'll tell you what, though, he won't come near me again after what I did to him."

"I hope you're right, but I fear he might be quite persistent," Max said. "When I spoke to him, I saw that he had a pile of Rick's CDs with him, some of them very rare. He was taking notes, and I could see that he also knows the blonde girl. Could they be working together somehow? I didn't get time to talk to her properly last night because soon after you left, Rick came in and got ambushed by both of them. He legged it pretty sharpish, I can tell you."

"Yeah, and he had a real bloody go at me last night for not protecting him. I reminded him that this whole bloody charade is due to him and that I'll sue the pants off him if anyone so much as lays a bloody finger on me. That made him think! But you know, I think part of his horrible, twisted mind is actually quite enjoying this. He mentioned that he felt like a Beatle, and he wasn't too happy when I told him that would be the walrus."

Marguerite cheered up going down the hill. As he predicted, she pedalled so hard that the motor whined in protest, as did any pedestrians stupid enough to venture near the road.

"Hey, this is fun!" she yelled as another near victim fled the scene leaving a trail of shopping behind them. "I just imagine them all as promoters," she said to Max with a smile when they had taken their seats at Christie's Poison Café by the harbour's edge.

"Hot chocolate, please," said Max to the automaton-like waitress.

"A spritzer please," said Marguerite.

"Sorry, we don't have that."

"What, you mean you don't have any white wine or any sparkling water?"

"Yes, but no spritzer."

"You get the spritzer by mixing them together!"

"Sorry, but it is not on the menu."

"You're not on the bloody menu, but it won't stop me adding you to it!"

"Sorry, I am not serving abusive customers."

Marguerite gave a death rattle chuckle and stood up suddenly. The automaton, shaken out of her mechanisity, took an involuntary step backwards, connected her left calf with the harbour edge chains, and back flipped over the harbour wall. The harbour at low tide was neither very deep, nor particularly clean. The waitress surfaced through a pile of twigs and feathers that were resting comfortably on a thick patch of diesel.

"That's probably the smartest thing that girl's ever done," Marguerite said, as she and Max got up to leave. "Because if I'd done what I intended to do to her, the zoo would be one short of its full complement tonight."

They walked around to the other side of the harbour and settled at the A-Muse Yourself café.

"Funny bloody name, that."

"No doubt named for the band. They're locals to the area, although no one has a clue who the members are. Nice songs, but as individuals, they have all the personality of a row of binary numbers. Ok, let's try again. Hot chocolate, please."

"Would that be the hot chocolate with black holes or with revelations?"

Max took a deep intake of breath. "And what might be the difference?"

"The black holes comes with marshmallows on top, and the revelations with bits of chocolate flake."

"Glad to see this theme business has been well thought through. The revelations, please."

"And I'll have a spritzer," Marguerite said. "You know what that is? Good. And I mean a straight up regular, no amusing, funny, bloody names spritzer. Clear? `Cause I can reveal to you here and now that you will be sucked into a black hole of my own making if I get anything else!"

The drinks arrived, and the two of them sat companionably looking across the harbour, where there still seemed to be some commotion owing to the fact that the waitress had clambered up the side of a moored yacht and stuck her foot through the cover. The owner accused her in a loud voice of being a vagrant and told her to get off his boat. The waitress, equally loudly, told him that there was nothing in the world she'd like to do more than get off his rotten, stinking boat. A small struggle ensured that both of them ended back in the water, whereupon the harbour master shouted at them for illegal swimming and generally bringing the town into disrepute. The yacht owner then invited the harbour master to come down and say that to him in person, while the harbour master told him to stop fannying about and come up. Meanwhile, the café owner was shouting at the waitress for leaving all the tables unattended while she went for a swim with her fancy yacht-owning boyfriend.

"I'm glad that we managed to bring a little joy into their humdrum lives," said Max, breaking the silence.

"Humdrum lives, that's a line out of *Singin' in the Rain*, isn't it?"

"I'm truly impressed," said Max with a nod of the head. "You're not just the angry, screwed up, conniving, bastard child of a 70s rock star. No, what with your admiration for The Fall and literary film knowledge, you're quite the Renaissance woman."

Marguerite gave a strange, tinkling laugh like a huge chandelier caught in a gust of wind. Max wondered if the chandelier was now going to come crashing down on his head but, fortunately, he had judged the wind's strength correctly.

"I do have a Master's in Fine Art and Deconstructionism, you know."

"I never had any doubt that that was the case. It was clear from your love of The Fall. What I always liked about them was not just the deconstructionist lyrics, but the way Mark E. Smith personally embodied the spirit of human deconstructionism. Talking about The Fall, how about getting Brix & The Extricated as the support act for Rick?"

"That's not a bad idea, although I'm never going to give you any bloody credit for it. Any others?"

"Of course, The Damned would be great. Their keyboard player, Monty Oxy-Acetylene, does some great dance moves, too. Just a shame that Rat's no longer with them. Mind you, if Rat ever finds out that Rick set him up, then we'll need to find another headline act! Elton maybe?" Max said.

"You've got to be joking. Elton's not crazy anymore. Forty years ago, you'd have had to tie him up with Watford scarves to stop him performing on the rock as a full size, bloody gull, but not now. There's always Taron Egerton, though, as a support act. He'd be cheap, I'm sure."

"How about David Furnish?"

"He's a bloody advertising executive, Max! What's he going to do, sell the bloody rock?"

"Remember, Linda McCartney had to start somewhere."

"You're starting to worry me here. Stick to a vague semblance of reality for God's sake. I have enough problems keeping Rick coherent," Marguerite shot back.

"There's always Pierce Brosnan for a quick turn. If Abba could survive him singing, surely Rick can?"

"But we're not supposed to see if he can bloody survive. We're trying to make this a triumphant, career bloody topping occasion."

"Now who's talking about reality? God, you're not actually serious, are you?! That would put a totally different perspective on things! You could still use Pierce, though. Just think how good Rick would sound coming on after him. Admittedly, the RSPB may sue for the deaths of all those birds after Pierce, but surely that's a small price to pay?"

"Ha! Even Rick isn't that rich."

"What about local bands? There must be a few down in this part of the world? I can check it out if you'd like. A local band is much more likely to do the show on short notice and at a lower fee."

"You know, that's almost sensible," said Marguerite. "So stop it immediately! Sensible doesn't have any part in the music world, and you'll get me all confused and emotional if you go on like that."

"Consider it done," Max said. "I don't like being sensible at all, but sometimes it creeps up on you unawares, like the flu. I can't help always being right, that's just a preternatural thing, but being sensible is something to be fought against and controlled. Are you going to the fancy dress bash at the beach café?"

"Why would I do that when I've got Rick?" Marguerite asked.

"Oh, I thought it might be interesting. I'm presuming Rick will be off by the weekend, so it would give you the chance to have a bit of harmless fun. By fun, of course, I mean better than sitting in the hotel room watching the mindless drivel that replaced TV programmes about twenty years ago. The music's going to be provided by the tragic bloke running the songwriting course, so I predict something really quite special."

"Ooh, I do like a good car crash of a performance as it happens, so maybe I will come. Will you be there?"

"Yes, I'll be there from early on, as I'm helping Glen and Cee set up. You know that steak of yours? Glen gave it to the man you assaulted. It seems he managed to upset Glen a bit, can't understand how. But Glen's still a bit puzzled by the fact that even with all the tabasco and laxatives he stuffed it with, plus the sprinkling of eyelashes from when he used it to nurse that black eye you gave him, there was no reaction at all. The man must be superhuman, so you be careful if he approaches you again. Violence and insults against him may not work."

"Ha ha! Now, if I track down a potential support act, how would you like to phone them up on my behalf to check on their availability? Sorry, I'm going to re-phrase that. I will give you the details, and you will phone them, won't you?"

"Yes, sir."

"That's better. I'm feeling more like my old self. It's all the sea air making me go soft. I won't have it! Right, I'm off to talk to the publicity people. Total w*****s, the lot of them, 'specially the young ones who have never talked to a human being face to face, but unfortunately, we need someone with at least half a social media brain to pick this up. Maybe quarter of a brain. Is there a local paper?"

"Yes, but no. Take it as a no, unless you want to have the concert publicized several weeks after it has taken place. It used to be a daily, then a three times weekly, then weekly, and now it's timed to coincide with the arrival of Halley's Comet."

"You're very hard on the folks down here, aren't you? They can't all be that stupid, surely?"

"Sorry, I thought that I was being balanced. The place is coming apart at the seams. Hardly any kids down here get ten A* grades in their GCSEs, and that puts them in the bottom five percent of the country given modern grade inflation. OFSTED were all excited last year when they came down to test IQs and found a marked improvement, only to discover that they'd been taken to the zoo by mistake. The three-toed sloth has now got a scholarship to Cambridge to read politics; it seems sloths are under-represented there, at least the three-toed kind."

***

Max and Marguerite headed off in separate directions, Marguerite to a meeting with the w*****s at an office just behind the harbour, and Max cycling home up the steep hill past the bird place. The e-bike grumbled a bit, but with some judicious use of leg power, it tackled the steep hill in moderate style. Max wondered whether Fizz might donate the bikes to those helping to trial them. He, for one, would certainly be interested, as it would enable him to sell off the small oil well he had purchased to fuel the old Jag.

Just before the turning onto his road stood a beautiful old church that, naturally, was no longer a church. It had instead become a space for craftsmen to make and show their wares, and for young musicians to practice. It was almost too good to be true that the local council had given its permission for such use, and he imagined some clever person had got it listed officially as a drug distribution and needle therapy centre.

Max walked inside and was immediately struck by the architectural quality of the place. It was so aesthetically pleasing and restful that Max was shocked that it had not been knocked down and replaced by houses for rich Russians. Come to think of it, that would have made perfect sense, as there was a conveniently attached graveyard.

As usual in these places, the types of artisans varied considerably. An elderly hippy, with all the right peace and love credentials on his shirt, was making colourful wind chimes that would only ever be purchased by someone intent on declaring World War III on their neighbours. Next to him was a vacant looking potter who specialized in making gargoyle mugs under the misapprehension that an expensive and vile-looking receptacle, that is impossible to clean, will always trump a cheap regular mug that doesn't tenaciously display the history of every single drink ever poured into it in the possible hope that some archaeologist might turn up in two hundred years' time and make a documentary about it.

Artists abounded, most of whom would have been proud to aspire to amateur status. In addition, there were log carvers, bird bath makers, and, right at the farthest point, before what would have been the choir, was a young man with a strange set of objects. His sign simply read "The Love Shop." Intrigued, Max asked him what he was up to.

"The young generation don't really like to see each other, it's not natural, is it? But obviously sex is still an urge, yeah?" So, I've come up with an idea to get round needing to have someone with you."

"I hate to tell you this, but blow-up dolls of both sexes have been available for decades," said Max.

"Gross! No one's gonna want to sleep with something like that. So, what I've done is to create these little multi-attachments here."

"And that way you can...?"

"Yeah, you've got it, shag your phone."

Impressed as always by the blind and totally overrated optimism of youth and pondering the circumstances in which Apple could become a legal parent, Max sought out the views from the clock tower. He found more art works up there, including an anthropomorphized portrait of a recent US president, and noticed a small door with "Do Not Enter" written on it, that evidently led up to an enclosed rampart. Focusing on the keynote word of "Enter," Max pushed open the old wood and iron door and climbed the stairway, heavenwards.

Emerging into the bright sunshine, Max was pleased that he had a book secreted about his person, as this looked like a perfect spot for the pleasures of the written page. He walked the round of the walkway, stopping in front of a large, black umbrella with feet.

"Morning, Jessica," he ventured, with all the certainty of a dictator the night before the polls.

The umbrella shifted to reveal an ethereal face, on which a slightly dreamy smile dared to flicker.

"Oh, hello, I'm just here catching a few rays and enjoying the peace and quiet to read and think."

"Good book, is it?" Max peered over at her copy of *Vanishing Point* and reflected on the virtual impossibility of any ray of sunshine gaining access to Jessica's skin.

"Fine, but a bit too theoretical."

"You didn't notice the 'No Entry' sign downstairs?" he asked.

"Oh, sure, but I didn't think it applied to me. What about you?"

"I thought it applied to me alright, but I just didn't think it was reasonable. Different approach but same result. What happened last night after I left you in the bar?"

"Absolutely nothing. The crazy woman didn't re-appear, nor did William or Rick. That William is a strange one, isn't he? I find him quite amusing in his persistence."

"He's certainly direct. Didn't you find his approach aggressive?" Max asked.

"Oh, he's completely harmless, I know the type well. It's the ones that you never know what they're thinking that are dangerous."

"I've worked for several CEOs like that. Neither of them ever asked to sleep with me, but you never truly knew what they were thinking about when they talked to you. Disconcerting really. True sociopaths. Maybe they fancied me rotten. William's not even on the same register."

"Would you sleep with a CEO?" Jessica queried.

"Well, firstly, I'm not attracted to the current majority CEO gender and, secondly, why bother when I've got an iPhone?"

"So, you saw the young guy's stand downstairs, too!"

"Yeah, quite amusing. Now, tell me honestly, are you going to stalk Rick Wakeman?"

"Look who's talking about William`s behaviour! Nooo, I loved his music, and I just wanted to have a nice conversation with him about his inspiration and how he composes. There's nothing creepy in that, is there? Much creepier is that woman who hangs around him and who hit William. I think Rick needs proper protection, and I'm not sure William is up to the job. I'm going to take him up on his painting course idea, though. I love all those kind of funky, bar code designs he does."

"Yes, groovy, aren't they. Tell me, do you play any kind of musical instrument?"

"Not forever. I used to mess around with the bass, but I got kind of bored with it. I had a boyfriend who was a singer, and I took it up because it was helpful. But I got bored with him."

"I can see how he wouldn't fit into your action-packed lifestyle."

"Hey! Stop taking the piss," she said throwing a lazy looking but lethal left right combination.

"Ouch! You never did all-in animal wrestling as a profession, did you?"

"Ha, ha, Nooo! But I can look after myself, you know?"

"Of that I have no doubt. Would you mind massaging my arms, I've lost all sensation where you playfully tapped me."

"Sure thing. I do a good massage."

Jessica was better than professional; disconcertingly so, in fact.

When Max had returned gradually to his senses, he remembered to mention the e-bike to her.

"That's so nice," Jessica said. "What colour is it, and does it have lights?"

Max assured her it was black and light free.

"Then great. I'd love to be able to use it for my errands."

"You can feed the language students as well as the birds."

"You've lost me again. Why would I feed the language students?"

"Because they need it. Remember that none of them speak a single word of English apart from 'Coke,' and they're at serious risk of starvation, particularly after their teeth dissolve. You wouldn't want the deaths of hundreds of young people on your hands when you could have done something about it would you?" Max explained.

"But what about you? You could help just as much as me."

"No, that would be letting the side down. Remember that, like it or not, I'm British and therefore patriotically, nay legally, now required to regard all foreigners as surplus to requirements."

"You're being funny again!"

"No, this time I'm being deadly serious. Sorry. Tell me when you're ready to pick up your bike, and I'll walk to the hotel with you. I know where they are stored. Would you like an ice-cream as well? There's a van always parked on Devil's View Plain at this time of year."

"Not sure about the ice-cream, but I'll have an espresso if they do one."

"Mr. Whippy may not stretch to that, but I'm sure we can find something for you."

"You're serious, it's called 'Mr. Whippy?'"

"What else? In the Southwest, 'Mr. Whippy' is your childhood friend."

Arriving back down in the clock tower room, Max noticed some American tourists admiring the president's portrait. With an effort, he and Jessica squeezed past and went downstairs and out into the street.

"This way," said Max as he cut up through a drive and into a long garden. "It's a slight shortcut up to Devil's View Plain."

"But isn't this someone's garden? I mean, this is a gated driveway, and we are climbing over a fence."

"This is all a modern development. When I was a kid, there was a hotel here, and the owners gave me permission any time to cut up through the grounds. I can't help it if the hotel was later demolished and exclusive housing built on it, can I? It's a Max right of way, and it's important to maintain it."

"Help me over, will you, I'm not as tall as you are," Jessica asked.

"No, you are a bit on the scale version size, aren't you? I would like to introduce you to the e-bike girl, the one who is on the songwriting course at the Bay View. She's rumoured to be the shortest female in Holland. I mean to say, she's bigger than you, but then she is Dutch."

Jessica caught her foot on the top of the fence and tumbled onto Max, sending them both sprawling. The noise attracted the attention of a large, bull mastiff who charged down the garden emitting a victory whoop, and with the clear intent to reduce the visible human population to bitesize chunks.

Jessica dismantled him like a wrecking ball taking out a skyscraper. The dog toppled sideways under her touch and gurgled ecstatically.

A bearded giant with an XL shirt straining over an XXL stomach appeared at a distance and yelled, "Get them, Frodo! Go on, bring the bastards down! You're going to regret the day you were born trespassing on my property! Go, Frodo, get them, get..."

And he stopped dead in his tracks. The sight of his beloved assault weapon rolling helplessly on the grass left him transfixed. That was a mistake, as Jessica suddenly released the dog and screamed, "Go, Frodo, get him!"

Acting under his new empress's orders, Frodo locked onto his owner like a guided missile and hurtled towards him in a whirring torrent of paws, saliva and teeth. At the very last moment, the man realized that the battle plans had been changed and with huge effort, managed to emit the single word "Coo!"

Unfortunately, this is not a word that history notes as being amongst the top commands recommended to avert an incipient military catastrophe.

Frodo's teeth found excellent purchase in the ample, almost made to measure, calf of the man's left leg. The howl he let out would have put many a wolf-impersonator out of business, and it set off a chain reaction of barking around the district the likes of which the 101 Dalmatians Re-Enactment Society would have been justifiably envious.

"I suggest that we just stroll fairly quickly out of the front gate, looking neither to the left, nor to the right," Max said.

"That's out of *The Italian Job*," said Jessica with something approaching enthusiasm.

"Good spot. Nice to see that it's not just tremendously quiet French films from the 30s that you like."

"I like lots of things, you know?" again with her classic questioning lilt.

"I'm sure you do, and let's discuss them when we, have, safely, opened, the er, gate, and er, reached the safety of the er, public highway."

"Was that another attempt at Michael Caine?"

"You win a free non-existent espresso at Mr. Whippy!"

"Oi, what's all that row going on!?" said a bright blue denim, white trainers neighbour leaning out of his window and gesturing with a large black can of lager.

Max gave a classic would-you-Adam-and-Eve-it shrug and lobbed back, "Got himself a much younger girlfriend. A real animal. Some people, eh?"

The man turned his head and shouted inside the room, "Charmaine, this bloke here says that your old man has got himself a piece on the side."

A terrifying woman in her mid-40s with black eyes and vertical, black hair blocked out the window, leading Max and Jessica to take instant remedial action by ducking beneath the wall and legging it crab-like for thirty metres until the slip road up to Devil's View.

"You lead an exciting life," said Jessica, panting amusedly.

"I promise you that it's not like this every day. The excitement sort of has to come to me. I'm much too lazy to go and look for it."

To Max's dismay, Mr. Whippy was not in his usual place in the central grass reservation. Instead, a stylish, brown van with go-faster wings that definitely stole something from Dame Edna Everage's glasses was in its place, the name "Van Chocolat" emblazoned on the side. A super-friendly, mini version of Richard Branson, with swept back, blond hair and a smile that would have relegated the Cheshire Cat to a footnote in history, beamed at them in take-no-prisoners style.

"And what can I get the lovely lady?" he gleamed.

Jessica was about to ask for an espresso but changed her mind, fearing that the disappointment delivered thereby would be an unfair return on the man's uber cheeriness.

"What would you recommend?"

A glint came into the man's eye, a bit like a child-catcher whose prey has conveniently stepped into its net. He started to recite a Bible's worth of available hot chocolate drinks before finishing his delivery with the killer, "But I can highly recommend our new St. Lucian 100% Gustronaut Special. It's just sublime, and I can offer a special fifty percent discount on the island-size version."

Sold.

"Why is it called the Gustronaut Special? He's not called Gus, is he?" Jessica asked.

"I doubt it. Much more likely it's named after a local kids TV rabbit character from decades ago called Gus Honeybun. Of course, he might be a descendant. The teeth are impressive."

Van Chocolat Man handed over the drinks, exuding the kind of enthusiasm you would normally need a special license and a locked room to own. "I'm genuinely excited to hear your reaction. Here at Van Chocolat we use only the finest cacao beans and no additives or preservatives. It's all about the cacao!"

Max took a sip of his drink. He hadn't realized that St. Lucia was such a big island; it seemed more like a continent's worth of luxurious frothing liquid that he was holding. He swirled the nectar around his mouth and was struck by its magnificent richness and depth of flavour. This was no packet of sugary brown dust powder mixed with hot water, but real, genuine, melted 100% chocolate. The drink had a slight bitter note, but the taste balance was so good that it was a revelation. Almost a taste bud revolution, in fact, as Max could see testified to by Jessica's look of pure joy and disbelief.

"Whoa!" she grunted in a voice three octaves below normal. "This stuff is just awesome! Did you know about this guy before?" Max shook his head. "I don't believe you, I bet you did. And how you found out about my love of chocolate I'll never know. You're a real dark horse, Max, and I'm going to have to keep an eye on you!"

Suddenly animated, it was hard to keep Jessica quiet. Having hugged Max so hard the breath was squeezed out as far as his toes, she bounced around like popcorn in a frying pan, little explosive giggles surfacing from time to time as she expounded on every topic from the editing techniques used in the film *His Girl Friday*, to the joys of walking barefoot at night in Geneva.

Seeing the reaction, the man in the van came out to thank them for such a positive endorsement. Jessica shook his hand so hard it matched the colour of his teeth, and for a moment, his smile was a frozen rictus of exquisite agony. However, being a real trooper, he fought through the pain to hand over some Van Chocolat badges and a free sample box of miniature bars. Jessica reached back for his hand, but this time the man managed to evade her clutches. Instead, she playfully poked him in the ribs, and he folded seamlessly in two while still managing a broken laugh.

Out of the corner of his eye, Max could see William emerging in the distance from the coastal footpath, accompanied by the sound of the shutters being pulled down on the observation look-out tower. Now didn't feel like the right time for another chat, so Max urged Jessica to polish off her drink and head towards the hotel. Jessica was so buzzy that she chose to take the grass bank down to the road, grabbing at Max and shouting, "Let's skip!"

It was more of a slide than a skip, but just as fun, though Max's e-bike might have had other ideas about that. A couple of kids walking on the road below were surprised by the sudden intrusion in their midst and looked embarrassed. *People should act their age* was definitely the silent aura being given off.

They entered the lobby, and Max hung around as Jessica headed to the bathroom. He never ceased to be amazed at how much time women spent in there. Personally, he liked a nicely turned-out bathroom, with a bit of joie de vivre about it, but not enough to dedicate large chunks of his day to visiting it like a wet-room art gallery. However, it did give him an idea. How about if art galleries had whole rooms with paintings of bathrooms on the wall? It would provide a sort of comforting, home from home feeling for the fiercer sex.

An arresting vision in an orange lycra top, with unsustainably baggy, formerly cream, jogging trousers and two-tone shoes entered from stage left.

"Hi, Max," Rick said. "I got a call from Squiggs that our, er, F-something friend was doling out e-bikes, and I thought I'd get my annual exercise strolling over here to check them out. Do you know where she's put them?"

"Yes, they're just around the side of the building. Fizz has anticipated your every need, so look for the slightly larger bike with a bottle of Moet in the holder."

"Splendid. By the way, thanks for your mechanic recommendation. The chaps are doing a great job overhauling the old steed, but it's taking more time than expected because they're having to get a joiner to make some of the parts."

The two men went in search of the bikes, and Rick was soon gallivanting happily around the hotel garden paths. Max went over to chat to the gardener.

"Hello, sir, we've almost finished the gate. The manager is going to ask the young lady to open it tomorrow. We're going to hang it first thing in the morning when the paint's dry. Young Boris is down there now putting a second coat on the outer gate, as well as yours."

Max turned and saw Jessica coming around the side of the hotel.

"Hey, there!" she yelled at Max, emerging into the light of the footpath just in time to collide with Rick.

The impact knocked him sideways into a flower bed full of what Max imagined, and very quickly had confirmed, were thistles. "Aaagh!" shouted Rick in pain.

"Here, let me help you," Jessica offered.

"Aaagh!" shouted Rick in fear. He desperately scrambled on his hands and knees across the bed to where the bike lay.

"Just stay still a moment, and I can rub you down," Jessica said helpfully.

Rick scuttled away from her grasp at epic speed, like a crab reading the menu and discovering it was the first course. He leaped on to his bike. "Aaagh!" he cried again in both fear and pain and hurtled down the lawn towards the gate. For a big man, he once again proved the consummate athlete. Flowers beds were skirted, garden statues slalomed, a pond jumped and, back wheel in fully controlled skid, the two open gates broached to perfection. In fact, it was all tremendous until he tried to negotiate the S-bend stairs down to the beach and encountered a party of hikers.

"There's another bloody pervert in them bushes, Mavis," exclaimed an elderly local to his beloved as they passed by a few minutes later. "I think the council should put up a sign to stop them. You remember, like them old 'No Camping' signs."

***

Back at the hotel, Max was commiserating with Jessica. "You really seem fated to terrify the man and, you know, you look nothing like Ronan Farrow, really you don't, so I don't get it."

"It's just not fair, and I don't understand it. Has anyone been saying anything to him about me, do you think?"

"Police? FBI? TripAdvisor? Who knows, you could be on the wanted list in fifty countries, although, on reflection, with a combined total of just under an hour in those countries, you'd hardly have had time to do anything really bad, would you?"

Deftly placing himself for safety reasons behind a finely rendered statue of George Harrison, the recently anointed Patron Saint of Gardening, Max added placatingly, "Seriously, I imagine that's it's just a misunderstanding. Just like you may be completely wrong about the blonde woman who hangs around with Rick, too. And William may just be a dull finance guy who aspires to paint and has nothing at all to do with any of this."

Max felt a certain relief in coming clean. He liked all these characters and realized that any one of them might cause him a serious injury if they found out that he'd been, well, potentially, kind of, misleading.

"Of course that woman's a stalker, it's obvious! And I'll bet it's her that has been bad-mouthing me to Rick. As for William, I'll test him about Rick. It's very difficult to conceal knowledge if you have it, so I'll see how much he really knows about Rick, and that'll prove one way or the other if he works for him. But he looks like a manager to me."

Max glowed inwardly. Mead Bay wasn't such a bad place after all. "Come on, no point in moping. Let's get your e-bike."

The e-bike seat was set too high for someone of Jessica's height, so Max suggested they walk both bikes down to his house so he could adjust it.

The back door opened, and Scabies let out an excited moan of anticipation on seeing Jessica. "He seems to like you," Max said as Scabies collapsed and transformed himself into a fur rug on Jessica's touch.

"It's nothing really. I like all animals."

"Right, well, I'll leave you playing with the rug, and I'll go and look for a spanner." He rummaged around in a bottom drawer and came out with a spanner that bore a remarkable resemblance to John Lennon. "This is pretty rare," he said proudly. "Yoko only authorized 500 of these special Lennon `Spanner in the Works` tools to be made."

"I'm not surprised, what's a spanner got to do with John Lennon?" Jessica asked.

"It doesn't, that's the whole point, but it is a play on a nonsense piece of writing that Lennon did in the 60s. So, it's like a double joke."

"Yes, but only if you know what it was he wrote in the first place and can then make the connection."

"Philistine!" sniffed Max haughtily and went off to adjust Jessica's nuts and bolts. When he returned, he found that she had made her way upstairs and out onto the terrace.

"It's kind of dreamy up here," she said lazily, the effects of all that hot chocolate miraculously dissipated.

"You're welcome to pop over any time while you're still in Mead Bay. Even when I'm not in, you can still get in through the bottom gates and use the ground floor terrace. You don't like gardening, do you?"

"I love it. When I was a kid, we had a huge garden, and I spent most of my time out there planting stuff, climbing trees, pulling the wings off flies."

"What!?"

"Just checking you were listening. Actually, I didn't plant much stuff, but I've always wanted a garden."

"Then you've come to the right place. I've always wanted a gardener! You see, although I'm high on the theory of glorious garden creation, in practice I am a follower of the modern Swiss approach to building, gardening, society, you name it."

"Which is?"

"Cover everything in concrete."

"Ah, yes, now you mention it, I've heard that's the case."

"New Zealand, though, must have been an amazing place to grow up. So much open space and greenery," Max ventured.

"Yes, it was pretty cool, before those damned hobbits moved in."

"But weren't they always there?"

"No way! The Shire used to be in England, but it got so built up that they emigrated."

"Fascinating, and that's where Peter Jackson found them?"

"Oh, no, Jackson is a hobbit."

"You're kidding me! The guy's frigging enormous."

"That's the McDonald's generation for you," Jessica retorted.

Max's phone went, and he ran downstairs to find that the buzzer had caused enough vibration for it to fall off the table onto the kitchen floor, where Scabies was pushing it around with his nose in the hope that it might turn edible.

"Get off, Scabies. Yuck!" as he picked up the pre-licked device. "Hi, Max here. Ah, yes, Sven, great to hear from you. Yup, ok, so you are moving to the Sedgemoor. Fine. Do you want to pop up for a coffee, er, if you're not too tired? I've got a friend here, and I'm sure she'd like to meet you. Good, see you in ten."

He washed his hands and phone and rejoined Jessica, who was thumbing through a paper folder. "Do you list all the films that you have?" she asked.

"Yup, I'm a bit nerdy that way. Thought it would be a good idea to keep track of them all since there must be about 700 or so."

"Seven hundred and sixty-three."

"There you go. It's always useful to be able to throw that into conversation as an ice-breaker."

"There's some cool movies in here. *Ice Cold in Alex*, *Local Hero* and *Blazing Saddles* I haven't seen for years. You couldn't make a film like *Blazing Saddles* today, though."

"No, of course not. Too much leather. Why don't you hang around for a few minutes if you've no immediate errands to run? There's this nice Swedish guy I met jogging earlier today when I was out on the e-bike. He's just moving hotels to below here and is going to pop up for a coffee."

"Sure, but then I need to go. Erran, um, things to do. Don't look at me like that, Max!"

A few minutes later, the sound of Sparks singing about the hippo in their pool signaled Sven's arrival.

"Great location," said Sven, now dressed in Scandy casuals.

"Jessica, this is..."

"Hi, Sven."

"Hi, Jessica, good to see you again."

"Hold it! Hold it! How did you guys meet up?" Max blurted out.

"Mead Bay in Saskatchewan, wasn't it?" Sven said.

"But Jessica was only there for about ten seconds a decade ago! And what were you doing there, Sven?"

"My company was doing some surveying for oil."

"But even so, to remember someone from that far back and when you only met for a fraction of a second is amazing."

"There are not many people who do one-legged, crane impressions in Saskatchewan," Jessica said.

"Ah, of course! Sven, what is it with the hopping?"

Sven laughed generously. "Oh, that! I damaged my knee ligaments skiing, around the time I met Jessica. The doctors told me I would need surgery, but I wanted to avoid that at all costs, so I developed a technique of hopping onto my bad leg to strengthen it. It's become a sort of habit now and, er, obviously a kind of trademark."

"Ok, so that explains why Jessica remembers you, but how come you remember her? I mean, I know she's loud, in-your-face and violent, but apart from that?"

"She offered to massage my leg."

"Yup," said Max nodding his head. "What coffee would you like?"

"Do you have an espresso?"

"You're in luck. I was forced to buy a machine a while back for a German coffee addict who was renting out a property I owned. You'll have to make it yourself, though. I don't have a clue how it actually works."

Sven headed off to the kitchen, and Max called quickly after him, "You might need to dust it a bit first."

"Nice dog," called up Sven from the kitchen. "I would love to have a dog, but I'm always travelling on business, and then when I'm back home, my social life gets kind of hectic." He returned upstairs and joined Max and Jessica on the terrace. "This coffee tastes a bit like it was discovered in an Egyptian tomb."

"You're a very lucky, man. Only my closest friends usually get the rare Egyptian brew. If you look on the packet, you'll find it's authenticated by Professor Mary Beard. She used to drink it as a child."

"Thank you, I'm honoured. I know Mary. Nice lady. Still very energetic." He winced at the taste but kept drinking.

"Sven, this company of yours, you really look for oil?" Max asked. "I mean, Mead Bay is famous for many things; seagulls, old people, Class A druggies, Muse, I could go on, but oil?"

"We are now owned by a wealthy Swedish American family who believe in taking more of a spiritual approach to the search for oil. We do use science, of course, but also consultants with special skills. Yuri Geller has been successful on a number of occasions in helping us."

"So, who are you using for Mead Bay, I'm curious?"

"A man called Mark Berry. He's not always very easy to understand, but our owner sees him as a kind of shamanic talisman. Apparently, he calls the spirits by doing some kind of robotic dance."

"I'm sure he's full of spirits," agreed Max with gravitas. He sneaked eye contact with Jessica, who emitted a whelping laugh.

"I think I'm going to like it down here," said Sven. "The lady who owns the Sedgemoor is very lovely and is going to give me a great deal. Also, there's lots of places to run, and it's full of language students. Do you run, Max?"

"As it happens, yes, I do shuffle around three or four times a week. If you want to hook up, that would be great. I've a feeling that jogging with you could be a life enhancing experience. Jessica, do you jog?"

"No, I do my speed walking every day, though."

"By which you mean night, I suppose?"

"Sure. It's much quieter, and I can really concentrate on what I'm doing."

"Maybe I could come with you one time?" Max ventured.

Jessica tensed involuntarily. "I'm sure you wouldn't enjoy that. I'd just cramp your style and get in your way."

Max let it drop but smiled at her questioningly. "I thought I'd let you know, Sven, that your girls are going to move into the Mead View Hotel. I spoke to the manager earlier, and he confirmed it. That should be fun. There's also a really nice Dutch girl staying there who's on a songwriting course and who I'll introduce you to, just in case you've never met her. Oh, and before I forget, there's a fancy dress party on Saturday night at the beach café!"

"Hey, this sounds cool. I like fancy dress parties, and I always bring my costume with me."

"Now that's impressive."

"I find that it helps get the conversation flowing with the ladies."

"So, who are you coming as? Bjorn? Benny?"

"Elvis."

"Elvis!" Max exclaimed. "Sven, I don't know what kind of girls you're trying to attract, but I need to warn you that you may be in for a shock. You should remember that Mead Bay is still full of women who were alive when Elvis started. They are the original super fans. One glance at you and every old biddy who is still ambulant will totter determinedly in your direction from miles around like the zombie apocalypse. Death by blue rinse is a terrible way to go."

"I am confident I can handle the situation."

"Well, you're a braver man than me, but then, so is any man. What about you, Jessica, any ideas about a costume? Joan of Arc? The Grey Lady? The Ghost of Christmas Pas.. "

"Ouch!"

"Sorry, Sven that wasn't meant for you. Collateral damage," Jessica said.

Sven picked up the drinks coaster that had bounced off his head. "Hit on the head by Alex Turner, a genuine life enhancing experience. Who are on the other coasters?"

"It's a noughties collection. There's also Amy Winehouse, Lily Allen, Dave Grohl, Meg White, a Cee Lo Green double coaster, and Charlie Watts."

"That's got to be the most bizarre collection in the world. I mean, seven coasters, not six or eight, including a double coaster and…Charlie Watts! Where did it you get it, Max? It's unhinged but brilliant!"

Max reached over to a nearby table and chucked a box in Sven's direction.

"Well, well, well, personally chosen and curated by Pete Doherty, who'd have guessed it?"

"And what are you going as, Max?" asked Jessica penetratingly.

"That's a closely guarded secret. It could be any of the characters on these coasters, or it might be Donald Trump, or even Attila the Hun, who knows? But I bet you will not be able to guess on the night."

"Will you be masked then?"

"Sven, if I wasn't masked my stunning good looks would announce my arrival a clear half an hour before I turned up."

Jessica twittered convulsively, or was it derisively? Max wasn't sure.

"So, Sven…" Max was interrupted by Sven's mobile ringing.

"Hi, Annasofia, sorry, Annabel, how are you? Yes, I've moved hotel. No, not tonight. I need more sleep. Tomorrow? Ok, let me check my diary. I can fit you in at 10:40 tomorrow morning if that's ok? Annasofia? Oh, she's the, um, hotel owner. Very strict, so I'm afrai… yes… I know you can be very strict as well but not tomorrow, Annabel. Now? No, I'm afraid that is impossible. I am in a meeting." He rang off and turned to Max and Jessica, eyes raised. "Sorry about that. Business colleague. We're working on a project together. Exploration stuff."

***

Sven let his eyes cast around the terrace and the living room behind it. "This is a cool place. You're not a musician, are you?"

Max shook his head. "Oh, no, just an unemployed architect. I torture an acoustic guitar from time to time, but only when no one's around to report me. What about you?"

"I have some keyboards, but they have more dust on them than your coffee machine. I travel too much. Someone told me you can buy travel keyboards, and I might look into that."

"I have keyboards here that you are welcome to use while you are down here. My Dutch friend also plays a bit, so you may be able to play duets with her."

"I don't have much confidence in my musical abilities, even though I love music," Sven said, looking somewhat wistful. "The keyboards don't respond to my touch in the same way as..."

"Don't worry. You'll be in good company. I see distinct possibilities for musical murder to be committed here assisted by copious quantities of alcohol. We have two keyboard players, a bass player, and a guitar destroyer. I can sing well enough with advanced auto-tune, so all we need is a drummer. I'm sure you can provide some backing singers Sven?"

"Yes, of course, but are you serious?"

"Perfectly, although I very much doubt we'll ever get everyone in the same room, let alone playing the same tune, so don't get your hopes up."

"Hey, I never said that I'd play bass!" yelped Jessica. "I told you that I hadn't played for years and besides which, I'm busy and may be leaving any day."

"Don't worry, there's no pressure, I was just floating some vague thoughts to vague people."

"I'm not vague!"

"Sorry, but you'll have to clarify that, Jessica."

"Double ouch!" Sven yelled. "That was the Cee Lo Green! How about, Jessica, if next time you aim the coaster at me? That way you might actually hit Max."

"Sorry, Sven, I might try that. Does your head need a rub?"

Max collected up the coasters and put them and other throwable objects on the far side of the terrace.

"How do you fancy helping me get the train running, Sven?" Max suggested.

"I can do that," chipped in Jessica. "I was always fixing my dad's car when I was a kid."

"I can fix a wooden boat," Sven said. "I have one moored in deepest, darkest Sweden."

"Hmm, difficult choice. How about if Jessica helps with the train, and you let us use your boat sometime, obviously after you've rendered it sufficiently pristine? That sounds fair, doesn't it?"

"Done. But what are we talking about, a Hornby train?"

"Of sorts. But you can sit on this one."

They all trekked out into the garden. "Amazing," Sven said, grinning. "That's just such a cool thing to have in a garden. Maybe I could ask my colleague, Annabel, if she'd like a ride?"

"Be my guest, although I will now also expect waiter service on your boat," Max said.

"Your pickled herring will be served to you in bed with fresh filmjölk. How does that sound?"

"Absolutely delicious. Unfortunately, and it devastates me to say this, owing to some soon to be acquired allergies, I will have to forgo the pleasure of the pickled herring and filmjölk and just settle for plain dull, old, fried eggs and bacon, with a flute of champagne."

"An espresso is fine for me," Jessica interjected.

"Hah! So, you're committing to the trip. Sven, you heard it here. If necessary, which is likely to be the case, we can now chloroform Jessica to get her there and then tie her to the mast."

"That would be distracting and maybe get in the way of sailing the boat. How about on the front of the boat?"

"Yes, yes, we can discuss the details later. Jessica, what do you think?"

"That you are completely mad! I haven't committed to anything. I just accepted the theory of the idea."

"But you don't deny that we'd need to chloroform you to get you to come, even if you did commit?"

"Ok, well, that may be true. But I won't be tied to the mast. I would want a nice comfy deck chair, a large umbrella, a supply of chocolate and daily access to a port for carrying out errands."

"You got that, Sven? By the way, I'd also prefer Yorkshire breakfast tea, not some ersatz Swedish equivalent from Marstrand. Now, to work! What do you make of the engine, Jessica?"

She pulled off the canvas cover and opened up the cowling. "So, it's a petrol engine."

"Is it? Is it?" Max ruminated. "That's good to know."

"And it looks as though some idiot has tried to put coal into the tank. We'll have to clean it out. Do you have a spare shirt? I don't want to get coal on my clothes."

"No, of course, it might show up as a lighter shade of dark," Max answered. "I'll see what I can find. Sven, could you also have a look in the shed and see if there's any petrol in there? If not, would vieille prune work? I've got a spare bottle."

Returning a few minutes later, Max handed a large, white T-shirt to Jessica which she slipped on over the top of her clothes.

"Who was this designed for? I could camp out in it," she said.

"Sorry about that. I was traveling First Class on American for business and made the schoolboy mistake of asking for a medium. You make an attractive tent, though, and it shows just how dark white can be against certain backgrounds."

Between the three of them, they managed to upend the engine, drain it and clean it out with a combination of a cloth on a stick and a hose. It took some time, and soon Jessica's shirt was back to her favourite colour, although, interestingly, the grime refused to attach itself to her porcelain features, something that could not be said for Max and Sven. Jessica then carried out some advanced techie operations like checking the oil and filling the tank. "Where's the starter button?" she asked.

Max looked in vain for a button marked "Starter." "What is the point in machinery that doesn't mark things clearly? How about this?" A jet water shot out at Sven, catching him in the mouth. "That must be like a kind of drink fountain for the driver, I guess," said Max thoughtfully as Sven coughed and spat out brackish, oily, liquid. "How about this one?"

A piercing whistle shattered the calm of the day causing all of them to jump suddenly like politicians realising they've accidentally told a truth. Scabies howled in sympathy and retreated to the safety of the house.

"Boy, that was loud!" Max yelled.

"Get out of the way, Max, before you press something that sets off a nuclear explosion," said Jessica, rubbing her ears and yawning copiously to try to restore a semblance of hearing. She pushed him aside and leant over the dashboard. "Right, I think the best way to switch on the engine is to turn the key." The engine ignited smoothly, and Jessica looked at Max with studied contempt.

"Oh, well, that's easy, isn't it? I mean to say, I thought we were looking for a starter button, and I think you'll absolutely have to admit that there isn't one," responded Max with a triumphant ring to his voice. He then re-established himself astride the train, and Jessica hopped on behind. "Away we go, ride 'em cowboy!" he whooped, releasing the brake and turning the accelerator handle. The track ran straight for 40 metres on either side of the lawn, then turned sharply at either end. Max reflected that it might have been advisable to cut the overhanging branches as he and Jessica were whipped mercilessly. The first turn required careful navigation, and the squealing of wheels on rails brought about a sudden vice-like grip around his ribs as Jessica clung on.

"This is fun!" she shouted into his still partially deafened ears, proceeding to whack him on the shoulder like a racing jockey encouraging his steed. The strike made Max jerk to the right, fatefully upsetting the laws of physics, causing the train to jump the rails and plough a furrow across the grass straight towards the gate.

The gate opened abruptly, and the Mead View's assistant gardener, Boris, appeared for an instant to say, "You'll be pleased to know, to noooo!" before being mown down. He tried valiantly to leap over the train, but this kind of thing requires dedicated training to enable the legs to obtain the requisite spring and timing, and to ensure that the spring then takes advantage of the training. Somewhat foolishly, Boris had omitted the crucial train jumping exercises from his regular gym circuit sessions, causing his leap to fall somewhat short of the required professional standard. His trajectory instead brought the softer, looser, hanging parts of his anatomy into contact with Max's hard, protruding upper reaches.

Max reeled from the blow but still had the sense to sound the whistle as the train hurtled through his gate and the still opened outer gate, whereupon the steep camber of the road helped turn it away from a stunning, but nevertheless once-in-a-lifetime, scenic, cliff plunge. He tried desperately to apply the brakes, but with no rail to apply them to, all that could be heard was a kind of redundant buzzing noise.

"Use your feet!" he yelled at Jessica as they plunged down the side road towards The Darwin Hotel.

Both of them tried, but the road was comically uneven, and each bump threatened to remove their feet. At the bottom, Max closed his eyes as they dashed through the intersection with the main beach road and rocketed across towards the entrance of The Darwin. Here, Max made an enormous effort to use his feet to turn the train away from the brick wall to the left of the entrance. Bits flew from his leather shoes, but he succeeded in averting disaster, only to be flung off onto a patch of grass, leaving Jessica to coast down the drive to the hotel.

Emerging from the hotel entrance, freshly showered, wearing a white suit and light brown brogues, and sporting a large plaster on his nose, Rick sniffed the air and decided to take a seat on the terrace. His equilibrium had been severely shaken by plunging headfirst into the bush by the carpark and then having to suffer the indignity of being dragged out by a group of pensioners who clearly thought he was a banker short of a funeral. He stepped off the pavement to cross the driveway and was vaguely aware of movement to his right.

"Help! Out of the way! Rick!!"

Rick turned, his jaw instantly dropping to subterranean levels and his blood crystallizing with shock.

"Shiiiiiiit!"

He recovered and was up to full speed in an instant, but the train bore down on him relentlessly. "Get away from me, you crazy lunatic. You're mad, you're mad, you're..."

And with that, Rick parted company with solid ground as he tripped over the far curb, collided with a drinks table, and was launched over the terrace wall into the pool some three metres below.

"Mummy, mummy, the fat man burst my inflatable duck!" wailed an inconsolable child. Her cry of anguish went temporarily unanswered as Mummy and all the others around the pool coped with the immediate aftermath of being hit by a tidal wave of water.

As the water started to subside, an old man cried out, "It's the dirty tramp that we just pulled out of the bushes! Mavis, get back!"

But he was too late, as Mavis had already picked up the pool rake and was hitting Rick on the head with the kind of power that suggested a former life as an Olympic marquee rigger.

Back up by the hotel, the train had slowed on the upslope at the end of the drive, and Jessica was able to step off unscathed. Max came panting up behind her, covered in grass and soil, with Sven, who had chased after them, bringing up the rear.

"It's great to see the train working so well. And I won't charge you a penny for the bonus off-rail tour and direct delivery to your hotel door," Max announced.

Jessica stood up looking spectrally windswept and smiled elatedly. It suited her, and Sven gave her one of his best schedule-being-freed-up grins.

"Well, that was fun! Short intensive trips are the way ahead. No wasting time. Perfect!" Jessica exclaimed.

"Only I wouldn't count on developing a beautiful relationship with Rick now that you've run him down twice in the last couple of hours," Max added. "Having said that, you are adding a certain undeniable spice to his life."

They peered cautiously down towards the pool where Rick, in a moment of clarity, had managed to grab the pool rake and tried to wrestle it away from Mavis. This had worked out less well than hoped for, as she was now in the pool and hitting him directly.

"My ducky!" wailed the infant.

"My wife!" yelled the old man.

"My stalker!" exclaimed Rick catching a glimpse of Jessica above him before disappearing beneath the water under the weight of the angry duck-less child who had climbed on his back.

"Is that Rick Wakeman?" asked Sven with something approaching awe. "He's so much more active than I imagined for a guy of his age. That's really cool. Can I suggest that we steer the train back to its home station before any awkward questions are asked? Jessica, I presume that you are on a tight schedule, so I'll just say au revoir. And here's my number. I'm staying about

100 metres up the road, so any time you want to drop by is fine. I'll always make myself available."

Jessica raised an eyebrow at Max and whispered, "He's a nice guy but just not my type. I'd also be worried that he might try his crane mating dance on me. It's weird enough with his clothes on."

Pushing the train back up the hill was far more difficult than its free-wheeling descent. It might be small, but it was also very heavy and very low to the ground. Fortunately, some conveniently located child labour was induced to push it in return for sounding the whistle.

A Swiss couple, walking through the cliff car park, heard the constant ear-splitting noise and rushed for the nearest cover, anticipating a nuclear strike.

"Oi! Oi! Oi! Get the bloody hell out from under my van," shouted the postman, on the way back from a fortifying cup of tea at the beach café.

"Sorry, but we must take cover. If we survive, we will be able to come out in a week's time."

"What do you mean a week's time! I've got lunch and two tea breaks to take, dogs to avoid, and even some deliveries to make if there's time."

"There will be no more deliveries. No more post. No more dogs."

"What do you mean no more post, no more dogs? What are you telling me? Is there a strike or something?"

"Yes, yes, a strike now. Very dangerous. Death to everyone. Just cockroaches and Keith Richards left."

"I knew I should never have left the army," the postman moaned. "What's the Post Office coming to? It's got no right to go all militant on me." And with, that he crawled under the van.

"Here, take a match," said the Swiss woman. "Whoever gets the short one will be eaten by the others in the event of starvation. It is efficient, no?"

As Max and Sven steered their mini charges through the maze of gates, they found Boris sitting on the ground, rocking back and forth and groaning sorrowfully.

"Don't worry, Boris," Max said, "you didn't damage the train at all and, let's be honest, there are too many children in the world already, so you're not going to miss out on much. What you need is a nice warming cup of my Georgian tea, and then do you think, just as a personal favour, you could flatten out the lawn where the train has carved it up?"

Train back under its cover, cleaned up and re-installed on the terrace, Sven imparted some of his life philosophy to Max. "I see it as my duty to be there for the ladies, you know. They give so much in life that I feel a need to give back. Sometimes it is not so easy, though, and I find myself being spread too thin. I have a big apartment with four bedrooms, so that no one has to be on top of me at the same time. They are kind of like comfy waiting rooms. I don't like jealousy, but occasionally it happens. I would love to be settled down and have planned children, but somehow, I find it difficult to commit. I keep thinking that maybe there is someone I have not assisted yet, and this saddens me. But I guess we all have our own problems."

"Yes," Max responded. "You could be a sad, single person with a tree-climbing dog and no ladies to help at all. I have several loser friends like that, poor bastards. Tchah!"

Max's mobile beeped, and he saw that Fizz wanted him to make a reservation at the Italian restaurant at 7:00, for eight people. Unfortunately, Stevo had decided to come along with Saff, but fortunately, Usan had declined, as apparently restaurants sought to impose on people by forcing them to choose food from pre-selected menus.

"You could join us if you like. Bring the girls, too," Max said to Sven.

"That would be great. I will see who is available, but maybe just one tonight?"

"Ok, I'll book a table for ten people. Would you like an e-bike? My Dutch friend works for an e-bike company and is trialing them while she is down here on her course."

"Neat!"

"Right, meet me at the hotel at 6:30, and I'll introduce you and fix you up, figuratively speaking. It's just over there up the hill."

Sven strolled off. It interested Max that he had not mentioned at all where he was actually working while in Mead Bay, nor what his work schedule might be. But then maybe he had more pressing matters to attend to.

***

A walk for Scabies seemed an unavoidable necessity, and soon the woods beckoned. At least today was a normal walking day, with no people distractions. Scabies was concentrating his efforts on squirrel catching, oblivious to the fact that dogs climbing trees was several evolutions away. That being said, he could on occasion claw his way several metres up a trunk before his frantic scrambling gave way to a slow, backward dive that left him puzzled and winded, though not enough to prevent several dozen repeats. In many respects, his abject failure was fortunate for him.

Max had once watched a neighbouring cat pursue its squirrelly prey up to the spindly swaying top branches of a tree, only to find that once it got there, what had appeared fluffy, cute and snack-like on the ground had metamorphosed into a psychotic, sabre-toothed killer that quickly skinned its pursuer's nose before effortlessly leaping to another tree. The cat, in the meantime, bloodied, battered and utterly defeated, found out that its retreat was severely hampered by branches so thin and unaccommodating that they simply refused to keep still long enough to allow for any purchase. Having used up eight lives, it finally arrived back on the earth an hour later, pledging to dedicate its final life to the fruitarian cause. In fact, in its final years, the cat insisted that it be recognised as a squirrel on the grounds that it possessed four legs and a tail, and identified as such.

On his way home, Max dropped by the beach café for a few minute's rest and relaxation looking at the sea. Secreted around the corner, in the sun but out of harm's way, sat Rick, nose deep in the biography of Steve Howe, the longstanding Yes guitarist. He looked up and guiltily turned the book over.

"Good book, that?"

"Ah, you noticed. I was reading it to check what nasties may have been laid at my door."

"And? Any tiny todger-type references?"

"That would at least be something. In fact, I'm not bloody mentioned at all!"

"Don't worry about it. At least now when you come to write your own autobiography you won't be embarrassed to call it *Yes, It's Me.*"

"Too right. Great title, too. You don't mind if I nick it? Says it all, really."

"My pleasure. What brings you down here?"

"I'm seeking shelter from that mad, blonde menace. I mean, I've had some crazy girls after me in my time, but none that's run me over with a bike and then chased me down with a train! Frankly, my nerves can't stand the excitement. I'm covered in bruises, running out of clothes, and, on top of that, all the guests in the hotel think I'm some kind of deranged drugged up nutter who plays inappropriate practical jokes and is of dubious moral standing. Back in the 70s, I would have been delighted to receive their disapprobation, but nowadays, I just like to drink a nice glass of Chablis and play Scrabble peacefully. I don't even resort to using only rude words anymore, which is why I am so completely rubbish at it."

Rick sipped his tea and continued, "I've got to stay down here a few more days until the van is ready, but I'm thinking of moving hotel to the Mead View to get a bit more peace and quiet. I mean, to say there's also that strange, red-faced bloke who pounced on me last night at the bar. Squiggs tells me she had to flatten him for inappropriate behaviour, although I will admit it takes a very brave man to trifle with her."

"That may be a good idea. Apart from the songwriting students and a few international, beach volleyball players, you are likely to be youngest person staying at the Mead View."

Rick's ears pricked up.

"Beach volleyball players, now that sounds like my kind of scene. Such technical skill and athletic something or other. Yes, that could be just what I need," and he hummed a few bars of "California Girls."

"One double traditional English breakfast with added chips," said Cee appearing from the kitchen entrance of the café.

Rick glanced furtively around him. "I'm not only trying to avoid stalkers. Managers, too. A man's entitled to a decent meal occasionally, but Squiggs seems to think that I need to be like Mick Jagger." He snorted contemptuously. "The man can't even play the piano decently, so why I'd want to be like him, God knows!"

"Cee what are you doing hanging around? You looking for an autograph or something?" Max asked.

"Why, are you famous, Max?"

"I'm shocked that you should have any doubt about that, but I was actually referring to Mr. Wakeman here."

"Did you really travel to the centre of the Earth?" Cee asked him.

Rick paused the fork with three chips on it just in front of his mouth. "In my head, yes, of course. But the idea came from Jules Verne."

"And was he in a band with you?"

Rick sighed, put the fork down and glanced up at Max. "Where's a decent stalker when you need one?"

Glen came out and chivvied Cee, "Come on, lass, there's a load of people in the queue waiting to be depressed. Morning, Rick!"

"I was just waiting to take the money for his first double breakfast," Cee argued.

"Oh, don't worry about that, it's on the house for Rick. Did you like the extra eggs? I thought I might as well give you all six from the box. How's preparations for the concert going? I think this could put Mead Bay back on the map, you know."

"Squiggs is down talking to the promoter and publicity people today. I'm hoping that it will all be fine. I've decided to perform *Journey to the Centre of the Earth* in its entirety."

"When did you decide that?" enquired Max with unmasked concern in his voice.

"Just now. I feel that this is a special place despite the mad entourage I'm attracting. Where else can a man get four breakfasts on the house?"

"Ah, wow, well, I think the full *Journey* would be absolutely amazing, but doesn't it sort of require a narrator and a full orchestra?"

"If we can build a stage on that weird-shaped rock, then rustling up a narrator and orchestra should be a mere bagatelle."

"You do want to live long enough to perform, don't you?" Max enquired. "Haven't you forgotten your manager? She was none too chuffed when you decided to perform on the rock instead of at the café. How do you think she'll feel about adding in a few barges and a hundred extra people?"

"Squiggs can do anything."

"Exactly. That's just what I am worrying about!"

"You think she might cut up a bit rough?"

Max yelled, "Glen! Glen! You didn't fiddle with Rick's breakfast, did you?! On your honour now! Rough! I think she'll spread you thinner than Madonna's voice! I'd move to the Mead View immediately and tell Squiggs through a chain of untraceable intermediaries that you've gone skateboarding with Ben Stiller in Iceland. In fact..."

But Rick was already off, leaving a trail of dust behind him although not, Max noticed, his second double breakfast.

"Do you think he's going to eat the plates, too?" asked Cee a bit later as she came out to clear up and found a table devoid of all matter.

"These rock musicians are a bit eccentric, so you can never be sure. But, live and let live is what I always say," Max said.

"Do you? You mean you never feel the need to say something else? I envy you that certainty. I'm not sure of anything at all. Maybe I'm just a figment of my imagination."

"Or a peachment. How do you fancy a bit of singing?"

"I don't know any songs."

"How about 'She'll Be Coming Round the Mountain When She Comes?'"

"But will she? What if they're wrong, and she comes by the road, and there's no one to meet her? She could starve."

"That Glue Theory degree really affected you, didn't it? Now, without analysing the song at all, do you know the words to 'Yellow Submarine?'"

"Yes, I know both of them. That was easy."

"Glen! New waitress please. This one's over-cooked!"

Max sat for a few more minutes and wondered who could replace Rick on *Grumpy Old Men* once Marguerite had filleted and fried him. Maybe David Crosby? No, too controversial. Ringo Starr? Way too grumpy. James Blunt? Yes. He was definitely knocking on a bit now in years and, what with the hits a dim, distant memory, like a pre-wigged Elton John, he must surely be grumpy?

He rang the Italian restaurant, booked a table, then puffed his way up the steps and back home. Time to settle down for his afternoon read, but the Andy Fletcher dancing tome still didn't appeal, and he couldn't face the dark depravity of *Death Ray*. At somewhat of a loss, he checked out a large stack of books that had never got past the Amazon unwrapping stage. John Lydon's *How I Ate the EU Butter Mountain* sounded appealing, but a slim volume entitled *I Wandered Loaded on a Cloud*, the collected poems of John Michael Osbourne caught his eye, and Max lay back on his sofa and prepared to be transported skywards.

In fact, he went to sleep within minutes, waking with a start to find Scabies persistently nose-nudging his hand, concerned that his dinner might be forgotten. As he fiddled around preparing le dîner du chien, Max made a note to carry the Osbourne book with him on future travels as a sleep talisman. He looked in the fridge to see if there was anything obviously out-of-date with which to spice up the meal. Some packaged salad had turned to mush and smelled vaguely compost-like, so Max mixed it in, adding a splash of Lea & Perrins sauce to give the finished meal a certain je ne sais pas.

Just time left to delicately place a dart in the left eyebrow of his former boss before having a shower, shave and dab on a splash of Purple Haze. A tasteful, grey *Beano* T-shirt with blue Gnasher emblazoned on the front, a maroon felt jacket and proper, brown, lace-up Italian shoes completed the look. Jeans, of course.

***

At six, Max texted Fizz to say that Sven would be meeting them at the hotel to pick up his bike, and just before six-thirty, he made his way out through the garden and up the hotel path.

Fizz was outside in the courtyard, her hair tied back and a hint of eye glitter catching the late afternoon sun. "Nice outfit."

"Thanks. You're looking pretty zippy yourself. The Italian restaurant will swoon at our entry. How's the course been today?"

Fizz rolled her eyes. "We were asked to pair up again to listen to each other's favourite music and why it inspired us. I was with Neil, the Welsh farmer, today, and all he did was play me Manic Street Preachers songs, raving about the bass player and how maximalist his minimalism was. It was fine, but I did get preached at, manically. That being said, I loved the keyboards on that album with the very long name. It just took their music to another level."

"I'm sure Nick Nasmyth will be delighted to hear of your entirely correct assessment of his contribution to the Manics sound. He's a sprinkler of musical fairy dust, and that's a rare quality to have. Brian Jones used to do the same for the Stones. Nick swims better, though."

Sven arrived, dressed entirely in khaki, with a green jacket. No others were in evidence.

"Hi there, Sven, this is Fizz. Fizz, no doubt you already know Sven?"

"No, I have not had that pleasure," said Fizz bluffing seamlessly.

Sven looked pained. Max could see his mind working overtime trying to place her and a sense of despair creeping up on him.

"Didn't we meet in Amsterdam?"

"No, never been there."

"Swaziland?"

"Never been there either."

"Swindon?"

"Come on, Sven, no one meets anyone in Swindon!"

"Oh, um, well, pleased to meet you. And a real surprise to meet someone new."

"I always try to be someone new. I find it very renovating. Can I show you to your bike, young sir?"

"Fizz, I presume we are going to walk down if everyone's going together? You don't have enough bikes left for everyone," Max observed.

"Good point. But we can send down Sven to order the drinks ahead of us. You can manage that can't you, Sven? What name is it under, Max?"

"Max and the Musicians. I thought it had a nice kind of ring to it, even if its veracity could be challenged."

Stevo appeared, bearing Saff, who looked spectacular. "Hi, Sven!" she trilled in surprise. "Fancy meeting you here again. It's been ages since that party in Swindon."

Sven radiated happiness. Stevo radiated toxicity, but still managed a nuclear winter smile and a guillotine nod of the head.

Max and Fizz drank it all in and shared a conspiratorial glance.

Six-thirty arrived, and Sven set off on his e-bike while Max, Fizz, Stevo, Saff, Jeff, Neil, Magnus, and Dev, a late-comer to the course, set off in undisciplined order for the restaurant.

As they passed the site of the dog-in-garden encounter, Max screened his face while furtively glancing in the direction of the house. A big man with his arm in a sling sat outside, looking forlorn and smoking a cigarette in the corner of lips sporting a noticeable cleft down the middle.

Max and Fizz chatted to Dev, a London-based industrial chemist and calypso and reggae buff. "I want to get myself some real steel drums. My girlfriend has threatened to beat me if I do, and that's an added incentive. The problem is that getting genuine Trinidadian steel drums is difficult without actually going there. I love Caribbean music, but I'm lazy and prefer to take my holidays in the Dordogne. I dream of buying a chateau and sitting on the roof playing stuff like 'Obeah Wedding' and 'Pressure Drop' to the surrounding countryside."

"A fine aspiration if I may say so," Max said. "Count me in among the guests. I'm very partial to a bit of Slinger and Fred, especially when served up with a glass of Pécharmant and some Cabécou with toast and honey."

The restaurant was large and semi-circular in shape, with scenic images of the Italian countryside on the walls and colourful tablecloths and glasses. As usual, it was busy, one of the few places in Mead Bay where families with children of school rather than retirement age would come.

Sven waved energetically from a large table set back in the corner, with bright red, wall bench seating down one side.

Max pushed ahead to nab one end of the table, with Jeff and Fizz on either side of him. Stevo squeezed in next to Fizz, with Saff by his side and Neil beside her. Magnus faced Stevo, and Sven faced Saff, with Dev next to him. The other end of the table was left empty, awaiting one of Sven's entourage to grace the stage.

"I hope everyone likes Prosecco," announced Sven. "I have ordered a few bottles for the table."

Everyone but Stevo was well up for that, but Stevo pronounced that he only wanted sparkling water.

"The old system can't take it any longer, I guess?" said Jeff. "All those wild parties back in the 60s!"

"I like to look after my body," Stevo opined, aiming a knowing smile at Saff, "and I'm afraid I can't remember the 60s."

Magnus laughed. "They always say that if you can remember the 60s, you weren't there. You must have had a great time, man."

Stevo started to look riled again. "It's nothing to do with my memory but to do with age. I was playing with little kids in the 60s, not playing music."

The table quietened.

"That's actually pretty disgusting, mate," called out Jeff. "It might have been the 60s, but it doesn't excuse that kind of behaviour. I've got small kids myself and the thought of you playing with them..."

Stevo exploded, "You think I`m a f*****g paedophile?!"

At some point in time during any given evening in a busy restaurant there is always a moment when there is a collective lull in the conversation. Tonight, the words "I'm a f*****g paedophile" had found that lull, and two hundred hostile eyes focused on Stevo, their owners mentally assigning themselves to a limb, or part of one.

"I was only three bloody years old at the end of the 60s!!"

The table fell momentarily silent with this revelation, and it was a few seconds before Dev could add, "So, the drink and hard drugs came later then, did they?"

Stevo ground his teeth, offered up what was meant to be a cool and withering smile and drawled out sarcastically, "Like yeah, man, I used to put away a bottle of Jack a day and hoover up more coke than a Pepsi addict. Took me years to clean up."

"And such a shame that it wrecked your career," sympathised Neil, reaching across Saff and placing his hand on Stevo's forearm.

"My career is bloody fine, thank you very much, and a lot better than yours!"

"So, you suddenly know all about sheep farming, do you, Stevo mate!

Thinking about it, though, you probably do know more about it than music. You wouldn't last five minutes in the Manics. Nicky Wire would blow you off the stage!"

Jeff reached over and restrained a frothing Stevo in his seat. "Now then, now then, no need to get all uptight about things, eh? Just a little light-hearted banter to brighten up the evening. I'm sure we're all good friends, aren't we, and we won't say anything more about the past. Sure you won't have a glass of Prosecco, Stevo? Armageddon is coming sooner than you think, and you might as well enjoy life while you still can."

Peace was temporarily restored, and a young waitress came to take orders. Several bottles of red wine descended on the table, and Stevo was prevailed upon to have a glass.

Saff was straight into deep conversation with Sven, and Stevo's fragile ego forced him to turn his attentions to Fizz. "You're really coming along very well, you know. I can stop, er, spot talent a mile off, even when it's well buried. And a nice, er, smock you're wearing. These vintage clothes boutiques are really in fashion."

Fizz, who was wearing her best, new, white-frilled Gucci shirt, batted her eyes seductively in his direction. "You're so kind to take such an interest in me. Tell me more about *Dalwhinnie Platform*. Such a good album, and I felt that the critics missed the profundity of your messages. 'Noodly' seems such an unjust comment to make, don't you think?" she addressed to the table.

"Noodly, surely not?" took up Max. "Tell me more, Stevo. I thought that was your *Endless Rivers of Grey* album back in the 90s?" And with that, he innocently took out a notebook and pen and looked across journalistically.

Now, *Dalwhinnie Platform* was a sore point for Stevo. He felt it was his finest work and had been mortified when it got no reviews at all. In desperation, he had approached the station master at Dalwhinnie for a comment and had thought long and hard about whether he could actually use "F**k off my platform, you English c**t!" somewhere on the CD sleeve.

"Ah, yes, you're referring to the light-hearted comments of my good friend and buddy, Stuart Maconie. That was such good fun, I couldn't resist using them. Ha! Ha! But with *Dalwhinnie Platform,* I felt that the depth of the music was such that I wanted the public to discover it without written preconceptions, no matter how good they might be. So, I decided to forgo all reviews and to let the album creep gently into the public domain like an, er, tortoise poking its head out of a shell."

In the dark, on an uninhabited island, he might well have added.

"And I hear that you are going to be playing this weekend at the Fancy Dress Party? Will you be treating us to the whole album?" Max asked.

"Oh, yes, what a good idea!" cried Fizz. "What the tourists down here need is a good dose of culture."

"I so agree. Far too many times you hear those dull old hits. Time for something a bit more edgy and out of left field, something to let the people rise up and celebrate." Max looked first to Fizz and then to Stevo to see if more was required. But no, Stevo was in the bag and *Dalwhinnie Platform & Other Love Songs* was set to be launched on an unsuspecting Mead Bay audience.

This task achieved, Max sat back and took in the conversation around the table. Jeff was busy advising Magnus to buy a crossbow and was sketching different types on a table napkin.

"But why do I need a crossbow?" Magnus mistakenly asked.

"When society collapses, you won't just be able to pop down to the shops. You'll need to hunt your food. A crossbow will allow you to hunt silently."

"So as not to scare away the other animals?"

"So as to prevent attracting the attention of any other survivors who will then come and kill you," Jeff answered. "Now, crossbows are highly regulated at the moment, but see here...," he said, drawing a series of diagrams, "you can place the main bow in a specially constructed exhaust pipe to get through Customs. Then the bolt itself can be hinged and fits into a small thin tube like one that holds a cigar." He sketched some more. "And as you can see from this sketch, you insert that up your backside at the angle indicated. But, for Christ's sake, don't eat any muesli before you travel, or it'll ..."

"Be a case of Usain Bolt," finished Max, helpfully.

Magnus inched away from Jeff and made a note to lock his hotel door, visions of becoming some part of Jeff's long term provisions plan floating uneasily through his head. He bumped up against Sven, who was discussing exercise regimes with Saff.

"You need to exercise all of your body and not just your arms and legs. I have these finger strengthening and dexterity exercises that allow me to hold myself in a press-up position on my fingertips with one hand while unbuttoning all my clothes with the other hand. I can also do the reverse, and this enables me to concentrate fully on other matters until the very last minute without wasting any time."

Next to Sven, Dev was disputing Neil's claim that Nicky Wire had more soul than Familyman Barrett, while Stevo was trying to talk across the table to say that neither could hold a candle to Nick Beggs.

"Nick who?" they both chimed simultaneously.

"Kajagoogoo!"

They looked at him blankly for a moment before a flicker of recognition came into Dev's eyes. "Oh, you mean that song from *Mary Poppins*? Can't say I noticed the bass player, but you got to love the movie."

"Oh, yes," said Neil. "And by pure chance, it's Nicky Wire's favourite movie. That and *The Exorcist*."

Max's attention was now drawn to Saff, who was demonstrating her double-jointed fingers to Sven.

"And I can put my legs behind my head, too. Look!"

Everyone did. In the restaurant.

It's not often that a waitress returns to serve a table to find herself looking at a head peering through a pair of bare feet. But Beata, known as Bella in the restaurant on the grounds that the average Brit wouldn't be able to tell the difference between one foreigner and another, took it all in her stride.

"More wine?" she asked, filling up Saff's glass and placing it between the toes of her right foot.

"You've done this before," said Fizz, as Saff emptied the glass without spilling a drop.

"I've got a beer trick I learned in the army that I can show you," piped up Jeff. "Get me a pint of beer and another empty pint glass."

Beata willingly obliged, strangely attracted by Jeff's 'Come up and see my long-term food storage unit' eyes.

Max whispered to Fizz, "This is a good one. I've seen this trick done before. What he has to do is hold an empty pint glass in his mouth, fill it with beer from a full pint glass, then manoeuvre it on top of the now empty glass, turned upside down, and drink the full pint without spilling a drop. It's brilliant and all to do with balance, suction and angles. You watch."

Not only the musicians' table, but practically every other table and the staff, gathered round to watch this stunning trick. The applause was profound and the resulting free drinks for the table a well-received reward.

***

Several hours later, the group staggered out of the restaurant.

"That trick was something else, but I'm worried about what Jeff's secret unit got up to in the army."

"I agree, Fizz," Max said, "and I'll be the first to admit that I've never seen the glasses being eaten afterwards. Life must have been really tough in there. I recommend neither the trick nor the subsequent consumption of a mafia don-sized Diavolo pizza topped with extra chilies, washed down by a vat of prunes. Might be best to keep in front of him at all times tonight and to block the gap under your door with a towel when you go to bed. Given what he has eaten, Jeff needs to be viewed as a fully primed and potentially lethal weapon."

Entering through the doors of the Mead View Hotel, the first sight they beheld was a harassed looking hotel manager pacing up and down. A wave of relief came over him as he spotted Fizz.

"Ah, Count..., Madam, there you are. I hope that you had a pleasant evening and not too taxing? Let me offer you a complimentary grappa on the house. This is a very special and made by my grandmother in Pozzallo. And you, sir, you are also welcome to a glass."

Max sniffed the glass and moved instinctively away from the candles on reception before knocking it back in one and carrying out a controlled gasp.

The manager then said, "The reason I wanted to catch you, Madam, is that tomorrow we open the new gate, and it would be huge honour for the hotel and me personally if you would carry out the small ceremony."

Fizz looked suspiciously at Max, who smiled innocently back and said, "What a splendidly appropriate request. If I had a hat, I would doff it in your general direction. May I also attend, and at what hour of the morning?"

"Thank you, sir, I am delighted to have you in attendance. Nine o'clock is the time set and no need, Madam, for a long speech."

Max sidled away after the rest of the group, who had adjourned to the hotel bar, with Fizz in hot pursuit.

"You're up to something, I can smell it! Who gets asked to formally open a garden gate in a run-down hotel unless there's some kind of evil scheme behind it? Don't smile sweetly at me like that. I'll make you pay by singing outside your window every morning. It will destroy you!"

"See you around nine! And don't forget the speech."

Max turned and left the hotel with some unrecognisable and presumably un-googlable Dutch words ringing in his ears. He skipped lightly down the hotel garden path and into his garden.

"Max!" came a coarse whisper from the darkness.

Max stood stock still, straining his eyes into the gloom. A large bush started to move towards him, which was somewhat disconcerting, although scientifically fascinating.

The bush transmogrified into a familiar shape. "I've been here for two hours, and I'm freezing. Several string drinks will be required," Rick moaned.

"String drinks?"

"Sorry, I meant strong. Just a mental typing error brought on by the cold."

"No problem, come along in. I'm pleased that you find my garden after dark such an interesting place to pass your time. What inspired you?"

"The desire to remain alive for a few more hours! It's terrible, Max. I checked out of the hotel like you suggested, but the Mead View is now completely booked out with bloody beach volleyball players. I even offered to share a room, but I don't think the manager took my suggestion seriously. He had the nerve to tell me to 'pizza off.' I was going to argue the toss with him, but then I saw Squiggs coming up the drive on her bike, and I legged it. She can't have believed the skateboarding story I left with The Darwin reception and must have been checking out nearby hotels."

"You actually left a message telling her you'd gone skateboarding with Ben Stiller in Iceland? Rick, that was just a figurative suggestion."

"I was rattled and terrified of bumping into her before checking out. I couldn't even remember Ben Stiller's name, so I said I'd gone with Rat Scabies."

"You know, I think you should give up music and just concentrate on your glittering new career as a fugitive."

"Now is not the time for levity. There are twenty missed calls on my phone, with a rabid manager at the other end of it that makes Boudicea seem like Ghandi. Do you have a bed for the night?"

"But of course. Always happy to help out a condemned man. And at least my Scabies will be pleased to see you, provided, of course, you don't nick his bed again."

"Thank you so much. I will dedicate my next work to you."

"I'm touched, but let's hope that it's not your gravestone, although that might be a first, so I wouldn't like you to rule it out entirely."

Inside the house, Scabies was less forthcoming than expected, preferring to keep close to his blanket. Max scouted for wine and found he was running a bit low on the decent stuff.

"Chateau du Cèdre 2016 Extra Libre suit you?"

"I like the sound of the extra libre bit," Rick answered. "Pretty sure that's a Cahors. I played a concert on the main square there about fifteen years ago, with my mate, Francis Cabrel, and they served us up this inky black stuff afterwards that I thought was oil. Ruined my trousers but tasted great."

Max felt it best not to ask about the trousers and confined himself to settling Rick down in a very old armchair that stains could only enhance. "Not got any green sausages today, but I have found some greenish chicken bits and a powder dip of, well, it's not marked, but I'm 100% certain it's beetroot."

"That'll do nicely. It'll count towards my five veggies a daaaaargh!"

Max turned to see Rick rapidly necking the whole bottle of wine in deep, sighing, gulps.

Mildly concerned, he slipped back downstairs to search for the missing label. A few seconds later he called up, "Don't worry, Rick, the chicken is supposed to have that greenish tinge, and it's very nearly in date. And the beetroot powder, in case you're puzzled by a slightly unusual taste, turns out to be mascara. No idea how it got in that cupboard. Gave up the drag act years ago. Look, anyway, it's eco-friendly, vegan mascara, so it probably still counts as one of your daily five. I've got squid fritters marinated in marmite if you'd like?"

Rick had a sunken look in his eyes, but there was a rather fetching hue to his lips.

"Glad you've kept to your Cahors and trousers pairing," Max observed. "I'm afraid that we've now run out of the Chateau du Cedre due to its sudden popularity, but I do have a reserve crate of the Bruno if that would suit you?" Without waiting for a reply, he went off to fetch some, leaving Rick absent-mindedly dipping more chicken in mascara.

"I was once told that I looked a bit like a basset hound by members of the band," Rick said looking ruminatively at the label on the new bottle.

"But that would be in the 70s, wouldn't it, when I imagine you were all imbibing sizeable quantities of the non-vegan mascara?" Max plonked himself down in an adjoining but cleaner chair. "Did you enjoy playing in those days, or was it one long chore?"

"It was fantastic! I mean, where else could a bunch of ugly misfits, with myself as an honourable exception, of course, get to do what we liked, when we liked, and occasionally get paid for it, too?"

"And laid."

"The icing on the cake. Pure gravy."

Max wasn't sure that gravy with cake was a good combination, but in a prog rock band, who knew?

"The other thing is that I grew up as a kid obsessed by wizards, and there I was, able to dress up as one and live out the dream thirty years before Harry Potter came along. I bet JK Rowling had me subconsciously in mind when she came up with the idea, not that I want to take all the credit. Got to take my hat off to Harry, though. That Voldemort would've had me for breakfast."

"On the contrary," Max said, "having seen your performance at the café this morning I rather believe the reverse. With you in the novels, I fear old Voldy would not have survived much beyond your first joint meal encounter, and JK would be several billion pounds and a Twitter account the poorer."

"I'd like to have played Quidditch, though," Rick mused. "I'd have made a good blocker, I think."

"No one would have sight of the goal with you around. But what about attending all those classes like Potions and Dark Arts? You'd need a good Hermione to help."

"I'm not worried about potions. I'll eat anything. You'd make a good potions master, Max. It's extraordinary what dangerous substances you can produce from a seemingly ordinary fridge. As for Dark Arts, I'm already good at those. You need Dark Arts expertise to keep lead singers in check. And I've been lucky enough to have had a good few Hermiones over the years, although come to think of it, not all of them may have been called Hermione."

Rick yawned, and Max pointed him down the corridor to a spare room.

"Much obliged."

Rick having shuffled off, Max tidied up and flicked on the television. He usually checked what day of the week it was by seeing which railway journey former politician turned colour-blind activist and serial trainist, Michael Portillo was taking. Today he was in Canada, so that meant it must be a Wednesday. Max watched Michael happily chuntering away while reading a dog-eared Bradshaw's rail guide from a former era. Why the BBC couldn't afford to buy him a new one, goodness only knew.

***

Max must have dozed off for a while and was awakened with a start. The front door was being banged furiously, and a familiar, shredding voice called out, "Max! Max! Let me in! You've got that miserable old git in there, I know! I've checked every other bloody hotel, hostel and paper bag in Mead Bay, so he must be here. Leaving me bloody messages about going to Iceland, well, I can tell you who's going to be on ice very soon!! Let me in!! Rick, you're dead!! Dead, do you hear me!!"

Max debated what to do. Scabies was howling in anguish, and in a few minutes Marguerite's voice alone was going to shake the front door off its hinges regardless of what he did.

While he was thinking, the spare room door shot open, and a wild-eyed Rick propelled down the corridor like a high velocity blancmange. "Hide! Hide! Hide!" he yelled, and with that, he started to bounce around the house like a pinball.

"On the roof, Rick, quick!" Max opened the terrace door, dragged a small step ladder from a cupboard and placed it against the wall. The immediate roof above the terrace was flat, and Rick was up it faster than a John Prescott left hook.

Putting the ladder back in the cupboard, Max descended the stairs and nonchalantly opened the door, swiftly standing to one side to allow Hurricane Marguerite to pass. Pass in a literal, not actual sense, as it was clear that the storm was very much still a work in progress.

"Where have you got him? I'll paste him over the walls for ignoring me. I spent all day working my bloody guts out to save his bloody concert, and he sells me some crap about skateboarding in bloody Iceland. Fact: no bloody skateboard has been built that could take his weight! Fact: the only time he met Rat Scabies was when Rat spat on him outside the 100 Club in 1977! Fact: I'm going to bloody kill him!" These facts established, Marguerite came down several notches on the Beaufort scale and accepted a glass of wine.

Max then tried to cover, "As it so happens, Rick did drop by earlier, I presumed on his way to Iceland, but left rather quickly. What has been going on? You look a tad upset, M."

It looked for an instant like Max was going to be plastered on his own walls, and he braced himself for the experience. Instead, the sound of rocks being crushed to their constituent atoms emanated from Marguerite's mouth and, when all the atoms had finally been liberated, she took a deep breath and sat down on the floor in the middle of the kitchen.

"I'll have another glass of that basset hound stuff, please."

Max reached over.

"That's fine, leave the bottle." She knocked back the first glass in a single go and was halfway through the second, when she sat back and re-engaged. "Well, you know I was going to talk to the publicity kids, then after that I went to see our idiot promoter. And he only tells me straight out that the concert can't go ahead. For bloody bird protection reasons!! I mean I went ballistic. 'No bloody birds live on that bloody rock,' I told him. 'They just shit on it!!' But it turns out, that the rock's not the problem, but the bloody woods just behind the beach. There's apparently some stupid twatted bird called the Lesser-Spotted Brown Drudge that only breeds there, and the RSP bloody B doesn't want thousands of people traipsing down there and disturbing the little f****rs. So, I said, 'Why don't you just pay off the Council boys like usual, or just shoot them?' He then tells me that the local Mead Bay mafia have nothing on the RSPB. Said that if you cross them, it's odds on that you'll find yourself forming part of the foundations of the new extension to their Centre for Conservation Science. I told him that was a better fate than he was going to suffer and, OK, I admit I shouldn't have hit him as hard as I did, not with a kettle anyway, but it felt good."

"So, it's all off then, just like that?"

Marguerite continued, "This is when it starts to get bloody weird. The promoter phones me from hospital a couple of hours later saying he wants to see me. Seems he only had a mild concussion from the kettle hitting him, but the fact it had just boiled burned his assets a bit."

"Strikes me you'd be well rid of this wimp."

"My thoughts precisely. Anyway, being the reasonable woman that I am, I went to see him. Even bought him a new kettle, a plastic one this time with a child safety catch in case anyone hit him again. Then I made him apologise for earlier on, 'cause you can't just let that stuff go, can you?"

Max settled on the floor beside her and looked interested, both because he was, and also for safety reasons.

"So, he tells me that although we can't use Shark Rock, we can have

Devil's View Plain provided that we agree to put the local Mead View Orchestra somewhere on the bill and give 30% of the profits to the Mead Bay Conservation Fund."

"What Fund? Never heard of it."

"I gather that it's been set up to enable the council to knock down those old fashioned Georgian and Victorian buildings and replace them with modern Swiss-lite style."

"So, concrete?"

"Yes, but with less expensive, instantly biodegradable concrete."

"And the Mead View Orchestra?"

"A sadistic mix of centenarians and kids who murder classical tunes for pleasure."

"Bloody hell!" Max responded.

"And I haven't finished. After giving me this load of tosh, he springs it on me that the concert has to take place a week from bloody Sunday and not in five weeks' time! Oh, and just to top it off, the council doesn't have enough money to pay for any of the staging and equipment!!"

"Wow! What else did he say?"

"Nothing. I found out that even a plastic kettle can knock someone unconscious if you use two hands."

"What a disaster. And it all looked such fun. Totally mad, but fun. Glen will be so choked. We've all kind of forgotten that he was the one who wrote to Rick in the first place and proposed to have an International Rick Wakeman Day. And Rick was chuffed enough to agree and actually looked excited about it."

"Not so excited that he hasn't done a bloody runner!"

Max coughed gently and, weighing up the pros and cons and deciding that it was only Rick's possible demise that would result in his actions, said, "It looks as though you never got the initial message he left for you at The Darwin?"

"What message?"

"He was so overwhelmed by the concert idea that he told me he had decided to perform *Journey to the Centre of the Earth* in its entirety, with full orchestra and narrator. I might have gently suggested to him that he make himself scarce while you got accustomed to the idea. But now there's no need for violence, as it's all over, and so I'll come clean with you. Rick tried to check into the Mead View, but it was full, so he came here for the night, as your instincts correctly guided you."

"So where is he now?" Marguerite asked.

"On the roof, wearing a pair of boxer shorts."

Max had never seen anyone laugh as much. Marguerite shook so violently with laughter that her diaphragm eventually went into spasm, causing her to gasp for breath. Coughing and crying, she eventually lay on her back exhausted, gurgling weakly and moving her head from side to side as if trying to deny what she had just heard.

When Max reached over to pull her upright, she was like a rag doll.

"You're going to have to warn me next time you pull a stunt like that. Too much anger followed by too much laughter can kill a girl, you know. Max, why are you looking so strange? If didn't know better, I'd say you were thinking."

A small smile crept into the corner of Max's eyes. "Taking everything into account for a second, is it feasible to host a concert on ten days' notice?"

"You're worrying me. Stop thinking at once!"

"But could it be done? Maybe as a day festival with Rick headlining? 'Rickstock.'"

"Laughingstock you mean! Look, it'll cost loads to get the staging and lighting and sound set up, and that's if you can get it at all. Then there's the backing musicians, let alone a narrator and bloody orchestra. Rick's usual guys are all off on other jobs at the moment, and you can't just put on one of Rick's shows with no rehearsal, and that includes him. And then what about an audience? Where are we going to rustle up several thousand people at short notice? Nah, the whole thing's a wash out, Max. The only positive thing is Rick sitting up on the roof freezing his nuts off."

Max thought a while longer and tried a different tack. "Look, and bear with me now, how bullet proof is Rick's reputation?"

"As what?" Marguerite retorted. "As a Grumpy Old Man, it's cast iron. As a musician, he's, ah, I see what you're driving at. You mean can his reputation handle a disaster of biblical proportions?"

"Exactly."

"I hate to say it, but the word Yes comes to mind. If the punks couldn't kill him off forty years ago, nothing can now."

"So, look, it's a win-win situation, isn't it? Why don't you give it a shot? You can work the publicity angle to play down expectations but at the same time take pleasure in winging it royally and, as the pièce de résistance, you can bully Rick something rotten for the next ten days on the grounds that this was all his idea!"

"You're a wicked, wicked man, Max Ahrenbee! And I do like a wicked man." And with that, she grabbed Max and applied considerable pressure to his lips. Max decided resistance was futile.

***

Max awoke with a dull, aching pain located where his head used to be. He was sprawled across the living room carpet, his arm draped over something soft and warm. Scabies, as it turned out. Marguerite was wrapped up in a blanket on the sofa. Also Scabies's. Empty bottles featuring basset hounds proliferated. His mouth felt like a dried riverbed that had previously flowed with glue. He spat out. Hair of the dog. An intense buzzing noise persisted, and, realising eventually that it was not coming from him, he crawled with his eyes shut over to the window. He then rested with his head on the cool ledge for about a minute before cranking open his eyelids a fraction of a millimetre.

"What on earth?" Max's eyes were now wide awake as he focused in on the whining sound. On his hands and knees in the middle of the hotel lawn, was the hotel manager, wafting the grass with a small hair dryer. Max was not the only spectator. He could see curtains twitching all over the hotel, and a group of staff talking in low, concerned voices up on the terrace. The manager looked up and shouted at them. Five minutes later, there were six members of staff, including the chef, advancing down the lawn inch by inch, with their singe of hairdryers sounding like a squadron of angry hornets.

"What the f*** is that noise!" said Marguerite sitting bolt upright, then realising that she had left her head on the sofa. "Oh, God, I hate basset hounds so much and, and what is this? Yuck!! I'm completely covered in dog hairs, and the smell!"

She tore off the blanket and walked unsteadily over to Max, who backed away.

"Keep away from me, Marguerite. I won't be hugged by a blonde Labrador impersonator, not until they've had a shower anyway."

"What are those people doing?"

"Drying the grass, of course. It's one of the services offered as standard in top Mead Bay hotels. The clientele down here are so old that any dew could cause death by pneumonia. Another custom down here is to have a ceremony for the opening of new gates. You are going to be lucky enough to see this in an hour's time if you can manage to squeeze in a shower and breakfast first. I have some shorts that might fit you with a belt and you can choose your own T-shirt. Meanwhile, I will see if the washing machine has a fumigation setting for your other clothes."

Thirty minutes later, Max and Marguerite were mixing orange juice and head restoring pills when the noise of the hair dryers stopped.

"Thank God for that. I thought that noise was never going to end," Marguerite declared. But the respite was fleeting and was replaced by the sound of pounding interspersed with shouting. "Sounds like an earthquake. The house is shaking. Jeez, at this rate, the roof is going to give in. OH, MY GOD, THE ROOF!! RICK!!"

Max and Marguerite looked at each other in wide-eyed horror.

Just for a second or two.

Max recovered first. He'd learned a thing or two from senior management. "Well, he might have reminded us earlier, don't you think? I mean, what kind of lunatic voluntarily spends the night on a roof in May, as opposed to say August, without so much as a blanket to keep warm? It's frankly irresponsible behaviour for a man who's headlining a major festival in ten days' time. A lot of people are relying on him and just imagine if he caught a cold? Right, I suppose we should let him down before he wrecks the house."

Max and Marguerite pulled open the terrace door and went out.

"Cup of tea, Rick?" Max offered politely.

"Cup of tea! Cup of tea! Cup of tea!" Rick repeated like a parrot, an iced parrot.

"Great, I thought you'd like one. If you'd just like to come down, Marguerite will explain to you about the new concert details. What happened to your boxer shorts?"

Somehow during the night, Rick had parted company with his only item of clothing and now presented an interesting public figure. Clearly, he had found somewhere to lie near the chimney that had sheltered him, and it seemed likely that the shorts had formed some kind of thin, makeshift pillow. A significant amount of roof pitch had also attached itself to him, to the extent of black hands, feet, posterior and left side. Max was not sure he was suitable to allow into the house in that state and told him to stay where he was. He asked Marguerite to chuck Rick a bar of soap and then disappeared for a minute, re-appearing on the lawn with a high-pressure garden hose in his hand.

"We're just going to give you a quick hosing down to wash of the worst of it."

Rick was still looking dully at the bar of soap in his hand when a jet of icy water hit him full amidships.

All activity in the hotel garden ceased to be focused on the lawn. A clutch of staff hair-drying a lawn simply could not compete with the wild new rooftop dancing act.

Two large, familiar Londoners were walking past the house with their wives. "Hey, Rat! Great moves, mate! See you've ditched the dog. Doesn't he like heights or somefing?"

Rick came down the ladder to scattered applause from hotel guests and passers-by alike. His face wore a stupefied expression, and he kept muttering "cup of tea" in mantra-like fashion. A blanket was placed around him, to a howl of dismay from Scabies, and a cup of tea poured down his throat, before he was led to the shower room and thrust in.

"I think it's safe to leave him in there for a while," said Marguerite. "No harm done."

"No, the roof looks ok. Thanks for asking, though. Shall we go and see the gate ceremony?"

"I thought that was a joke?"

"Oh, no, it's very real, although I suspect that Rick may have stolen the show a bit. He moves well for an old boy, doesn't he?"

They made their way carefully to the hotel, going the long way round, despite Marguerite's moans. "Sorry," Max said, "but the hotel manager doesn't know that I live just below him, and there's a good reason for maintaining that lack of knowledge, quite aside from any awkward questions that might get asked about people dancing naked on the roof."

Fizz was hovering nervously around the top end of the hotel garden. "What's going on, Max? Oh, hi, Marguerite, good to see you. The manager asked me to put on my best clothes for this ceremony and to say something about cultural ties and world peace. I'm seriously worried about his mental health. Did you see him drying the lawn earlier?"

"I'm sure it will all work out fine. Don't sweat it, have fun, and just pretend you're a famous person like, oh, the King of the Netherlands. He must open lots of major buildings, so regard this as a piece of cake. We'll support you, and then you can come round to my place afterwards. Marguerite is going to tell Rick about the all new, totally revamped concert details, and I'm sure she won't mind you being there, will you M?"

"No, the more the merrier. You might just be able to help us out."

Fizz was about to ask what the King of the Netherlands had to do with anything but, fearing the answer, just said, "I don't like to ask, but was that Rick on the roof a few minutes ago?"

"Oh, that!" Max said. "Yes, he's working on a new piece of music about the Summer Solstice and wanted to flesh, er, act out some of his ideas. I think he's hoping that Julian Cope will do the actual naked dancing in any live performance, but personally, I think he's showing a real talent in that area."

Just then, the manager walked up. "Ah, Mr. Ahrenbee, so nice that you could come. And who is this lovely lady in the, ah, Stranglers T-shirt and combat trousers?"

"Let me introduce you. This is Glenda Jarvis. She works as the firm's enforcer. You know, bad debts, that kind of thing. She's very efficient, 150% recovery rate. You noticed the shirt, well, she's a 7th Dan Shidokan karate expert. Only she and JJ Burnel have reached that level in the UK. Both her bark and her bite are lethal, and her strangling's well up to scratch, too. We wanted to talk to you later about something, is that ok?" He tapped the side of his nose and walked off, leaving the manager in a sweat of consternation.

"What was all that bollocks about, Max?" Marguerite asked.

"It just occurred to me that the hotel could help out with the catering for the concert and, well, just let's say I have some influence on the manager that might ensure a better price."

"How come you never thought about band management, Max? You're completely wasted on architecture."

"I don't know, Marguerite. Architecture's a tough profession. Most of those empty column spaces are put to good use, you know."

They walked down towards the garden gate area, where a fair crowd of hotel guests had gathered, along with an ancient brass quintet. Only Jeff from the songwriting course was there, though. He collared Max. "That was fun last night, wasn't it? And it didn't end when you left either. We've got a free day today as our esteemed course leader is somewhat incapacitated. Seems it's true that he was never much of a drinker, but he made up for it last night. About two o'clock this morning he tried to show us that Saff was not the only person who could put her legs behind her head. God knows how but he managed it, but suddenly, there he was lying on the floor with a foot around the back of his bonce. And, um, that's exactly how he stayed. It took the ambulance an hour to get to the hotel, by which time his trousers had given up as well. The medics called in the police as they thought he was deliberately exposing himself. Still, I think the course may be better off now, as he's no longer speaking to Saff on account of her copping off with the Swedish bloke. But it wasn't very smart of him to yell at her when he was lying exposed like that on the floor. He sounds uncannily like Jimi Somerville this morning. It reminded me to add 'Smalltown Boy' to my playlist."

The quintet blew something that might have been a fanfare, and the hotel manager craved everyone's attention and asked that they have a glass of the complimentary champagne in their hands. "When I was a small boy in Napoli, my mother would always say to me, in between the sound of birdsong and gunfire..."

"Get on with it, I want to go out!" cried an irascible and unfeasibly mobile guest.

"Yes, precisely. She would tell me to get on with my life and be proud to serve others. She told me to..."

"Open the bloody gate, will you!!"

"Exactly. To open the gate and get out into the real world. To follow..."

"Jesus!!"

"Jesus and his ways of giving to the people."

An empty glass of champagne whizzed past his head and smashed against the wall.

"And this is what I have endeavoured to do in my own small way." He cleared his voice. "Today, after 150 years, we are replacing the garden entry gate to the hotel. A gate which is like the entrance to the soul of this place. We do this to honour every guest who ever stay in this magnificent edificio, and as our contribution to global sustainability and, ah, world cultural cohabitationing. We welcome today now our very special guest who will open the new gate and to whom we dedicate ourselves. She is a person of the highest quality and breeding. A fine musician, supporter of the arts and ah, justa very good indeed. I give you the Cow, um Cow, ahem, lady from Arnhem."

And with that, he bowed and handed a pair of kitchen scissors to Fizz who was wondering what kind of alternative universe she had fallen into, and whether to kill Max now, or after the ceremony was over.

"Well, well, this is indeed an honour. When I was a girl, my father used to call me his little princess, but I realise now that becoming the Cow Lady of Arnhem was always my true destiny."

The hotel manager smacked himself on the head in mortification. "Princess! Princess!!"

"I am not sure to whom I owe this honour," Fizz continued, "but I have a pretty damn, er, pretty good idea, and I will be thanking them very personally afterwards."

Max started to edge back into the crowd.

"So, sustainability and world," Fizz went on, "what was it, cultural cohabitationing; a lovely word that I guess can mean whatever you like. For me, I dream of a sustainable world where we all travel by e-bike and get rid of those horrible polluting cars. As it happens, I have details of a fantastic such e-bike, one that has been personally endorsed by the Duke of Attenborough, and I can very much recommend that you all purchase. The hotel manager will be circulating details, and discounts will be available for everyone who can recite the Dutch national anthem. For those of you who are perhaps a little longer in the teeth, I can assure that we do provide stabilisers and a nice little plug that will re-charge your pacemaker while you are cycling. Now, as for cohabitationing, I have a dream of a world where bats are free to mingle with humans without insensitive vampire jokes being made, where bats can hang undisturbed above beds and on curtain rails, a world where bats replace cats as a girl's best friend. Bats are so much more sustainable. No scratch marks and fur everywhere and no bodies of dead mice littering up your kitchen. The hotel manager will be handing out details of where you can purchase bats for your home. These bats are bred and endorsed by the Duke of Attenborough, and he would like me to add that he is only keeping a small amount of the profits to ensure the sustainability of his chateau in France. The rest of the profits will be donated to the British Inland Revenue. So, there we have it, e-bikes and bats; that is my vision for the future. And now, without further ado, in the name of all the cows in Arnhem, I would like to declare this gate open."

With that, Fizz cut through the cloth, and a stunningly bright orange wonder was revealed to the world. It had been the senior gardener's idea to use luminous paint, given the age and eyesight of the average guest.

"Wow, I am so impressed," said Fizz standing back in amazement. "And this coat of arms in the middle must be those of Arnhem unless I am much mistaken? And the female gargoyle in the top right-hand corner with the coronet on top must be, ah, yes, silly me."

The band struck up a spirited version of an old Musical Youth number as the applause rang out and the hotel staff served up more champagne. Fizz looked around with hawk-like eyes and spotted Max buried amongst the guests.

"Max. Oh, Ma-hax, my little sweetie pie. Come to Fizzie!"

Max grabbed hold of the hotel manager and engaged him in conversation. "A splendid event if I may say so. And so clever of you to tee things up for the countess in that way. E-bikes and bats, now that's what I call a philosophy. By the way, do yourself a favour and learn the Dutch national anthem, old chap. I can see a glittering future for you. How does 'Keeper of the Royal Bat' sound?

"But she is a princess and why you not tell me that?!"

"I told you she is very low key. That just kind of slipped out, and I know you can be relied upon not to say anything. Shssh. Now, to business. There is going to be a major rock festival on the plain in ten days' time. The headline act is a personal friend of the countess, and this is a tremendous opportunity for the hotel and for you. It may cost you a bit, but think of the publicity and the opportunities that will come from it. You may be able to have this hotel permanently full of rich, successful, attractive, young people in the future if this goes well. It's a once in a lifetime thing."

The manager opened his mouth, but nothing came out.

So, Max continued, "But not a single word to anyone at the moment, especially not the current owners. The concert is a secret until we tell you it isn't. Now, I will be sending Ms. Jarvis to talk to you about what is required and what we expect. She will be your main contact."

"Mr. Ahrenbee, but this is so amazing and wonderful. Oh, my mother she would be so proud! You just leave everything to me. It will be stupendo! I am the solo of discretion. I cannot thank you enough," and he started to kiss Max's hand.

"Reserve your thanks for the countess, she's just coming. And remember, we are relying on you not to fail."

Fizz caught up with them at this point and was about to share some thoughts with Max when the manager intervened, grabbed her around the shoulders and started kissing her cheeks passionately. Max winked at her as she glared at him over the manager's shoulder and shot off to safety, parting with, "I think you'll find that life is going to get much more interesting around here. Seriously, Fizz, you'll end up thanking me for all this, really. Just think how many e-bikes you are going to sell! See you in thirty minutes at HQ for a debrief. Weapons to be left at the door, please. Violence is severely overrated, you know."

Fizz struggled to free herself from the manager's embraces but to no avail.

"Oi, wait for me!" shouted Marguerite, running to catch up with him. "That was fun, wasn't it? I mean, where did she make all that stuff about e–bikes and bats up from? Really taking the piss she was and good luck to her. Imagine calling someone the Cow Lady of Arnhem and then asking them to open a bloody garden gate? I would have hung the manager up instead."

"Don't do that," Max warned. "He's going to be very useful to us. He is now more convinced than ever that Fizz is some kind of Dutch royalty, and what's more, I've told him that she's a personal friend of Rick's. He's expecting you to talk to him about catering arrangements, and I made it quite clear it might cost him a bit but that it would be good publicity for the hotel. So, don't go offering him any money unless you have to, and be nice but firm, if you get my drift?"

"Oh, I get your drift all right. Good cop, bad cop routine, right?"

"Right! Ok, shall we go and see our veteran musical property and put him in the picture?"

Pushing open the back door of the house, Marguerite shouted for Rick, but there was absolute silence. Max also noted that Scabies was not in his usual position.

"You don't think he's taken the dog for a walk, do you?" Max asked.

"No pun intended, but do you see any pigs flying? More likely he's still in the shower."

They climbed the stairs and found the bathroom door open but no one inside. However, the sound of gentle snoring was coming from the spare room, and, pushing the door open, a hint of grey-blond hair was just visible at the far end of the bed, while at the near end, Scabies was equally fast asleep.

"I suppose he didn't get all that much sleep last night and what with the energetic workout this morning..." Marguerite said.

"Let's give him until Fizz extracts herself from the hotel manager and turns up. I could do with ten minutes down time myself, come to think of it."

Max and Marguerite took themselves back to the living room and cat-napped for a short while before the front doorbell rang, and the sound of Cee Lo Green's "F**k You" jolted them out of their seats. Opening the front door with some trepidation, Max was relieved to see Fizz had brought Jeff along with her. Jeff wasn't generally a dangerous guy, except when making long term food plans, so Max felt relatively safe.

"Fizz, so nice that you could come. Long time no see. Did you use the new gate to get here? Splendid. Jeff, can I get you a mid-morning cup of something?" He was prepared to keep up this inane level of bonhomie until he had exhausted any immediate structural re-arrangement plans Fizz might have for him. But instead, she was sweetness and light itself.

"It's ok, Max, no need to drown us in happy, crappy garbage. It doesn't suit you, and anyway, I've decided to spare your life for the time being. I had the chance to think about what you said about this being a great opportunity for my company's e-bikes. You are completely right. I've already sold twenty in the last thirty minutes, and we only go into full production in three months' time. In fact, I'm going to call my boss this afternoon to see if I can negotiate some commission."

"Don't forget your friends," risked Max.

"I won't, although we may have somewhat different ideas of what a friend is. And what have you done to the hotel manager? He seems always to be on the edge of a total breakdown. I need to know what you told him about me!"

"You over-estimate my powers of influence greatly, Fizz. However, it might just be that the manager believed you to have some distant links with the Dutch aristocracy. I feel no guilt on the matter now, however, because you managed to elevate yourself to princess in your groundbreaking gate-opening speech."

"But I only said that my father called me princess. Surely, he didn't think that I...? He did!"

"And as it happens, that suits us all very well with regard to the concert, as your favourite hotel manager is likely to assist us on your behalf."

"Wait a minute! That doesn't explain why he would help with the concert 'on my behalf.' What else aren't you telling me, Max?" Fizz demanded.

"Only that you were a friend of Rick's. Absolutely nothing else, I promise, or may God strike me down with a feather duster."

"Marguerite, is that an English term?"

"Don't ask me. I'm from the North. Sounds vaguely English, though."

"Jeff, has Fizz told you about the concert?" Max asked.

"Rick Wakeman? Shark Rock?"

"Yes, that's it. But we've got a big surprise for you both. For ornithological reasons, the concert is being re-located to Devil's View Plain a week on Sunday. Marguerite and I were hard at it last night, er, going over the initial plans, but there's a huge amount to do, and your help would be most welcome wouldn't it, M?"

"Not just welcome, but essential."

"And what did Rick think about the changes?" Fizz asked.

A large figure wrapped in a *Who's Next* duvet appeared at the stairs. "What did Rick think about what changes?" he yawned sleepily.

"Hello, Rick. Sleep well? Just finalising the plans for your concert. You did want to perform *Journey to the Centre of the Earth* with full orchestra and narrator, didn't you?" smiled Marguerite with all the innocence of a baby kitten.

"You mean you're not upset at all?" said Rick.

"Ha! Ha! Moi? No, of course not. It's a super idea, but I just need your confirmation in writing for the, er, promoter."

Marguerite handed up a piece of paper which Rick leaned on the edge of the bannisters and signed, unread.

"Right, lardy pants, now you're for it! Get dressed and get practising. You're headlining a day-long festival in ten days' time on Devil's View Plain, accompanied by the Mead View Orchestra. Got it?

Silence.

"Rick, pick that bloody duvet up!!" Marguerite yelled.

"Yes, Rick," Max joined in. "Fizz is just an innocent girl from Amsterdam and as for Jeff, you might give him food provision ideas unless you cover up quick. M, go and slap him, will you?"

A few minutes later, Rick was on the sofa nursing his jaw.

"It was for you own good, Rick. You looked like you might faint, and a quick slap at least gave you a good reason to fall over."

Rick looked discomfited. He started to squirm on his seat, and his hands became active in making circles in the air. Eventually, his mouth opened, "I'm not f*****g doing it! You've stitched me up, Squiggs. How can I be expected to play in just ten days' time? I'm a professional, you know. I don't just turn up and play unrehearsed. What about my reputation? And who is the Mead View Orchestra? Never heard of them! No, no, this won't do at all."

"You signed a contract, and it's you that wanted to play the whole bloody piece!"

"I'll be ill. You can't force me to do this. I'm an old man. There are rules, conventions, treaties..."

"Hmm," said Max. "I fear Rick might well become ill if his defamation of Rat Scabies gets out. Rat's currently a very unhappy man, and I believe that he is prepared to pay a lot of money to be able to have a quiet little chat with you." He thrust a copy of the Rat Scabies article under Rick's nose.

"You bastards! You wouldn't!"

"Ok, that's settled then," Marguerite announced. "Rick, you get dressed and I'll talk to the promoter, if he's conscious. Let's reconvene here at 12:00 if that's fine with you, Max? In the meantime, get your thinking caps on, ladies and gentlemen."

An hour later, at the beach café, Rick was starting to recover his equilibrium, aided by a double English. He waved his fork in the air by way of illustration. "You know, I think this might just work. The Shark Rock idea was all very well in its way, but it was always going to be hard work getting the staging right. I kept telling Squiggs, but she had her heart set on it. Nine days is a bit tight, though. But, if the orchestra's up to scratch, we should pull through. You don't by any chance have a CD of *Journey*, do you, Max? It's been a while since I played it."

"Another breakfast, Rick," said Glen in the form of a statement.

"So kind. I need to keep my strength up for what's to come. Squiggs won't have this all her own way."

"By the way, Glen, you couldn't pop up to my place at 12:00, could you?" Max asked. "You know where it is? Good. Look, there's been a major change in the concert arrangements, and as you're the one who inspired it, it's only right that you should know what's going on. Plus, we're going to need your help."

"Can I help, too?" asked Cee, poking her head around the corner. She cleared her throat and sang in a completely unexpected semi-operatic voice,

"She'll becoming round the mountain when she comes

In a yellow submarine, yellow submarine."

"Where on earth did you learn to sing like that?!" Max asked.

"Oh, my mum was a big Freddie Mercury fan. That song 'Barcelona' was her favourite."

"But this is brilliant. You sound like Monserrat Caballé, and with a wig on, Rick looks like her. Fizz, you told me that Cee had potential, and you were right. With a voice like that, maybe we can find her a place on the extended bill?"

"And I could do survival classes and give cross bow lessons," added Jeff with unbridled enthusiasm.

"Lovely, Jeff. Super. You do understand what kind of festival it is? Still, who knows? We may need someone with your underground skills."

***

At 12:00, the team gathered around Max's dining table and looked expectantly at Marguerite. "Tomorrow morning all hell is going to break loose," she began. "The publicity kids are working their little Millennial socks off to put together a live concert site for 9:30 a.m. At the same time, announcements are going out on every piece of social and anti-social media we can access, and I've called in a lifetime's worth of favours to get half the radio stations in the country to shout out for the event. So, first things first, what are we going to call the bloody thing?"

"What about the original idea of 'International Rick Wakeman Day?'" said Rick. "It has a nice, catchy ring to it and says it all, really."

Marguerite answered, "Sounds too much like a memorial. Let's make it sound like you're still alive shall we, even if it's a moot point?"

"How about 'Wakeman's Not Dead!' then, with someone entertaining like Sir Brian Blessed as narrator?" volunteered Max.

"I like the Brian Blessed bit. Hold that thought," Marguerite said.

"Something a bit more trippy, such as in 'Rick's Like Really Awake, Man Festival?'" Jeff offered.

"Much too 60s," she replied.

"Then how about just 'The Centre of the Earth Festival' (with Rick Wakeman)?" Max said.

"I like it," Marguerite decided. "That'll do. But, let's just hope it's not so deep underground that it's dead and buried before we even start."

A glass of port was poured out for everyone, as no wine, basset or otherwise, was left.

"To 'The Centre of the Earth Festival!'" Max toasted.

"Cheers!"

"Right, now down to business," Marguerite picked up. "I reckon that the plain can cope with about 3000 people. As for price, I'm thinking £99 a head for ordinary tickets and that we should cordon a section off in front of the stage for a Gold Circle. Price, £199, and maybe a Silver Circle at £149. We need security to stop non-paying punters creeping in. Jeff, does that sound like your kind of thing? Fizz, you need to keep the hotel manager onside. Play up the royalty stuff. Promise the manager a knighthood and a free night in Amsterdam, with men, women, animals, whatever floats his boat. I'm going to be leaning on him hard for a lot of free food and drink, so I need your back-up. Sharkies can have its own feature stall, and we need other food stalls, too, all on the left side, away from the standing area. We'll take a big chunk of their money, but Sharkies can have it for nothing. Glen, can we call it Rick's Café for the day? Good. The stage needs to be the cliff end of the plain to allow maximum numbers to use the grass. The stage is going to have to be much bigger than usual, to accommodate the bloody orchestra! Support acts, Christ! Don't even know where to start there. We can update the website when we have some. But they've got to be cheap! Max, I want you involved in everything as a kind of project manager/fixer in addition to me. Right, any comments?"

"Er, what about rehearsal space for me and the orchestra?" chimed in Rick.

"I'm sure if we make the Arts Centre in the old church a reasonable offer, they may let us use that," said Max. "They've still got a fully functioning organ which Rick can use before his own gear turns up."

"Great suggestion," said Marguerite. "OK, let's go over everything again. I may be Rick's manager, but I'll be the first to admit that I've never organised a festival before, let alone start to finish in just over a week. As Charlie Croker said in *The Italian Job*, 'It's a very difficult job, and the only way to get through it is we all work together as a team. And that means you do everything I say.' Got it?"

"I don't think he said 'Got it.'"

"Shut it, Max!"

"Or 'shu...' ok, ok, got it, Charlie!"

The rest of the afternoon was spent drawing up lists of things to do, ripping up those lists, drawing up new lists, ripping those up, trying to do without lists, and then drawing up new lists on ripped up paper. During this creative process, enough port was sunk to empty a large container ship, and the list of things to do became increasingly, artistically, avant-garde in layout and varied in content.

"Green sausages are very important for the orchestra's morale, served up with nut wine and chocolate digestives," said Rick solemnly nodding his head.

"And if I place a trebuchet in the far corner, I think we can protect the whole exposed left flank," Jeff said.

"And Rick can make his entrance onto the plain on a sponsored e-bike, wearing a bat cape."

Max snapped out of his reverie. "Sponsorship, that's it! Fizz, your company could make a killing out of putting up some sponsorship money. How about it? And there must be other mugs who would be interested, surely? I'll take a look at it with Marguerite."

By five o'clock, nature had run its course, and even the most left field ideas had dried up.

"I need to get some fresh air," said Max. "Anyone take a turn on the plain with me?"

To his surprise, Rick staggered to his feet.

"Might as well have a proper look at the site."

"Perfect. I'll buy you the best hot chocolate you've ever had when we're up there. It's good for clearing the head, too."

***

"Ah, this is the life," said Rick, standing by the cliff top railing looking out to sea. "Couldn't have picked a better spot for a concert if we'd tried. There's loads of space for concertgoers, and all that fresh air will be good for them."

"Too much fresh air might be a problem," noted Max, feeling the breeze.

"At this time of year, it should be perfect, and a bit of breeze will mean we don't need fans for the performers, including me. That reminds me, we should have some kind of backdrop to the stage to give it some class."

"Nice idea, but we should concentrate on making sure we have any sort of stage before we worry about the aesthetics."

"I've full faith in Squiggs and the team. Now, what about the hot chocolate you were promising me? There's a man with an unfeasibly large smile looking at me from in that van over there."

"Ah, yes, that's Van Chocolat Man."

Max ordered the same as the previous day, and Rick had the Tanzanian 80% with added cocoa nibs.

"My goodness, this is something else! I could live off this hot chocolate!"

Max was aware of Van Chocolat Man trying to catch his attention and left Rick a second to see what he wanted.

"That's not who I think it is, is it?"

"If you think it's Marilyn Monroe, then no."

"I had a certain be-caped 70s keyboard player more in mind."

"Well, I think you're very wrong to have him in mind rather than Marilyn Monroe, but you are correct."

"Splendid! Splendid! And what's he doing down here?"

Max told him, upon which the man's smile threatened to white out the vicinity.

"Can I come and see you a bit later, at your house? I might have some, ah, mutually beneficial proposals."

Max very much hoped that he would.

Rick had meanwhile wandered off, drawn by the Coast Watch building. The old keeper came down and started to chat with him, and Max observed them happily engaged in conversation. After a while, some chocolate biscuits appeared, and the two of them headed into the building, Rick waving to Max as he did so. Max strolled over and was stopped in his tracks by the sight of William emerging from the triffid bush, carrying a bucket and brandishing what looked like a nine-iron club. He waved at Max and held up the bucket.

"Forty-six balls, and I'll bet there are at least as many again in there. I've filled my bucket, but I'm going to come back tomorrow morning. That was an excellent tip of yours." He paused a second before continuing, "Was that Rick I saw with you? What's going on?"

Max decided to put William in the picture about the concert.

"And he wants a stage backdrop? I would be very happy to do that for him, although of course, I want the copyright in my work and in any related merchandise. That's only fair."

"You know, I think that's a brilliant idea, William," said Max, with a huge internal grin. "And there's no time like the present. Rick's in the Coast Watch hut, so I suggest you go straight in and make your pitch. Don't take no for an answer!"

William strode off, and Max went to sit on a nearby bench to better enjoy the entertainment. He heard raised voices, a scattering of furniture and then absolute silence. A couple of minutes later, a jubilant William emerged waving a piece of paper.

"I really can't believe it. Commissioned! Rick looked very stressed when I came in. I imagine the pressure of the concert. And the old Coast Watch man had some kind of fit and kept asking me not to use my golf club. Poor old boy's obviously nuts, and I tried to demonstrate that there was no space to swing it properly. Unfortunately, he moved, and I caught him slightly on the chin. No real harm done, though, and Rick just agreed to all my terms without any push back. Even the merchandising! With a theme like Journey to the Centre of the Earth, I can give full reign to my artistic vision. Max, I can't thank you enough."

With that, William scurried off and left Max alone. He was aware of two anxious faces peering down at him from the first floor, Coast Watch window, and a few seconds later, an ashen Rick emerged onto the plain.

"I see you've engaged William to do your artwork. I admire your grand gesture in support of the abstract artists of this world."

Rick wiped a shaky hand across his brow and slumped down on the bench. "I consider myself a very lucky man to have escaped so lightly. When he came in with that golf club and assaulted old Jim, I thought my time had come. Jim tells me that he's a notorious gangster from the West Coast of Scotland with a penchant for using human flesh and blood in his paintings. Do you think he'll do the same with the backdrop?"

"I doubt it. He may drink the blood of his victims, but it's a waste using blood to paint with, and William doesn't like to waste anything. He's very tidy, very clinical."

Rick shivered perceptibly. "To think that I was sharing a hotel with him and that crazy woman, too! Doesn't bear thinking about, does it? Do you think he's looking to take all the concert proceeds? I gave him any merchandising linked to his artwork, but what if he wants it all? I suppose I could give him Squiggs, but she'd only be enough to cover a small canvas."

Max replied, "I don't think you need be worried about that. His one true passion is art, apart from depopulation of course, and you've caught him at his most altruistic. But best maybe let me deal with him?"

"Absolutely. I can't be stressed going into a major concert, and besides which, I need to focus on rehearsals with the orchestra. It's strange that I've never heard of them before, though. Are they good?"

"Breath-taking from what I've heard."

They ambled back down to the house, where Fizz opened the door. "Marguerite and Jeff are asleep, and Glen has gone back to the café. I wondered if you'd like me to take Scabies out for a run?"

"I'll come with you," Max said. "First, though, do you think you might exercise your abundant charms on the manager to find Rick a bed? He's terrified by Jessica, and now William, and I haven't the heart to tell him that they're relatively safe."

"I'll see what I can do, but it is pretty full with leggy beach volley ball players, all of whom are much taller than me. As a back-up, how about asking Sven if there's room at the Sedgemoor? I know Rick's not a girl, but with his long hair, Sven might never notice."

"That is actually a very good idea. About the hotel I mean." Max dialled a number on his phone and waited. "Hello, Sven? Have I called at a bad time?"

The sound of intense male and female panting could be clearly heard, climaxing with, "Oh, my God, Svenny, that was so hard!"

Max was quietly impressed.

"Hey, look, I'll call you back. Sorry for disturbing you both."

"No, no, that's quite alright," panted Sven. "We've just got to the top of Murrain Drive, and it was a really tough climb."

"Ah, fine. Look, well, er, slightly disappointing, but never mind. Do you think there's space at your hotel for Rick? He's got problems with stalkers. Not something that's ever troubled you I imagine? Excellent. Do you have the number? I'll give her a call now." Max rang off and immediately re-dialled. "The Sedgemoor? Great. I understand from one of your guests, Sven, that, yes, yes, he is a very nice gentleman. No, I think all those ladies are work colleagues. Um, can I just finish? He mentioned that you still had some rooms free, and I have a distinguished musician who is in urgent need of a room for the next week while he prepares for a major concert here in Mead Bay. Rick Wakeman. R-I-C-K. Wakeman. W-A- ... he's very famous. He was in Yes. Y-E-S. No, Yes. Yes! Rick Wakeman. Rick, oh, bugger it, Elton John! Sssh, no publicity! He's heavily in disguise. Big blond wig and quite tall. Yes, I know he looks small on TV, people always do."

Max turned to Fizz. "That's sorted, I think. Rick, can you let Marguerite know that I've got you booked into the Sedgefield under the name of Mr. John. Nice and anonymous, eh? I'll also drop by the old church now and see if I can get the ball in motion. I'll call M later, so she can follow up."

***

A little while later, accompanied by the dog, Max and Fizz set off. Scabies was unhappy because the woods were in the opposite direction from where they were walking, and he whined piteously.

"For God's sake, grow up!" Max admonished.

"You've hurt my feelings. You know I'm height sensitive."

"I'm talking to the dog."

"And that's supposed to make me feel better? Anyhow, I'm not going to let it bother me because it looks as though I am going to be on a great commission to sell the e-bikes. I phoned head office while you and Rick were out having fun, and they're going to confirm it tomorrow. They're also pretty keen on the sponsorship idea, too, although we don't have much money yet."

Scabies decided that if he wasn't going to the woods, then he would make his protest by stopping at every single lamppost, gate entrance and clump of grass sprouting out of a wall for a thorough exploration and watering.

"Imagine if humans did that all the time," said Fizz reflectively as Max yanked Scabies away from his latest prize.

"For some humans that would represent evolution. Have you ever been to Paign..."

"Hello, Max."

Max and Fizz stopped dead in their tracks and looked around. Nothing.

"I recognise the voice and distinct lack of any physical presence. Where are you, Jessica?" And with that, Max made a show of looking under Scabies, and searching his pockets. A tinkering laugh rang out.

"Very funny, Max."

Max honed in on the tree before he discerned the shadowy human form sitting in it. "You've picked a nice day for it. I find that the English weather is often off-putting for even the most ardent bibliophile arborist. What are you reading?"

"*Peace.*"

Max positioned himself under Jessica and saw a huge book balanced precariously on a branch. "*War and Peace*?"

"I'm only covering the peace bits. It makes it so much more readable."

"You're on to something there," said Fizz, craning her head upwards.

"Jessica, this is Fizz."

"I've heard so much about you from Max," said Fizz, extending her arm and shaking Jessica's foot.

"But there's nothing to tell."

"Max can talk a lot about nothing, believe me."

"Shall we come up?" Max asked. "I haven't sat in a tree for several decades. Very remiss of me, I know, but life got in the way."

The tree was on the old church boundary and could be accessed by a side gate. Even with some low branches for assistance, it was not a straightforward climb up to Jessica, and Max was surprised that she had managed it. Eventually, and with the donation of some skin from his ankle, Max made it onto what was admittedly a luxury branch. Fizz was soon with him and admiring the view.

"I love it up here. This would be Holland's highest natural point. My parents will be so jealous. It's a shame we can't get Scabies up here, though. He looks sad," Fizz said.

Sad was perhaps not the right word to describe Scabies's repeated manic attempts to launch himself bodily up the trunk. In fact, he only gave up when, with a yelp, he snapped a nail and thought it wiser to find a comfy, sun-kissed grave to settle on instead.

Max felt in his element. "I love the fact that we can see the road and the church grounds, but no one can see us. Have you got anything we can throw, Jessica?"

An elderly couple, standard Mead Bay fare, exited the old church and took a turn towards the graveyard. Max waited until they had reached the first headstone and called out, "Welcome to my grave," using his best Hammer Horror voice.

The couple looked for the speaker and laughed at each other.

"You laugh at my death, and yet, not long you, too, will be here beneath the earth."

The laughter died and a look of fear transfixed their crumpled faces. They turned and retreated fast. Max called out after them, "Return. Return. You cannot escape your fate," accompanied by an eerie booming laugh.

Fizz cuffed Max lightly on the shoulder. "Max, you shouldn't do that, you know. They might drop dead with shock."

"But what better place to do it than in a graveyard?"

"You have a ready answer for everything, don't you?"

"Yes, but only time will tell if it's the right answer."

An atypical younger tourist, with a small child, walked by on the road. "Mummy, can I have an ice-cream?"

"Only if you're a good girl."

"But I am a good girl. Always."

"Now you know that's not true, Trudi. You hit that little boy just now at the beach when he didn't want to play football with you."

"That wasn't me, Mummy. That was his sister!"

"Now, Trudi you know what happens when people lie. Something bad always happens to them."

"But do you ever lie, Mummy?"

"No, Trudi. I learned from my Mummy always to tell the truth."

"But what about the time you threw away Daddy's old football boots, and you said they were stolen."

"That's not true, Trudi, and you know it. They were stolen, and may the good Lord strike me down otherwise."

War and Peace from ten feet proved an admirable substitute for the good Lord.

"Drat it!" said Jessica.

"Are you sent by the good Lord?" asked the little girl, looking up into the tree quizzically.

"We're more of an independent angels' outfit," said Max, "But we have similar views on lying, and we like to do things by the book."

"It's a very big book."

"No bigger than the lie, little girl, no bigger than the lie."

The three of them shinned down the tree, retrieved the book and fanned the mother back to a semblance of consciousness. Fizz then zipped into the church and bought an ice cream for the little girl. "What are you going to say about this?" she asked with a hint of concern.

"That angels threw the book at Mummy for lying."

"You'll go far little girl. Keep up the good work."

The three of them entered the cool interior of the old church and looked around for a figure of authority to talk to. Today, the artists were absent, replaced by a group of elderly ladies torturing flowers. Max approached the nearest one to ask if she knew who had responsibility for hiring out the building.

"Oh, you're in luck. Mrs. F'ting-Brightly runs our flower therapy group and also happens to chair the Trust." She eyed up Jessica and Fizz. "Is it a pole dancing group you want to set up?"

Max restrained Fizz, who was doing a good impression of someone who needed restraining, and went over to where the Trust Chair, a handsome, well-constructed edifice in her early 60s, was somewhat exasperatedly explaining to a fossilised stick that she should not put the flowers upside down in the vase even if it did make them easier to get back out again.

"Ahem, Mrs. Fa..." Max stopped, transfixed. The name badge held him in a ghastly thrall. Fizz looked puzzled, but Jessica had already dissolved in cheeps of laughter and had turned away.

Mrs. F'Ting-Brightly turned round and saw Max struggling. "Oh, it's the name. Don't worry, I've heard all the jokes. I was 'Twice Nightly Brightly' at my girls' school, 'Rightly Brightly' when I joined the Young Conservatives, and 'Unsightly Brightly' when I broke my nose playing lacrosse at uni. No, I've heard it all, so don't worry."

"Ah, well, that's a relief, Mrs. Farting-Brightly. I was a little concerned I must admit."

"F'Ting, F'Ting, young man!"

"Gosh, yes, so sorry, like Fanshawe or Bouquet."

"What are you going on about? Are you alright? It's not a mental health group you want to use the hall for, is it? I've quite enough trouble with the so-called artists that loiter around here and with these kind of people," she said, waving dismissively at the flower torturers.

"No, no, not at all. Mrs. Fa, F'Ting, what are your thoughts on music groups?"

"I'm the founder and lead oboe player of the Mead Bay Orchestra. Why do you ask?"

An hour later Max emerged, bathed in sweat but wreathed in smiles. Mrs. F-B also emerged and slapped him on the back, winding him instantly. She was completely transformed.

"I say, what a wheeze! The Mead Bay Orchestra playing for 3000 people at a rock festival. Usually, we mangle a bit of Elgar and Handel in front of a handful of life's lost souls, but this is the real deal. This Wakeman chappie sounds wonderfully eccentric. Never heard of him, of course, but you tell me he went to the Royal College of Music, so he must be able to play a bit, mustn't he? Will we have to take drugs? I missed out on all that scene, but our conductor, Colonel Tripehound, told me marvellous stories about taking horse tranquilizers in Malaya. I do hope he's up to the job. Deaf as a post these days. But then, he is 91."

"That went smoother than expected," Max said to Fizz afterwards. "Just for goodness' sake, make sure the press doesn't get hold of her name. We can't have the first oboe player upstaging Rick. Might do to ensure he has a spectacular cape nonetheless."

Max called Marguerite and told her the good news about using the old church for rehearsals. He gave her Mrs. F-B's number. "And they'll do it for nothing she assures me. Perhaps a small rider for the colonel, er, from the vet?"

"What's this about her name, I don't get it? I can laugh at anything rhyming with Brightly, but I can't mention farting? Is she incontinent or something? No, don't bother going over it again now. See everyone tomorrow morning at 9:00 at your place to wait for the website go-live and the first radio announcements. The publicity kids are sending out the script to the radio stations as we speak. I suggest everyone gets an early night. I've already sent Rick to bed. He was rambling on about being forced to employ some Scottish gangster to paint the stage set, and I'm getting seriously worried about him. Oh, and Max, make sure there's something to bloody eat for breakfast, will you? Something normal people would regard as food."

"You heard her, Fizz, an early night."

"I heard real food for breakfast. Do you have any?"

"Perhaps a quick top up in the village might be in order. Do you two want to come along and supervise? We could then have a curry at the restaurant a few doors down from the Coop."

"Nothing I like more than a good, spicy curry," said Fizz. "That and sushi."

"I can meet you there," said Jessica. "I..."

"We know."

Max and Fizz walked in silence back towards the house, taking a detour via the café in order to see if Glen could make the 9:00 meeting. However, he had already left for the day, so Max left a message with Cee, who was clearing away the tables.

"I don't see why I have to put all the tables away when I'll just have to bring them all out again tomorrow."

"Theft?" said Fizz.

"Most of our customers find it difficult to even pick up a knife and fork, let alone a table. No, it's just an example of the pointlessness of things, and if anything's pointless, you can be sure it's me who's doing it," she sighed.

"Better now? Why don't you hide them so that everyone thinks they've been stolen? Then you could be the heroine who finds them?" Max suggested.

"But can I trust you not to tell on me?"

"Good grief, of course not. We'd shop you straight away, wouldn't we, Fizz?"

"But then I'd get fired!"

"You've got it! But at least it wouldn't be a pointless action. It would be an action with real consequences. It could change your whole life."

"Mmm, you make it sound so appealing put that way, but I guess I'm not adventurous enough."

"Don't worry Cee, your concert debut a week on Sunday will be the adventure of a lifetime."

Cee looked at Fizz in a horrified manner. "He is joking, isn't he? Please tell me that he's joking."

"Ok. He's joking."

Max turned to Fizz as they climbed the steps up towards the house. "That was kind of you. Can't have Cee panicking, can we?"

"Why are you looking at the hedge?"

"Just checking it. You know it's recently become quite a place of pilgrimage."

"I'm not into hedges myself. Too clingy."

"Of course, you're Dutch. Grass and weed are fine, but you guys are too lightweight for the full hedge experience."

The village Coop was quiet, and Fizz went around efficiently picking up proper food, carefully replacing all the items Max had already placed in the basket.

"What's happened to the crumpets?" he asked.

"Not good for you. I've bought what claims to be wholemeal buns instead."

"There you have it, 'claims to be.' You don't have that problem with crumpets. They are what they are. Simply full of pure, unadulterated, crumpetty goodness and overflowing with fresh, healthy, damp prevention holes, just begging to be smothered by glorious natural free-range products like butter and cheese."

They checked out without the crumpets.

At the Kentswood Tandoori, given the time of day, it was pleasantly full and child-free. Two mandatory pints of Kingfisher in various states of undress sat on the table, with Fizz noticeably undressing hers faster, as if in anticipation of the Chicken Phall she had just ordered. Max had stuck with his favourite plain Chicken Tikka, with plenty of brinjal bhaji and lime pickle.

"Do you think Jessica will show?" Fizz enquired.

"I reckon yes, but not until we've ordered dessert. She can't cope with the pressure of confirming her arrival to coincide with everyone else, nor of being expected to eat courses in normal order. Once she's here, she'll be fine, but if you tell her in advance she'll have a good time, then she'll worry. I think she feels guilty if she feels too happy, so happiness needs to happen to her unexpectedly."

"But she still enjoys sitting in trees, taking late night walks in potentially dangerous places and chasing rock stars."

"And are you adducing this as evidence of her just being a regular kind of girl? What about you?"

"I'm just a super, super, normal, regular, dull girl."

"That's such a shame. But it's a killer title for a book about your life. Or at least a pamphlet. I can see Keira Knightley starring as you and Xavier Bardem as your boyfriend in Azerbaijan."

"Tajikistan," Fizz corrected.

"Sorry, Tajikistan. Act One, Scene One, a young Fizz, played by a suitably made-up Warwick Davis, walks across her parents' lawn and out of the back gate. The police locate her and bring her back. Her father, played by Robert De Niro, tells the press that, 'We were so worried. Nothing like this has ever happened before, and with Holland being so flat, she could have walked to the coast and fallen in the sea.' Act One, Scene Two, Fizz as a young woman is telling the story to friends and marvelling about her exciting childhood. Promising, don't you think?"

"You can write the screenplay, but I really want Jennifer Lawrence."

"Well, ok, I think De Niro has more gravitas, but we can try."

"And Warwick Davis?"

"Fantastic actor. In real life, he's rumoured to be Liam Neeson."

As predicted, Jessica arrived for dessert. "Have I missed anything?"

"Only a minute alphabetical dissection of your character. We haven't got past A yet," Max said.

A piece of keema nam landed on the waiter's head, having missed Max's. "Good shot, madam. We pride ourselves on the aerodynamic shape of our products. Would you like another one? A whole keema nam goes much farther, you know."

Jessica felt somewhat obliged to accept his kind offer, as well as to order a significant portion of the menu. Naturally, it fell to Max and Fizz to eat most of the food, with the result that they could hardly breathe by the end.

"I don't think I can face riding back on the bike, just in case I explode," said Fizz undoing the belt on her trousers.

"Can I suggest we adjourn to the pub and a nice comfy sofa seat for a few minutes?" Max replied. "I don't think I can even make it as far as the bike."

They sat back in the pub looking like two members of Mr. Creosote's extended family, while punters eyed them nervously and congregated together outside the potential fall-out zone. Jessica, not being in the same delicate state, was now on an up and managed to find everything amusing, constantly nudging Max or Fizz and laughing at their groaning reaction.

Desperate for any distraction from the feeling of having consumed a hot beach ball, Max explained to Jessica about the concert changes. "William has also taken it upon himself to paint the stage backdrop. He could do with help I'm sure, so this could be a golden opportunity for you to do some painting while probing his hidden depths."

A flicker of a smile registered on Jessica`s snowy features.

"That might be kind of fun."

"Yes, and I think that there's a very good chance William will introduce you to Rick. I mean, if William is who you think he is, then Rick can't rightly refuse can he?"

After an hour, the hot beach ball had reduced to a warmish football, and Max and Fizz felt able to venture out to the bikes. Jessica opted to walk alone through the woods.

"Do you think Stevo will be up to playing at the fancy dress party after his injuries last night? It would be such a shame if he had to cancel, although maybe Usan could step in?" Max asked.

"Don't even go there! I'll make sure he's there, even if it's in a wheelchair. In fact, that might come in useful afterwards," Fizz answered.

Max felt worn out but not actually tired when he got home. Requiring something restful, he put on some Bocherini string quartet music in the background and listened to an old CD audiobook of Robert Hardy reading Patrick O`Brian's classic *Master and Commander.* Such was the power of Hardy's mellifluous tones that he had never managed to get beyond the end of Disc One before dropping off to sleep. It used to be Max's go to listening on long flights, and there was a time when he could recite at least the first 45minutes and 16 seconds by heart.

It was three in the morning when Max awoke and crawled off to bed, relieving the exhausted quartet. As he closed his curtains, he could have sworn that he glimpsed an arctic fox slinking into the shadows on the other side of the street. Arctic fox-like, anyway. He wondered when Jessica slept.

***

"Nice pajamas," said Marguerite with a hint of sarcasm as Max opened the front door at 8.30 the next morning, sporting a pair of swimming trunks with "Hello" on the front and "Goodbye" on the back. "Very fetching."

"Given how I feel this morning, I should have put the 'Yesterday' ones on. Help yourself to whatever you like. Fizz bought some food that should pass muster. I'll see you in a bit after my shower. Could you let Scabies out the back, please?"

He returned downstairs to a house full of smoke as the recently arrived Jeff demonstrated his pan-blackening recipe for steak and sausages. "Jeff, have you invited the whole hotel? There's enough food there for an Axl Rose snack! At least I think it's food. Should it be that black?"

"There'll be no antibiotics in the new world, so it's important to cook your food very thoroughly. This will last for weeks without deteriorating."

"Jeff, don't give him ideas!" cried out Fizz. "It's bad enough the fridge being full of green sausages and chicken. I don't think black is a big step forward."

"I'll have some, Jeff," said Rick. "The circular black things too, please, which I'm guessing were once eggs?"

Jeff emptied a variety of black objects onto Rick's plate. They landed with a resounding clink, and then skittered across it.

"For God's sake, open the window a moment!" shouted Marguerite, "or the whole bloody house is going to look like a bloody advert for *Back in Black*."

"Sausages, Max?"

"Thanks. Mmm, like the crunchy texture. What's this black stuff on the side? Ah, black mustard, quite a novel concept, that. Not sure it'll catch on, Jeff, though maybe Heston Blumenthal... Tea anyone? I've got white milk, but Jeff, if you fancy black, then feel free. I run an open madhouse, so everyone should feel at home."

Despite Jeff's cooking attempts, or perhaps because of them, there was a light-hearted air at the breakfast table and a degree of excitement about the concert.

"Ten days, it's crazy!" said Fizz, quickly adding, "but I'm sure Rick will pull it off in style. I can feel that it's going to be a triumph. Max, why don't you get some bubbly out?"

He did.

"I give you Rick Wakeman, famous Yes man and Central Earth star!"

Everyone toasted Rick, then Marguerite, then everyone in turn, ending with a nod to Jeff's breakfast, as it fit the term 'toast' rather well.

"Ok, shush everybody, the first announcement is due on BBC Radio Two in a minute," Marguerite said as she turned on the radio and waited. Glasses were refilled and, as something resembling a song by the ginger-tattooed bloke ground to a halt, Zoe Ball took to the airwaves.

"And now for some genuinely exciting news! You've heard of pop-up books, you've heard of pop-up shops, but now we've got a genuine pop-up rock festival! Fresh from skateboarding in Iceland with his naked, dog dancing buddy Rat Scabies, yes, folks, you heard that correctly. Ha! Ha! Legendary keyboard wizard, former member of quintessential prog giants Yes, and latter-day king of *Grumpy Old Men*, the one and only Rick Wakeman is putting on a charity rock festival this Sunday, yes, that's in three days' time, on Devil's View Plain in Mead Bay down on the sunny South West Coast. The weather's set fair, so get your arses on down there!! Rick will be wowing the crowds with a no holds barred performance of his classic album *Journey to the Centre of the Earth*, accompanied by full orchestra and narrated by Sir Brian Blessed. Rumoured support acts include The Wurzels, Deacon Blue, Muse, Tori Amos, and there's even talk of Elton John putting in an appearance. I've got to say that I am deeply, deeply impressed by someone of Rick Wakeman's God-like status taking such an adventurous approach to putting on a festival. Glastonbury, eat your heart out!! Tickets are available right now on the 'Centre of the Earth Festival' website, so get yours straight away. Of course, I'd usually be getting tickets for free, but as this is for charity, I'll even buy my own! Full details of the charitable causes will appear on the website along with advice on where to buy a picnic rug and hamper. Watch out for those seagulls, though, and see you all in Mead Bay on Sunday!!"

Had a representative from the Guinness Book of Records been in Max's kitchen at 9:31 a.m. on that particular Thursday morning in May, they would have witnessed the first known occurrence of absolute zero, something previously thought to be scientifically impossible. The state of suspended animation lasted a full minute, until a loud crack was heard, accompanied by a muffled howl from Rick. "That sausage broke my tooth!"

Normally, such a statement might elicit a sympathetic response, but this was not normally, not by an abnormally long chalk.

Marguerite was silent. She buried her head in her hands, then jerked it upright and opened up her mouth as if to scream, then closed it again and returned her head to her hands. She repeated this action so often that it resembled a video loop.

Fizz looked at her nails, which admittedly did need cutting, and then the ceiling, which didn't.

Jeff muttered continuously under his breath about how unimportant a broken tooth would be after the apocalypse, and Glen looked like a man who had had it statistically confirmed that Burnley's chances of ever winning the Football Premier League again were significantly below those of the Boris Johnson Cabinet Party No-Stars.

Max, on the other hand, was wryly amused and a touch energised by Zoe's announcement. He rose from his seat, put on the kettle, prepared a pot of super strength Georgian Tea, laced it with irresponsible quantities of Buckfast Tonic and added a dash of Angostura Bitters. He hoped that the effect on the others would prove to be as enervating as Jeeves's special concoctions always proved to be on Bertie Wooster.

The effects were indeed gratifying, with a collective vertical lift-off occurring without so much as Nimbus 2000 in sight. The ensuing gasps and strangulated cries simply acted to cement the success of the moment for Max.

Eventually, however, seats were regained, and systems started to function again. Marguerite warmed up with a continuous thirty-second outburst that simply ran all existing profanities into a single word, as if Frankie Boyle had been cast as Mary Poppins and was trying out his own version of supercalifragilisticexpialidocious.

She continued on in fine machine gun fashion.

"ThoselittleMillennialbastardsaregoingtodiediedoyouhearmeandwhen theyaredeadiamgoingtobringthembacktolifeandkillthemagainandagainho wdaretheyannounceacharityconcertacharityconcertforfuckssakearetheym adyestheyarecompleteravinglunaticswhowillbankruptusbutnotbeforethey aredeadbymyhandforwhichiexpecttoreceiveanobelpeaceprizecanyouimagi neannouncingaconcertforthreedaystimethreedaystimethreefuckingdaysti metoarrangeaconcerthowcouldanyoneinthefuckinguniversebethatstupide venMillennialswhoaregoingtodie!?"

"My tooth!"

"A broken tooth is the very, very least of your problems, Wakeman. Stop whining, phone a bloody dentist and while you're there, see if he can give you a new brain. You're going to need one!"

At this point, Marguerite stormed out of the house, and Max quickly googled the publicity company before phoning up and advising them to barricade themselves in the office and hide all heavy or sharp objects. "You may think you know what anger is, but if anger is a drop of water, then you are about to be consumed by a flood on a scale that would have transported Noah's Ark to Mars in less time than it has taken me to call you a useless waste of space. What do you mean you thought your script would spice things up a bit? And where in f***k's name did all that stuff about Brian Blessed, Rat Scabies and the rest come from? It's all total bollocks! What? Brian Blessed heard the broadcast and has already accepted and wants green jelly babies and three bottles of 18-year-old Glenlivet?! Oh, God! I thought you were going to die, but now it's a certainty. How old are you? Twenty-seven? That figures. Look, as your last living act, can you contact Radio Devon and put out a call for anyone willing to donate staging, lighting, electrics, toilets, you name it. Oh, and I suggest you add on funeral services. Bye now. Say hi to Janis and Jimi."

He terminated the call and turned to Rick, who was rocking back and forth, holding his jaw. "Ok, you next." He picked up the phone again and dialled his local dentist, explaining the issue to the receptionist.

"Oh, my God!" she said. "I was just listening to Radio Two. How amazing! Get him to come down straight away, and we'll fit him in. It'll take no time to glue a new tooth onto his plate. Is gold ok? I've seen his capes."

Max called a cab and slipped Rick some neat Buckfast Tonic to swill around his mouth in the meantime. The good thing, he reasoned, was that with the pain from his tooth, it had not yet fully dawned on Rick that a journey to the centre of the Earth, starting immediately, might be a top plan.

Next, he said, "Glen, can you keep your phone line at the café open, so we can get hold of you and Cee if needed? If you need cover, then I'm sure Marguerite will square it with you. Jeff, have you ever played the alp horn in front of 3000 people? Fizz, I think we should pay a visit to the Coast Watch hut and then seek out William. Once Marguerite gets back from liquidating the publicity guys, she can take over again. This going to be fun. All together now!"

The doorbell rang, and the sound of Right, Said Fred being too sexy for their shirts bounced itself off the walls of the hallway. Max opened the door, surprised that Marguerite could have moved so fast.

"Hi, there! Is that Max?"

Max reached for his sunglasses.

"I just heard the Radio Two concert announcement, and it sounds like you need a sponsor. Remember me? I'm Gus Rabot. Van Chocolat Man."

***

Over the course of the next few hours, the exploding galaxies of rage originally emanating from Marguerite had subsided to mere bubbling volcanic lava flows, as she offloaded on anyone she felt might be to blame for the situation with clinical brutality. It was certainly going to be easier to reach the concert promoter and publicity team now they were sharing the same hospital ward. Instead of anger, there was now in Team Wakeman an air of grim determination, combined with a doctorate in gallows humour. Wakeman, sans team, however, was experiencing rising levels of free flow, toilet-inducing panic, which grew to toilet out-of-order levels after Rick met the Mead Bay Orchestra for the first time that afternoon.

"Good afternoon, Mr. Wakeman. I'm Maud F'Ting-Brightly, the Mead Bay Orchestra organiser, and this is Colonel Tripehound, our conductor."

Rick shook hands limply and looked for a quiet place to lie down and die.

"You take drugs, m'boy?" asked Tripehound conspiratorily. "I can get you some splendid horse pills if you like. Got a wonderful supplier in Widecombe. Help you ride the fillies, what!" he cackled, slapping Rick on the back and falling over in the process.

A near zomboid Rick was led to the organ, where he eventually recovered enough to introduce himself and suggest that they start at the beginning.

"I will do the narration myself today, so bear with me. It'll be ...," but the orchestra had already started, taking the colonel dropping his baton as a sign.

"Catch up, Wakeman, you're falling behind," Tripehound shouted as Rick scrabbled to find the right notes. This was always going to be a Herculean challenge, as the orchestra was playing something that sounded like a John Cage-Rammstein mash-up.

"Olé!" said Tripehound as the orchestra shuddered to a halt. "Gave you a great run for your money there didn't we, my boy? A few more run throughs and you'll be as good as new."

Rick appeared to be suffering from some kind of existential crisis. He sat there making angry gurning faces, then giggling manically. Every time the orchestra started to play, he was rendered helpless within seconds. All the orchestra was getting from him as direction was a series of "Three days! Ha! Ha! Ha! Three days!" accompanied by the discordant sound of his head banging against the organ keys.

Things were fractionally better back at the Mead View Bay. Following a short, one-way discussion with the hotel manager, Marguerite had herself an office, a phone and an Italian slave. The concert website now included this number, and offers of help were flooding in.

Max poked his head around the office door. "I think I've got security sorted out, M, and sponsorship is rolling in now that Gus Rabot has taken the lead. Turns out he's not just a one Van Chocolat Man. Owns a bloody fleet of them, plus, it seems, half the Caribbean. Fizz's guys are transporting down their entire stock of e-bikes, for sale at a discount, and they're happy to give money to the right charitable causes. On which point, perhaps we can have a word?"

Leaving Marguerite a few minutes later, Max went in search of Fizz at the songwriting course centre. He entered the back of the hall and observed Stevo holding forth, propped up by crutches.

Today's topic was the importance of adding a bridge to a song, and Stevo was already struggling.

Magnus was being vocal about the fact that many great Blues songs did not have a bridge and, as most modern music derived from the Blues, why should they start tinkering with things? Usan felt that any set way of writing music was artistically unacceptable and violated the fundamental right to be free of norms, while Jeff pointed out that not only was it difficult to play a bridge on an alp horn, but that songs that got straight to the point would be needed after the apocalypse to avoid communication misunderstandings, unnecessary delays and death.

Fizz was looking frustrated and was drawing a picture on her notebook cover of a figure that looked very much like Stevo, being attacked by vampire bats.

Max hissed her name from the shadows, and she excused herself, a look of relief on her face.

"Oh, my God, that was tortuous. And my fellow students are almost as bad as Stevo at times. I'm glad you came to rescue me. What trickery do you have in mind?" she asked.

"Trickery? What defamation! I'm as straight as the prime minister, and anyway, what I have mind is actually really simple. We've just got to get William moving on the backdrop, and I also need your help with getting the Coast Watch to agree to a temporary redecoration of their tower to make it more concert-friendly. I'll explain to you as we walk over."

There were already five Van Chocolat vans up on Devil's View Plain, all bar one playing *Journey to the Centre of the Earth*, the exception being the one nearest to the cliff, which, quite rightly, was playing *Close to the Edge*.

"Gus knows his stuff," said Max as the former waved at him cheerily.

"Come over a second. I want you to try our Wakeman's 100% Earth Special."

Max was more nervous than he let on, having visions of encountering a huge vat of hot chocolate into which four full English breakfasts had been blended. Instead, he was once again transported with delight.

"Don't let on," Gus winked, "but this is the magic extra ingredient."

Good, old Buckfast Tonic, thought Max.

Meanwhile, strange things were going on near the Coast Watch Tower. Huge pieces of cloth, many metres long and wide, were laid out on the grass, in the middle of which was the arresting sight of William, wearing only whitish underpants, running up and down with a massive paint roller. Close by, and covered head to toe in green paint, a man was dancing with jerky movements and shaking a pair of maracas.

William snatched up a large dressing gown as Max and Fizz walked toward him and momentarily abandoned his activities. "I heard the broadcast and thought I'd better get straight down to work. Jessica has offered to help me; she's just getting some more paint. For some reason, she doesn't believe that I only heard about the concert on the radio this morning and keeps laughing and hitting me every time I deny it. She wasn't a schoolteacher in another life, was she?"

Max made a slight head jerk towards the dancing man.

"Oh, he tells me he's an oil consultant. Heard the news on the radio this morning and insists that his dancing will ensure good vibes for the concert. I think he may be a few symbols short of the full weather chart, but maybe I can use him later on as a human roller."

"Keep up the good work," Max said. "We're just off to see old Bill in the Coast Watch Tower to ask him about some temporary decoration."

They knocked on the door, and after an age, a very cautious Bill cracked it open.

"Hello there, remember me?" Max asked. "I just wanted to speak to you about the rock concert that's taking place here on Sunday. You hadn't heard? Oh, well, in short, about 3000 people are going to descend on the plain for a day-long, charitable concert, and we want to paint your tower to look like some kind of underworld castle. Bright orange is the idea."

Old Bill gulped several times, and then let fly. "Of course you can't bloody paint the tower orange! We're a serious outfit, and I won't have drug-crazed hippies larking about taking drugs and..."

William walked over to join them.

"... and naturally I'm just having a little joke, and there's nothing nicer I can think of than having the tower painted orange. After all, we've all got to do our bit, don't we? Maybe you'd like to add some turrets as well?"

"That's a splendid idea. William, can you do turrets? One other thing. Naturally, we won't interfere with your Coast Watch duties, but we'd rather like to use your downstairs room as a sort of backstage changing area for the major artistes. Ok? Fantastic. The countess will be so happy about the orange, by the way."

Max pushed Fizz forward towards old Bill and nodded at him. Bill straightened like a ramrod and brought his right hand smartly to attention. "An honour to meet you, ma'am. Please come upstairs and take a seat. There's some very fine views of seagulls, and I bought some lovely Jaffa cake biscuits and an orange drizzle cake just in case you dropped by."

He shot off for a couple of minutes, returning with an orange-coloured tray, on which were set out the Jaffa cake biscuits, the drizzle cake and a plate full of marmalade sandwiches. "Paddington's finest, ma'am. I have also brought you a nice pot of Orange Pekoe tea, so that you'll feel right at home. I just like to say that I've always been a great admirer of Van Gogh, Vermeer and, er, Johan Crufts. Any colour of orange you'd prefer for the tower?"

Fizz felt rather sick when she left an hour later, suffering from a surfeit of all things orange. "God, the things I do in the name of the Dutch aristocracy. I think I really do deserve a title for my efforts. Max, do you have any of those nice, crunchy, salty black sausages left?"

Max's phone went. "Hello, Max, this is Sven. Heard the news about the concert and wondered if I could help at all? The volleyball girls are keen to help, too."

Max's phone went again. "Hi, Max, Marguerite here. Can you come over? We have the small issue of finding singers and a band in addition to the orchestra."

Max's phone rang a third time. "Max! Max! Max! This is Rick. Squiggs won't pick up the phone. The orchestra is a joke, A JOKE! Get me out of here! I'll do naked dog dancing, in fact, anything, abso-bloody-lutely anything but this. HELP!!"

"You're very popular," observed Fizz with a wry smile.

***

Scabies was unused to being abandoned for hours at a time and looked distinctly put out when Max and Fizz turned up later.

"We'd better take him with us when we go out again, "Max said. "Hey, Fizz, what about your course? I don't want to mess you around when you've paid all that money."

"Are you kidding?" she answered. "Aside from the unlooked-for orange OD, this is the most exciting thing that's happened to me since discovering a swimming pool in my basement! Besides which, if I can sell those e-bikes, I'm 100% certain that the company will reimburse me for the course."

"A pool in the basement? That's quite adventurous of you."

"Oh, I didn't put it in. It came courtesy of the previous owners. They just forgot to tell me about the leak."

The house phone rang to Noddy Holder's familiar strains. "Max, Glen here. I just thought I'd warn you that there's a bloke down here with greying, ginger hair looking for Rick. Looks like a demented Wurzel Gummidge. He's very angry. Something about defamation of character. I suggest he and Rick don't meet. Could he be a surgeon? He certainly seems full of detailed suggestions for re-arranging Rick's body parts."

"Thanks Glen, I've a pretty shrewd idea about who he is, and your advice is sound. Fizz, I'm going to see Marguerite. Could you speak to Sven and ask him to go up and see William, and maybe also Gus? That backdrop is going to take a huge amount of work, as is decorating the Coast Watch Tower. And as we speak, I'm wondering if the beach volleyball brigade could do an onstage display game?"

"Personally, I'm drawn to a good, old-fashioned, naked dog dancing display," Fizz answered. "Rick's so good at it, William seems to have no inhibitions either, and I imagine Sven would jump at the chance."

"Hmm, I'm not so sure. The Stranglers got arrested back in the 70s for naked, onstage dancing, and that was without the dog. We'd probably have the canine protection league to deal with nowadays. All these animal protection organisations are highly aggressive when it comes to errant human behaviour, or at least I hope so."

"You hope so?"

"Nothing, just a figure of speech."

"Can I take Scabies if Sven wants to meet up?"

"Be my guest. If he gets really naughty, just whisper, 'Pet food factory' in his ear. It usually does the trick."

"And Sven?"

"Marriage."

As Max walked up the corridor to Marguerite's temporary office, he saw the door open and the hotel manager slink out bearing an empty tray. "I am looking after her myself, Mr. Ahrenbee. I have offered free rooms to any VIP guests who come to the concert. We are full, but it will not harm some of our older guests to share a room for a few nights. More warmth and less lonely. Er, will you mention the hotel on the concert website?"

"Thank you. Of course we will. And I appreciate your approach to the guest bed situation. It's exactly the approach most rock musicians have adopted for years."

Marguerite was sipping a large glass of something white and eating neatly cut cucumber sandwiches. Three phones were on the desk, and all three were currently off the hook. "I needed a bloody breather. Switched my mobile off, too, to let me think. There's a load of local businesses that've offered support, but they need vetting, which is where you come in, Max. We've basically got the rest of the day today and half of Friday to sift and organise and then the afternoon and Saturday to get everything bloody built. I'm trying to think of this as a completely normal situation, but every hour or so I need to shout at someone, which is where that manager bloke comes in very handy."

"Happy to sort through the offers. I might pull in Fizz or someone else, too. Rick's in total meltdown over the orchestra, so I suggest that the hotel manager takes round a bottle of the finest of whatever he's got to make it seem as if we care. But in any case, I suggest you put out a call for some additional professional classical musicians as back-up. And what about the band? I see from the original recording of *Journey* that Rick used a bunch of mates, as he didn't want stars to detract from the music."

"That's true, or he could have just been skint, but it still leaves us needing two male singers who can hold a tune, a guitarist, bass and a bloody drummer. Any ideas before I take a trip to the hospital to help transfer our publicity team and ex-promoter to the morgue?"

"You could do that anyway for a lark," Max responded. "What I'll do is go and check out the songwriting course people. They may not be able to string two comprehensible words together, but one or two of them might actually be able to play something or, God help us, sing."

Marguerite looked sceptical. "I think there's more chance of all The Beatles getting together with Elvis for an evening of Mongolian throat singing, but we haven't got anything to bloody lose, so go for it. Right, I suppose I'd better put one or two of the phones back on the hook. This Sharpham Barrel Fermented White's not bad at all, by the way. We should stick some on the rider, provided Rabot's paying."

Back at the songwriting course, they were on a break, and Max took advantage to speak to Stevo. As he explained the predicament and alluded to what it might do for Stevo's career to have any of his students involved in the concert, he saw he was being held close to adoration.

"I'm not too shabby myself to be honest," Stevo ventured, "but I do know the recording, and it possibly needs a higher vocal range. Neil has a good set of pipes and Magnus, too, if you don't mind him sounding a bit Abba-esque."

"Ok, let's give them a go. They need to go to the old church at 9:00 tomorrow morning. You know, the arts centre place? I'll drop off a CD of the album a bit later. Who knows, we might even be able to fit in some of the others as part of the day, seeing as it's been described as a festival. How about you getting everyone on the course to contribute to an original group song? Something along the lines of sustainability, ecology, that kind of thing? Just an idea. Also, see if anyone has any party pieces they could trot out."

It was dusk before Max had finished talking to the long line of local businessmen who kept arriving at the hotel. The manager was delighted, as most of them dropped into the hotel bar afterwards for a drink. The new promotionally priced Wake Rick Up Before You Go Go cocktail was proving very popular and showed that even the worst advertising works if the product looks like a bargain.

Ipplepen agricultural construction company, Barn to Be Wild, were engaged to build the stage and were happy to do so for a ridiculously cheap price provided Rick sang the original song with suitably adapted lyrics that included references to "shedded wheat." Max agreed readily on Rick's behalf.

Lighting was courtesy of the Princeton Light-Fingered Company, a group of ex-cons who said they could get any kind of lighting equipment at short notice. That sounded ideal.

Other major contractors included sound equipment laid on by Whispering Bob Harris & Co. from Topsham and sanitation facilities by Pooh and Bear It from Bovey Tracey.

After the contractors, came a long line of food and drink vendors, most of whom Max sent in to see Marguerite. Gus Rabot also came by to help her out and to ensure his company's presence was not watered down by too many high-profile stalls.

Gus volunteered one of his vans to ferry concert performers to and from the hotel and the stage area. Although the total distance couldn't have been more than about 400 metres, it still sounded like a fun bit of added festivalia.

At seven o'clock, a shadow of the former keyboard wizard was decanted by Van Chocolat to Max's house, where another gathering of the clans was taking place. The Georgian Tea mix was not going to be sufficient to revive Rick, so Max sensibly announced a killer concoction with a Polish Spirit base. Actually, it was just neat Polish Spirit, but Max pretended it was mixed in case Rick's liver did a runner.

It took a combination of flattery, cajoling and, mostly, outright threats to stop Rick from upping sticks and heading straight home to Castle Wakeman. The final clincher was Max taking him gently aside and asking what time he should arrange a meeting with the Wurzel Gummidge character.

Ground down, and by now, grandstandingly grumpy, Rick started to treat the team to the story of his afternoon at the old church. However, the experience was so awful that within seconds, he had dissolved into hysterical fits of laughter, laughter which spread like contagion around the table. Those who knock the evils of alcohol clearly haven't seen the miraculously morale restoring effects that a bottle of Polish Spirit, or indeed two, can have on a small group of condemned people. Indeed, further buoyed by a monstrous delivery of chili pizzas, with a bakery's worth of garlic bread, within an hour of Rick's arrival, the whole group would have been prepared to pay Viagogo a king's ransom to ensure luxury berths for a Titanic re-enactment.

Rick even took it in good heart when informed that Neil and Magnus would be rolling up in the morning to try out for the male singing roles, and that the Brixham Fisher NKGP Choir would be providing choral back-up.

"NKGP?"

"'Never-Knowingly Gendered Persons,'" Max explained. "They used to be the Brixham Fisherman's Choir, but took the lead from the fact that their catch is becoming increasingly gender fluid."

Marguerite injected herself into the conversation, "I hate to add to all the enjoyment we're having, but we're going to need to sort out a draft running order by Friday night for the whole bloody festival. Gates, if we had any, are due to open at 12:00 on Sunday, with the first act on at 2:00, and Rick due around 8:30. That means six and a half bloody hours of time to fill, and we don't yet have any confirmed support acts, despite the information those unhinged publicity kids sent out to all the radio stations around the country. I've had a chat with Max, and we reckon part of that time can be taken up by Rick doing a pre-set, billed as 'Rick and Friends,' or something similarly daft. The only problem is that I'm not sure what friends Rick can blackmail to come, so we may have to define the term loosely. Don't look at me like that, Rick, unless you want another broken tooth! The idea is that the pre-set should just be an informal rock jam.

With a bit of luck, it'll help lull the crowd into expecting very little for the main set which, as things stand, is going to be very important for our collective health."

Rick was sent home to bed early, although later reports from Sven were that he had been prevailed upon by the Sedgemoor's owner to play "Rocket Man" and "Benny and the Jets" on her iPad Garage Band keyboard before being lured into her bedroom by a packet of unopened chocolate digestives and a six-pack of Babycham.

Max, having seen Fizz and Jeff off to the Mead View Hotel and Marguerite to The Darwin, tidied up and made a resolution to go for a morning run on Friday. This was almost unheard of in Max World, but as he had persuaded Sven and supporters to join him, there was plenty of incentive, and he thought the morning blast of fresh air would do him good. Having said goodnight to Michael Portillo, this evening sporting a turquoise jacket, yellow tartan kilt and blue wellington boots, he hurried upstairs at a record-breaking pre-midnight hour.

***

The morning saw a change of weather, and it was dark and wet as Max crawled into his running gear at 8:00. He swore to become a religious man, donate all his money to charity and dedicate the rest of his life to good works if Sven failed to show up. Confirming his view of faith, Sven showed up on the dot of 8:00 with a lycra of beach volleyball stars. Sighing, Max pulled his golf cap down as far as it would go and stepped out into the gloom and wet. Ludmilla, the Russian woman Max had first seen with Sven, spotted Scabies just as he was closing the door. She thought he was sweet and wanted to take him along. Max tried to explain that Scabies would have his own agenda, but she just laughed and slipped on his lead. Scabies, lured by her attention and attractive scent, was easy prey.

Max described a route, and they all set off. It became apparent very quickly that the volleyball women were much fitter and faster than Sven and Max, as Scabies found to his cost. The Labrador was too busy trying to stay on his feet and keep breathing to worry about lamp posts. Every time he slowed, he could feel the breath being cut off as his neck took the strain.

"Going for a run?" asked Mrs. Shevanksy.

"Going to shoot some doctors," replied Max, as usual.

"Keep it up!"

Max decided he liked Mrs. Shevansky. She had so much common sense for an old person.

As with Glorious Girl, there were distinct advantages to being slower than Ludmilla and her cohorts, and Max couldn't understand why Sven hadn't realised this earlier. Pride was a poor substitute for a beautiful view.

At the top of Murrain Hill, Max staggered to a halt. "Nice panorama across the bay," he wheezed at Sven from a semi-prone position.

"It would be a shame if we find oil here," said Sven, hopping in habitual fashion. "It would ruin the bay."

"I met your oil advisor today, and I think there is a significantly higher chance of finding fairies at the bottom of my garden. However, you should be aware that I am prepared to give your company a long-term option on said fairies should such an event occur."

After a short break, they all descended to the sea front, something Max found tougher in many ways than the ascent, given the pounding to his aging knees.

The beach café provided a welcome end to the run, and Glen was noticeably keen to provide the service, edging Cee bodily out of the way.

"And what can I get you fine ladies and gentlemen on this damp and grey morning? That's a very good crane impression by the way, sir," to Sven. "Are you coming as one tomorrow night?"

Ludmilla asked for some water for Scabies, although smelling salts would have been a better idea. She then plumped for the post-Brexit breakfast, which was kale soup, with Ray Mears's patented 'seven year' matzo bread on the side. Most of the others chose the same, but Sven and Max plumped for the old English.

"Do other cranes try to make friends with you?" asked Cee.

"Only the lady ones," replied Sven.

"How do you tell the difference?"

"I have studied a great deal and have an excellent book on cranes written by a British writer, Bill Veriodi. Do you know him?"

"No, I've never met anyone famous apart from Rick Wakeman. Do you think he likes cranes?"

"Do I like what?" asked Rick, materialising like an Indian guru.

"Cranes," clarified Max.

"Well, some of the big mobile ones are quite a sight."

"Aren't they all mobile?" asked Cee, somewhat surprised.

"Not the tower cranes; that would be a disaster waiting to happen."

"I didn't know any of this. You are all so well educated. I must buy the book," Cee said.

"Before you do that, could I have my usual?"

"Yes, Mr. Wakeman, two old English coming right up."

Rick turned and admired the view.

Max broke the silence, "Rick, let me introduce you to Sven, fantasy oil man and crane impressionist. Also, to Ludmilla and the international beach volleyball stars. They are keen to put on a display as part of Sunday's festival if that's ok?"

"I wish you hadn't mentioned the festival so early in the morning. I've come down here to build up my strength for today's ongoing rehearsal nightmare. That being said," he perked up, "it would be an honour to have you all as part of the fiasco. We can probably live without the crane impressions, though. Things aren't that bad yet."

Max bumped into William on his way back to the house, who was riding an e-bike so heavily loaded with painting canvas and materials that the tyres were flat. "I hope the rain stops soon. It doesn't help with my artistic creation. The good news, though, is that Jessica has come up trumps. She was on one of her midnight walks and managed to collect all this useable material. I was getting worried that we wouldn't have enough. She is a strange girl, though. Whenever I suggest we might pool our creative urges, she just keeps quizzing me about more and more obscure Rick Wakeman facts. She walks all night, and I spend all night up to my eyes in Wakeman trivia research."

At home, Max put on the local radio to see what news there was about the festival. He was pleased to note that it was a hot topic. Hot enough for the first major complaints to be aired from locals frothing with anger about the imminent invasion by unwashed hordes of mostly well-heeled, middle-class people to Mead Bay. Hordes who would disrupt the economy by injecting into it unreasonable amounts of non-benefit, non-drug money.

Vying for headlines with the festival, was a report about the overnight mass theft of sails from yachts in the harbour. Foreigners were quite rightly suspected.

Fizz called to say that she would be tied up for much of the day, as the songwriting group had gone into overdrive. For the first time, Max detected some genuine enthusiasm for her course and was delighted that she was so into it.

Up on the plain, the first workmen had started arriving, and Marguerite was pacing up and down shouting at people in expert fashion. The hotel manager, meanwhile, was running around at her command with an industrial tape measure, trying to get the dimensions for each piece of the festival jigsaw right. Max was impressed by Marguerite's ability to visualise the final picture from a large patch of empty, damp grass.

William had fortunately disappeared, probably in search of a dry place to paint. However, Sven's oil consultant remained a steady, metronomic feature on the horizon, like a trippy, hot-wired Duracell bunny.

Max connected with Marguerite and asked the hotel manager if he could spare the ground staff to paint the tower and make a turret. The suggestion was that the colour used on the hotel garden gate act as the model.

"We're expecting our first make-up artists later today," Marguerite grimaced. "We need to keep them well away from Rick, so I've told them he's rehearsing in a secret location on Dartmoor."

Max looked at her blankly.

"Journalists, Zombie Man! I will handle them, but can you get down to the old church to warn Rick and the orchestra about keeping their mouths tightly shut? We're already tightrope walking without the bloody rope, and we don't want to be doing it without the tights as well."

Max walked to the old church and entered to a cacophony of sound. It sounded more like *War of the Worlds* than *Journey to the Centre of the Earth*, but there was at least the vaguest semblance of progress being made.

Rick saw Max and called a temporary halt to proceedings. He was sweating profusely, but there was a determined glint in his eye.

"It's a catastrophe, but at least I've persuaded Mrs. Fart to dump the colonel in favour of someone who can stand up unassisted. In the meantime, I'm doing it myself from the organ loft. The singers are actually passable, and Stevo is at least adequate on guitar and happily character free. We've also acquired a good, young, bass player off the street, small chap in a big black hat, but we're still short of a drummer. Now, if I had six weeks to rehearse, we might get somewhere, but we don't, so I may have to improvise a bit. A lot. Can you order several cases of that Buckfast Tonic?"

***

The next day passed in a blur of activity for Max and his cohorts.

"Crisis? What Crisis?" said both Supertramp and some girl in *The Day of the Jackal*, probably not related. The truth is that when every living moment is a crisis, as had been the case in Wakeman World since 9:30 on Thursday morning, crisis existence and crisis management become the norm. So, when Max finally came up for air, around 6:00 late Saturday afternoon, he felt strangely out of sorts and slightly bereft. His last act had been to veto Sir Brian Blessed's enthusiastic suggestion that he scale the Coast Watch Tower and re-enact *Henry V* on the top of it.

"I've still got it, you know!" boomed Sir Brian.

Max wasn't sure what he'd still got but persuaded him to reserve it for the onstage performance.

The mobile rang, and a harassed sounding Glen was at the other end of it. "Max, can you pop down and lend us a hand setting up for tonight? It's getting out of hand."

Max was temporarily nonplussed, and it took him a few seconds to realise that Glen was talking about the fancy dress event.

"You're still going ahead with it, then?"

"Too late to cancel the bloody thing, and now half the world seems to want to come. We're going to have to put a rope across the entrance to limit entry and all. I could have charged £50 quid a ticket!"

Max slipped out of the house and down to the café, where Glen's legs could be seen staggering under a large stack of green chairs. The beach was full of people playing games and drinking in the late afternoon sun, and Max realised that he was seeing only a tiny proportion of tomorrow's festival crowd. "Where are they all staying?" he asked.

"There's tents all across the meadow and in the woods. The police have sensibly decided to keep a low profile," Glen said.

This was just as well because the first seagulls were starting to crash out of the sky, caught up in the voluminous clouds of marijuana smoke billowing up off the beach.

Max turned to see Cee also enveloped in smoke and coughing violently. "Absolutely vile and disgusting, I don't see what people get out of this stuff at all!"

"What in the hell are you smoking, Cee? I've never seen anything like it before."

"Grass, of course."

Max sighed and went to help Glen set up a circle of chairs around what looked like a wooden loading pallet. "What's that?"

"A wooden loading pallet. One of our suppliers lent it to us to act as a stage. It'll be fine provided Stevo isn't wearing stilettos." Apart from the chairs, there was a secondary bar to be set up, an attempt at decorations, "Some I had left over from Christmas," and a music system. "I'm prepared to play a little bit of Yes, but I don't want to scare the punters off, so it's mostly 80s and 90s stuff."

"Are you going to have a prize for best costume?"

"Hadn't thought of that. Maybe a signed copy of *Journey to the Centre of the Earth*? Is Rick coming down, by the way?"

"No idea, but don't worry, I'll sign it. The signature will probably be clearer anyway."

After an hour of sorting things out, the extension cable from the plug in the café to the stage area was not long enough, the glitter ball refused to turn and the café kitchen smelled like someone had had a bonfire in there. Glen wiped his brow and invited Max to share a drink.

"Can I have one, too?" asked Cee plaintively.

"Only when you've finished getting rid of that terrible stink you made."

They sat around the side of the café, looking out to sea and reminiscing.

"If you'd told me a few months back, when I wrote to Rick, that we'd actually be holding a concert for over 3000 people tomorrow, I'd have suggested you get your head examined," Glen said.

"And if I'd known, I would have definitely taken your advice. You know it's only six days since I stumbled across Rick in the car park, and yet so much has happened that it seems far more like a week." He glanced at his watch. "Right, I need to be off to see a dog about his dinner. I'll see you in a bit, Glen, but you won't see me!"

***

Originally, Max had intended to go to the party as Iggy Pop but was concerned about modern attitudes towards full-frontal, geriatric, male nudity. So, he plumped, that being the apposite word, for an old favourite.

Elvis left the building shortly after eight and shimmied down the beach steps to the café. Seven other Elvises of all shapes, sizes and sexes were already there, although only one fit the latter-day Elvis picture.

"Hi, Rick," Max said.

Latter-day Elvis jumped, nearly spilling his two glasses of wine.

"The two glasses of wine was the clincher, if you were wondering."

"Max? For God's sake don't give me away. I promised Squiggs I would go straight home after the final fiasco, er, I mean rehearsal, but I need some distraction, or I'm going to go crazy. Glen has promised I can hang out in the kitchen, which is just as well, as I'm famished. Two packs of chocolate digestives and a party size pack of Wotsits are all I've had since breakfast. If I don't get some proper food in me, I'll keel over."

He motioned quickly at a passing pirate. "Glen! Glen! You couldn't rustle up another breakfast or two, could you?"

"Extra eggs?"

"Please!"

With that, Rick disappeared, leaving Max to join the throng of perhaps a hundred party goers. Apart from the Elvises, there was the usual assortment of the common and the baffling. Amongst them, Max spotted William easily, as the latter's attempt at fancy dress was to wear his normal clothes combined with a hat with corks. He was busily showing photos to a Maid Marian who was rapidly running out of room to retreat.

A small ghost-like Elvis was blending into the background, and Max was just going to speak to her when he caught sight of Wurzel Gummidge. The latter was going from person to person in interrogative fashion. He was obviously getting nowhere, and Max could sense his rising frustration.

"Oi, short arse, seen Wakeman?" Gummidge asked with contempt to another small Elvis. A mistake, as it turned out, as Marguerite kicked him hard in the shins and let fly with something from the lost *Elvis Does Derek and Clive* tapes. Gummidge retreated fast, and Max quickly went over, identifying himself to avoid injury.

"I know who that was, Max, and he's welcome to Rick, but not until after the gig tomorrow."

William, now sans hat, wandered over.

"Well, good evening, good evening!" he said cheerily, addressing himself to both Elvises.

Max could see Marguerite tense as she recognised William. William being oblivious to her identity, continued with, "It's good to see Elvis making so many comebacks in one night." Not put off by the ensuing deathly silence, he turned to Marguerite and added, "Nice breasts, Elvis."

Max was impressively shocked and emitted a nervous laugh. William, sensing that his quip might have fallen on less than fertile ground, added quickly, and in the interests of complete clarity and full absolution, "I was being Australian!" He chuckled matily for the full length of time that it took for Angry Elvis's knee to connect with his groin and reposition his testicles as an extra pair of tonsils. He then dropped heavily to the ground like a felled kangaroo.

"I'm feeling so much better all of a sudden," Marguerite said. "Let's get a glass of something bubbly."

Glen's music choices were good, and the crowd was dancing with increasing merriment. While Max and Angry Elvis were dancing, they were joined by Ghost-like Elvis. Ghost-like Elvis had recognised Max through his disguise, but not Angry Elvis. Fortunately, the latter was also none the wiser about Ghost-like Elvis, though it made Max distinctly edgy. He looked round for evidence of Fizz in vain and saw no sign of her or her songwriting cohorts.

Just as he was about to give up, he noticed a group arrive together, and Fizz stood out in epic fashion, dressed as an orange, and wearing an orange fright wig. He flagged her down. "Hey, Fizz, didn't you realise that it was a fancy dress party and not a fresh fruit convention?"

"I will ignore that jibe. I am being both very patriotic and healthy, so don't knock it, Elvis!"

"Who's the drag queen?"

"Stevo. He's come as Frank n'Furter."

"But he's supposed to be performing, not enjoying himself. That being said, if I was him, I think I'd also be heavily in disguise."

"Oi, love! You can't go over there, that's for the band."

Stevo glared mincingly at Glen and said, "I am the band, Captain Pugwash."

After a double-take, Glen was all apologies.

"Sorry, er Stevo, isn't it? But you know, what with this being a fancy dress affair and all that I thought you might be one of the punters. No offence intended. You just set up and tell me when you're ready."

Stevo smiled for a second, and then his smile vanished.

"What do you mean no offence intended? I am dressed up. I mean, this is not what I normally wear. Do you honestly think I am a transvestite!?"

Midway through this little rant the microphone was switched on by a vigilant Cee, and the words "I am a transvestite!" blared across the terrace and onto the beach at ear splitting volume.

"Well, that's got their attention, Stevo," shouted Glen, giving a thumbs up sign. "On with the show, then." He grabbed the mike and announced, "Ladies and Gentlemen. Here to entertain you tonight, all the way from Transsexual, Transylvania, the seductively smooth and sensational Steve 'Stevo' Roberts!"

Stevo reached for the mike, missed, and then toppled sideways as one of his heels went through a gap in the makeshift stage.

Glen caught him and announced to a cheering crowd, "Sorry, wardrobe malfunction. Once again, I give you Steve 'Stevo' Roberts!"

Stevo staggered, grabbed the mike, and announced, "This one's for all you lovers out there. It's called 'Grey Eyes on a Grey Morning.'"

Max counted thirty seconds before the first catcall of, "Shut up and take your kit off!" cut through Stevo's delicate electric acoustic dirge. He ploughed on regardless.

"Just testing you with that one. Ha! Ha!" Stevo announced, now colouring to a tone that out-rouged his make-up. "Let's rock it up a bit for you groovers. This one's called 'Delicate Flower on a Windswept Arctic Beach.'"

A collection of minor chords heralded another mid-tempo pale wash of a song, made worse by Stevo trying to pull some increasingly desperate rock star poses as if to convince the audience that he was singing about triffids in a hurricane.

By now the catcalling and boos were drowning out the song, and Glen looked anxiously at Max.

"I thought that would get you going," said Stevo, having ground on to the bitter end regardless.

Glen sidled up to him. "Stevo, me old fruit, do you have anything maybe a bit more upbeat, anything at all? Even a cover version?"

"What about Nick Drake?"

"No!"

"Leonard Cohen?"

"No!!"

"Rick Astley?"

"Mate, are you trying to get us all lynched!!"

Abruptly, Wurzel Gummidge pushed through the crowd and confronted Stevo.

"Can you play the 'Ghostbusters' tune on your guitar, tosser?"

"Well, er, yes I expect so, but (getting annoyed) who the hell are you?"

"Just you shut up and play! I'll sing. Alright you lazy bunch of soft smug bastards. I hate prog rock, and I hate Rick Wakeman, so you can all f*****g hate him, too. Got it?! Ok, Shirley, take it away," he glared at Stevo.

Stevo dutifully started on the 'Ghostbusters' tune, and Wurzel rasped his way into a wholly new version. The transformation was amazing. Within a minute, all those peaceful, happily stoned, middle-aged, middle-class wine drinkers were pogoing and spitting like it was 1977. The call and response of,

"*Who you gonna kill*?"

"*Rick Wakeman*!"

was a joy to behold and might have gone on and on, had it not been for the swift intervention of Angry Elvis who, menacing the singer with both a red-hot toasting fork and a blood-stained kitchen knife, brought about the swiftly revised chorus of,

"*Who you gonna kiss*?"

"*Rick Wakeman*!"

which happily went down even better.

Glen put the sound system back on after one final chorus. "Boy, that was close!" he said to no one in particular.

Stevo looked crushed. Totally wiped out. Max and Fizz even felt the tiniest bit sorry for him. An idea which had been percolating in Max's mind came to the fore, and he pulled Stevo to one side, gave him a drink, and started to talk seriously in his ear.

In the kitchen Latter-day Elvis was sweating heavily as Mr. Gummidge came in looking for food. "Who are you, mate?" he asked with menacing suspicion.

"I, er, help out down here as an assistant chef," Rick answered.

"Right, mate. Get me some sausage, egg and chips."

"Ooh, er, right you are."

Rick began randomly emptying things into a pan.

"What are you, some kind of effing joker? Take the frigging plastic wrapping off the sausages first! Here, let me do it."

Glen walked in and looked on in amazement. "You are who I think you are, aren`t you?"

"No!" Rick exclaimed.

"Not you, Ri...oger."

"Rioger, that's a bloody weird name," Mr. Gummidge said.

"It's, er, Manx."

"Well, whatever you're called, you're a crap chef. I'll show you how to make a real sausage, egg and chips. First of all, you cover the sausages with brown sauce and brown sugar and add some nicely worked up gob. Next, next...I'll just take a quick break. See ya!" and he took two steps diagonally, swung his legs up onto the counter and slipped through the serving hatch, narrowly avoiding the toasting fork launched by Marguerite.

"That'll keep him away for now, but we'll need to bump up the security tomorrow. Right, who'll get me some sausage, egg and chips? I'm famished. Rick, get away from that pan! I don't want to be bloody poisoned. Glen, you've got my full permission to hit him if he causes any more trouble. Anywhere but the hands is fair game. Oh, and send him home at 11:00, will you?"

She turned to Rick. "And you go straight to bed when you get to the hotel. No bloody chocolate digestive orgies with the owner, right?! It's going to be long day tomorrow, and you need much more beauty sleep than most, and that's just to not frighten people."

Fizz popped her head round the corner. "Can I join you? William is making freshly squeezed orange jokes, and I need a break."

"Sure, grab a glass and have a sausage," Max offered. Seeing her suspicious face, he added, "They're not mine."

Rick started out of his daze. "That's not the crazy William you're talking about, is it? Max, he's not going to harm anyone, is he?"

"No, not today. Squiggs had a calming chat with him earlier. Really connected with his inner sensibilities in a powerful way." He continued, "Fizz, I've just had a little tête-à-tête with Stevo. For some reason, he feels that his gig didn't come off too well. Didn't show him in his best light. Didn't do justice to his songs."

"It came across as well as we hoped," retorted Fizz.

"Precisely. But it seems that our hopes and Stevo's were slightly different. The total humiliation bit apparently wasn't in his vision. Even when I kindly explained that this was the inevitable result of his singing his songs in the manner of his choosing, he struggled with it."

"Poor lamb."

"Nicely put. And I thought, seeing as we've slaughtered our lamb in a most satisfying way, maybe we could now help to resurrect it? Apparently, it's been done before."

"I'm intrigued, tell me more."

"That's a relief, as I was going to anyway. I think Stevo's style is all wrong..."

Outside, the fancy dress party was winding down, and Cee awarded the prize for best costume to South Park's Veronica Crabtree lookalike. Usan was not amused and refused to accept. This left Cee confused and anxious, and so she announced that Elvis had won. Glen shot out of the kitchen at this point.

"Are you trying to bankrupt us, Cee? The winner not only gets a signed copy of *Journey to the Centre of the Earth* but also a free as-much-as-you-can-eat breakfast. There's at least one Elvis here who I know would eat us down to the foundations of the building! I'll take over."

He cleared his throat. "Seeing as we're all here in advance of tomorrow's music festival, which is the celebration of a famous album, I think it's only right that the best costume prize tonight goes to someone who has taken that idea to heart. So, with no further ado, I have great pleasure in awarding the best costume award to the lady who has come dressed up in honour of The Fall's epoch-making eleventh album *I Am Kurious Oranj*. Fizz, come out of the kitchen and collect your prize, please."

A big round of applause broke out, with an added cheer by Marguerite, as a profoundly baffled Fizz emerged.

"Who are The Fall, for God's sake?" she hissed at Max.

"Mark E. Smith and yer granny on bongos," he replied helpfully.

"You'll pay for this!" she grimaced malevolently, before going on to thank Mark E. Smith, grannies everywhere, as well as all curious oranges.

To her utter amazement, some sage heads nodded and shouted out, "Here! Here! Good on that girl. She's a smart cookie, that one!"

Back in the kitchen, a beatific Rick signed a deluxe vinyl copy of *Journey* and dedicated it to "Finn."

"Don't worry," said Max. "It'll be worth a lot more now. Everyone'll think it's dedicated to Neil Finn."

It took a while for the party goers to wend their way home, largely because many of them didn't have a home to go to. Max hoped that those settling down on the beach had reckoned with the tide. He had half a mind to warn them, but then Herbert Spencer's phrase of "survival of the fittest" came to mind, along with Doris Day's "Que sera, sera," and he went back to helping Glen and Cee clear up.

Rick and Marguerite were sharing a bottle of wine on the terrace, and Fizz was struggling to get out of her costume. Jessica had simply vanished, although Max could sense she was not far away.

"Rick, give me a hand pulling Fizz's costume off, will you?" Marguerite asked. "She's glued it on. That, or too many chips tonight. Right, got her? Fizz you resist, and we'll pull. Glen, lend a hand, will you? Ok, one, two, three, heave!!"

Ten minutes later everyone was ready to leave.

"Fizz, you look really fetching in that outfit, you know," Max said. "Those scooped out half oranges are a bit snug, but they'll do the job, and the frying pan will be fine if you hold it close. But, be a dear next time and wear some clothes under your costume will you? Remember, Rick's an old man and hasn't unpeeled an orange for ages. We're lucky that the shock didn't finish him off."

Glen was allocated to walk Rick back to his hotel, while Max escorted Fizz up the steps. Marguerite crossed the road into The Darwin, and Cee was left complaining about having to walk home in the dark on her own.

"Never mind," said Glen, "you're not going frighten anyone if you keep quiet."

"Also, the spirit of Jessica will watch over and protect you," Max added.

"Who's Jessica?"

"A song by the Allman Brothers."

"And who are they?"

"That's easy, Cee. All men, but not all brothers. Good night."

As Fizz and Max reached the carpark, he heard voices coming down the steps from above.

"Quick, Fizz, you'd better hide for a second."

A moment later, an elderly couple from The Darwin appeared, nodded at Max and then stopped dead.

"Mavis, it's another one of them bloody foreign perverts in the bushes! A woman this time. Naked, too. It's disgusting, that's what it is."

Fizz emerged smiling and grabbed the old man in a powerful embrace. "Oh! Wilfred, where have you been? I was so worried. I've been waiting for you in the bushes just like you asked, and I'm wearing your favourite outfit."

She jiggled slightly. "And who's this old lady? Is that the auntie you were telling me about? I'm sorry, Wilfie, but it's too late to play now, so you'll have to wait until tomorrow. Night, night, Auntie! Hey, give me back my frying pan!"

But it was too late, and Fizz and Max rushed up the remaining steps, with Elvis's head now occupying a position of strategic importance. Behind them a Punch and Judy show was in full swing.

"So (bang) I'm (bang) you're auntie (bang) am I (bang)! I'll (bang) tell you (bang) what you are (bang)! You're (bang) a filthy (bang), rotten (bang), little (bang) shit (bang)! There's you (bang) telling me (bang) that you (bang) hate all foreigners (bang) when (bang) all you want (bang) is to give (bang) foreign (bang) floozies (bang) a good banging (bang)!"

"Ok, look, Fizz, do you want to drop by my place to put on some extra layers, make that any layers, of clothing? I'm sure Scabies will forfeit his blanket if you're careful not to mess it up."

They unlatched the back gate and began to walk along the garden towards the house when Max stopped suddenly. The lights in his living room were on, and he could see three, no four, Elvises, dancing around in gay, one could even say naked, abandon.

"So, that's where Sven got to! And I wondered who the hell all those other tall Elvises were! They all looked the same with the rest of their clothes on. But what are they all doing in my house?"

"I'll give you one guess," Fizz said.

The back door was shut, but the front door was cracked open. Opening it wider, a streak of black fur shot out at knee height and proceeded to roll over and over on the lawn in a highly agitated fashion.

"He's been at the whisky again," observed Max as he and Fizz entered and stood in the hallway. "What in the hell are they singing up there? It sounds like some kind of tribal sacrifice is going on. Fizz, what's that on your back? Look, there's something in your hair, too. F******g hell, the place is swarming with hornets!!"

Max sprinted up the stairs. "Come on, you guys, stop pronking and get out! Fizz, turn the hose on at the tap by the garage."

Fizz disappeared and Max picked up Scabies's blanket as four Elvis heads on naked bodies rushed past into the garden. Max started swooshing hornets off them with the blanket until Fizz came around the corner with the hose on full blast.

"Dance, Elvis, Dance!" she shouted gleefully as the freezing cold water hit them full-on, soliciting agonised yells.

With the blanket as a shield, Max ventured back into the house and set about opening the terrace doors and every available window. He then quickly snatched up T-shirts, shorts and towels, grabbed a few bottles of wine, and set about filling up the paddling pool.

"Well, this is cosy," volunteered Sven as he raised a toe out of the paddling pool and took a swig from an open bottle of Pécharmant.

"Yes, and perhaps now you'd like to tell me how you ended up here?"

"Ah, yes, I know it might have looked a little strange, and even very slightly suspicious, but we had your best interests at heart, Max. You see, we left the café a bit early as the girls do not usually drink, and I thought it would be good to go for some late evening exercise to freshen up."

"Dressed as Elvis?"

"I like Elvis."

There was no remotely rational answer to that, so Max motioned for him to continue.

"So, we were passing your house when I heard the dog barking like crazy, and what looked like a noisy cloud of smoke rising out of your chimney. I knew you were still at the café, so I tried the front door with my Swiss banker's card."

"And it worked?"

"Oh, yes. As you know, all bankers are crooks, so I had the idea that the card might have been designed to have other uses. It did. I let us in and heard a buzzing noise coming from the chimney. I was not scared a bit, but I suggested that the girls go and have a look while I guarded the dog. And then it happened."

"Yes?"

"The hornets' nest fell down the inside of the chimney, and they were not happy. At all."

"Maybe they are not Elvis fans?" suggested Fizz.

"We concluded that with amazing rapidity."

"So, you all stripped off and danced naked around the living room," concluded Max. "Now it all makes perfect sense of course. Obvious. Obvious," he said nodding, while looking at Fizz, tapping the side of his head and rolling his eyes in a manner suggestive of drink being the least of Sven's problems. "Now, ladies and gentlemen, if you'll excuse me, I must go to bed. Early start in the morning and all that. Please feel free to finish the bottle before you go, but no singing, please, although 'Blue Moon' is ok."

Max escorted a reluctant Scabies back into the house and tentatively started to close the windows. Unlike Elvis, however, a few persistent hornets refused to leave the building, including some in Max's bedroom. Reluctant to cosy up with these charming little insects, he grabbed a spare duvet from the airing cupboard and settled down for the night on the bathroom floor. It was a long night, with short stretches of restless sleep disturbed by vivid dreams of life-sized hornets playing lutes and all called Sting.

***

At six a.m., Max gave up, stepped into a cold shower and tried to freeze himself into some semblance of shape. He certainly froze. Scabies was less than amenable to being booted out at such an early hour to carry out his ablutions. He whined piteously and then promptly fell asleep outside the back door.

"Can I come in please?" called out a rather rough sounding voice a few minutes later.

"Is that you, Scabies?"

"No, it's not! Do I sound like a bloody Labrador!!"

"Oh, hi, Marguerite, welcome to Valhalla. Breakfast?"

"Not sure I can. I didn't sleep a wink, and I feel sick. What's more, I saw Rick's stalker and that way off the spectrum headjob painter heading off together towards the plain a few minutes ago. What with them and that certifiable bloke from last night, I feel like running away to Ibitha."

"Oh, come on now, nothing's that bad. Only the latter actually wants to kill Rick, and he may still prove useful to us."

"Max, your scheming positivity is sometimes way too much for me. We've got the dodgiest, most unrehearsed set list you can possibly imagine, a weather forecast for tonight that threatens to turn the plain into a giant swimming pool, stalkers, homicidal maniacs, randy Swedes plus a freaky, dancing oil consultant who thinks he's a peace guru. Now, on top of that, I've just heard that Rick's organ is playing up, and would you believe it, I've had Brian Blessed's agent on the phone asking if he can sing 'Climb Every Mountain' sitting on a bloke dressed up as Mount Everest. Help!"

"A mere bagatelle, my dear M. Given the fractional time we've had to put on this shindig, I think it's all going Aladdin Sane."

"Don't you mean Hun...?"

"No, it's not that good. But still, look on the plus side. We've got a major sponsor and, from what I can gather, some last-minute additional sponsors. We've got a stage, a unique backdrop, an orange castle, and far more lighting and sound equipment than can be legal. What's more, we have a full side field of concessions, great artist catering courtesy of the hotel, and more people turning up than you could possibly have dreamed of. On top of which, we've turned the tables on the local council by doing what they should have done, actually registering the Mead Bay Conservation Fund as a charity. I can't wait to see their faces when they realise that they're committed to spending every penny on preserving Mead Bay's classic buildings and public places. Ha! Ha! They'll go ballistic!"

"And come straight up and try to stop the festival. Which reminds me, do we have any security at all?" Marguerite asked.

"Oh, yes," Max smiled with evil relish, "and I don't think the local council is going to cause us any problems at all, not unless, of course, they're skilled in medieval warfare."

"What do you ... no, I don't want to know right now. I will have that breakfast if you don't mind, and maybe a small version of your patented pick-me-up."

The two of them lingered over their food, and Marguerite wore a sullen, gallows expression.

"Look," Max said, "if the worst comes to the worst, you can always write a book about this and sell the film rights. Just think, Scarlett Johansson could play you, James Corden could play Rick, and every other supporting cast member would be played by Michael Sheen."

"Including you?"

"Ah, no. I was thinking Owen Wilson."

"Who looks and sounds nothing like you."

"Yes, a distinct advantage."

"Right, let's stop playing games and get on with it. I'm just going to call Sven. He's responsible for making sure Rick is out of bed and ready to be picked up by Van Chocolat at 9:00. The plan is that he stays out of sight at the Mead View until we need him. I've got his stage clothes and make-up there."

"Make-up?"

"Of course, bloody make-up. There might be children and adults of a nervous disposition at the festival."

"What's going to happen with the organ? Doesn't Rick have some man who maintains it?"

"She's a girl, and she should be arriving at the hotel at 9:30. I've actually got every confidence in her. The problem is usually bits of food gluing up the keys."

Max locked up the house. "I'm sorry M, but I'm going to have to bring Scabies along. I can't leave him here all day, or there'll be a flood." He made as if to go out but stopped suddenly in his tracks, a grin breaking out on his face. "Just one last thing to do," and reaching over to the counter, Max picked up a suitable dart and chucked it at his former boss's face.

"Bullseye! Right in the vermin's forehead. Things are looking up!"

Entering the hotel by the back gate, Max and Marguerite were welcomed by the sight of fluorescent orange pennants strung from tree to tree across the gardens, with a huge banner staked in the middle, proclaiming "Welcome to the Centre of the Earth." Some familiar rock scene hangers-on could be seen taking selfies with the statue of the Patron Saint of Gardening, while others, having had an early start on the orange juice, were talking to it in earnest fashion.

The manager of the hotel was in the lobby in front of a huge makeshift buffet, on which there was orange pasta and, well, everything was orange.

"God, I feel queasy just looking at it," said Marguerite, and immediately slipped on her sunglasses.

The manager was as effervescent as the orange and seemed to have also acquired a matching tan. "Deelighted to see you on this historic day. I am so happy we take part in this concert. Even with the free rooms we take so much money last night at the bar that the hotel will be in profit. No need to go into the funeral business this year."

"Great to see you, too," Max said. "I hope you don't mind me asking, but are you wearing make-up?"

"Ah, no. Ha! Ha! I'm afraid in my enthusiasm to honour the countess and the big occasion I use perhaps a little too much orange colour in the food. I got a good deal online, and I didn't like to waste it."

"How much colouring did you buy?"

"One hundred kilos. But don't you worry. Is quite safe. Nobody dies, probably."

Further enquiries about the probability of the term 'probably' being probable were put on hold by the appearance of Fizz, sporting even darker glasses than Marguerite.

"Ah, Cow, er, Madam," stammered the manager. "And how are you on this bright sunny day? Some nice pasta for your breakfast?"

Fizz's grey pallor turned swiftly to green, and contrasted beautifully, Max felt, with the manager's orange.

"Coffee please. Just coffee. Black. Black you understand? Not any other colour."

"What's up Fizz? You didn't drink that much at the party. Surely this is not caused by your ill-advised communing with nature afterwards?" Max asked her.

"It's all Jeff's fault. I was creeping back to my room when he suddenly appeared and told me I should go to the bar, as there were lots of interesting people there from the music industry. Boy, was that a big mistake! These guys can drink for Holland, and I was stupid enough to join them."

"Do tell all, who was there?"

"Well, that's just it. I didn't want to appear ignorant, so I didn't ask, and no one told me. The only one I remember was this huge bear of a man who climbed up the curtains in a kind of Tarzan outfit spouting Shakespeare. Brian something. My God, he was hairy!"

"Ah, yes, that's Sir Brian Blessed, our narrator. Famous for his hirsuteness. He puts the 'la' in 'goril.'"

"And he poured about a litre of that special killer Wakeman cocktail into me. Called me a nice witch, or was it a wench? Doesn't really matter. At my age, I'll take any compliment. Ah, here's the coffee. Thank God!"

Suddenly, a large, fat, ugly, greasy-haired man, with pre-announced halitosis and a supercilious sneer, barrelled into reception. "Who's the organiser of this bloody shambles? I want them here right now."

"And who are you, sir?" asked the manager icily.

"I'm Crook, Councillor Bill Crook."

"And are you performing today?"

"No, I'm not performing you Eyetie idiot. I represent the events planning department."

"Then I'm afraid you are too late, sir. This event is already planned. Would you like a free cocktail before you go?"

"What do you mean go!? I'm not going bloody anywhere, Luigi. I'll have you on a plane back to Pasta Land so fast that your little wop feet won't touch the ... did you say free cocktail?"

"Yes, sir, just come this way. I will look after you very well."

The manager winked at the others and led Mr. Crook off to the bar. "You will not see him again," he whispered.

"One down, thirty-two to go. The roses will really bloom this year at the hotel," Max grinned approvingly.

Ensconced in the hotel HQ, Marguerite ran through the patchy set list, "I'm not sure all of these people are still alive, let alone coming," and took an increasing number of frantic calls.

Max, too, was receiving messages, one from Gus Rabot. He was sorry to presume, but was it ok for the Van Chocolat Steelband to play in the concessions area? Absolutely! In fact, would they like to be on the main stage? If so, Max would send over renowned calypso expert Dev Patel to meet them. Yes? Great!

"M, we've got another act!"

Fizz knocked and came in, looking pleased with herself. "I've finished another song, inspired by Burt Bacharach and Hal David, called 'Cows and Bats and Bikes.' Can I sing it this afternoon?"

"Hmm, really good, is it? Could you try it out on Scabies first? If he doesn't howl, then you're on. I've put him in that room just down the corridor."

Fizz smiled, whacked Max on the back of the head, and departed down the corridor.

"Scabies, oh, Scabies. Fizzie's got a treat for you!"

She pushed open the door and froze rigid.

"So, what's this treat you want to give me?"

"Oooooh f***k!"

"That's very kind of you, but I'll have to pass on this occasion. My sciatica's playing up. But come in anyway and have a cup of tea now that you're here."

On Devil's View Plain, the morning sun was defying the weather predictions, and an air of head-in-the-sand optimism reigned everywhere amongst the first arrived of the stallholders.

The steep slope of rough grass and undergrowth that bordered the long, left-hand side of the plain was cordoned off by thick new rope chains, while the footpath in the far right- hand corner behind the stage was blocked off by a temporary wooden gate with barbed wire on top. With the right-hand side of the plain consisting of one long, high stone wall, and the nearside being effectively fenced in by a string of cottages, the only clear way up was now by the entry from Devil's View Road.

On the huge stage, final preparations were taking place, with lighting and sound being checked, musical equipment lugged into place and orchestra seats lined up. It was a tough physical job, but all due credit to Gus Rabot for persuading the local infant school to provide their pupils in return for free chocolate for the teachers.

Behind the stage, the backdrop was being readied for lifting into place. A massive roll of canvas was systematically being nailed to wooden supports, before a rope and pulley system hauled the whole thing up and slotted the supports into holes drilled into the ground. William was overseeing the work, wearing an outfit that borrowed a lot from Henri Rousseau. "Wrong way up!" he cried at the foreman.

"There's a right way up?" came the baffled and somewhat vexed reply.

A small dais was also being completed off stage, sponsored by Kiruna Oil, and was just awaiting final approval by their esteemed oil consultant, who at this moment was being re-charged using leads attached to an old car battery.

A pile of sand had been deposited to the left of the stage, ready for the beach volleyball exhibition, and the players were running lengths of the plain, stopping occasionally to do squats and thrusts, all as part of their daily routine. An exhausted Zoe Ball was trying and failing to keep up in an attempt to carry out some form of interview.

She staggered over to the Kiruna Oil area. "Push off, Berry, my turn with the battery leads. Where do they go? Ooh, that's nice."

Back at the entrance, a queue was already forming, ready for the 12:00 opening. Pavement barbecues were in full swing, and brown-cloaked monks were proving very popular with their "Wake Up with Wakeman" Buckie Special. So far, twenty-six members of Shaz's Aberdeen Australian Ladies Didgeridoo Self-Defence League had volunteered to join the Order.

Although the queue had its fair share of grizzled prog veterans, there were a surprising number of under 60s, including a decent clutch of students who had rolled up to experience the delights of a festival for the first time, the Devon County Show being their only previous reference point for mass gatherings.

Back at the hotel, a gleaming Van Chocolat van drew up and no lesser a figure than Gus himself got out and opened the door for Rick to emerge. Admittedly, Rick's Teletubbies pajamas, combined with Laurel and Costello slippers, did detract a bit from the pomp, but then again, Rick was strictly off duty until the afternoon.

A few friendly voices called out to Rick as he entered the lobby, asking to be remembered, to which Rick smiled, waved and gave the standard line that Marguerite had beaten into him of, "No, I wasn't there at the time."

You couldn't be too careful.

Tea in hand a few moments later, Rick asked Marguerite about his organ being fixed (a marmite sandwich problem), and his costume.

"Are you ok with 'Van Chocolat' being written on the back? Gus'll give you a lifetime's worth of hot chocolate in return," she informed him.

"That's no problem at all. Be a pleasure. What a gentleman. Any, er, backstage extras?"

"Mrs. F'Ting-Brightly fancies you, if that's what you mean? Oh, and your stalker's around somewhere, too."

The door opened and Fizz came in. "Um, Max, er, Scabies really likes the song and thinks I should sing it immediately after the execution."

"What!?"

"Scabies really likes..."

"Yes, he does as a matter of fact."

On cue, Rat Scabies, wearing army fatigues with a green Stetson hat, strode in to gratifying dramatic effect. "Hello, you bunch of miserable scheming wankers. Not pleased to see me? Well, I'm very pleased to see you. Oh, yes, I am. Very pleased indeed," and he laughed like a chainsaw violently cutting through a particularly rough Canadian pine tree.

"Now," he continued, "I'll admit that my plans for Mr. Wakeman here were, until a few minutes ago, terminal. But, after having had a cosy little chat with my friend, Fritz, I've realised that keeping him alive is distinctly in my interests. I've got my autobiography coming out next month, timed to coincide with the definitive Damned retrospective at the V&A. So, Ricky boy, once you've changed your underwear, you and me are off to rehearse. I think you're short of a drummer, aren't you?"

Rick, mouth still gaping wide open, hands locked white knuckled in front of him, gasped a few times and tried to remember how to talk. "I'm, ha, well, honoured isn't the, but surely, if only, tremendous."

He tried again. "Great, just great. What an honour. No need for rehearsal, though. A talented drummer like you will breeze through the show. Oh, yes."

Scabies cackled, shaking his head in mock amusement.

"Oh, I'll have no problem at all playing your stuff, but that's not what we're going to rehearse. Right, let's be having you." He bowed formally toward Marguerite and said, "I give you my word of honour that he'll be onstage on time. And, if he's a good boy, all in one piece. If not, in little pieces. Can't say fairer than that, can I?"

Rick whined and looked pleadingly at Marguerite. She gave him a granite stare. "Don't look at me like that like, Ricky boy. You've made your bed, now you can lie on it, naked, clothed, dog or no dog. Off you go and just be grateful you've got a decent drummer for tonight." Turning to Scabies. "He's all yours. Now, Mr Scabies, you wouldn't mind just signing this, would you? It's for my nephew. Just make it out to 'Marguerite, with Love from Rat.' He's a bit sort of, er, confused."

"I told you he'd come in handy." Max smiled smugly after Rick and Rat had left the room.

"Do you think Rick will be alright?" Fizz asked.

"I'm sure he'll be fine. He's been in worse scrapes than this. In fact, come to think of it, Rat turning up might do his image a bit of good. Whatever you said to him, Fizz, you have my thanks!"

"I think my offering to give him a free e-bike had something to do with it. He's very keen on bats, too. Fricasseed apparently. I think it must be some kind of rare species?"

Marguerite's phone went off. "It's security. Jeff says the queue is getting so long he wonders if he can let in the gold and silver circles early to stagger things a bit. Sounds like a good idea. Max, do you want to go over and keep an eye? I need to sort out some stuff with the hotel manager and talk to the music press, as well as some of the bigger make-up artists from the dailies."

Max slipped out as the first of the journalists filed in. A vaguely familiar face.

"Hello, Miss er, um, ah, Marguerite. Hugh, from *Horse & Hound*."

"F**k off Grant!"

Fizz parted company with Max at Reception. "I've got a final run through with Stevo and the others. I can't believe that we're doing this, and nor will you when you hear us! God, I'm so nervous I must go to the loo."

A firm arm shot out and grabbed her. "Madam, it will be my pleasure to escort you. I just grab the polish."

As Fizz was marched to the toilet, Max exited the hotel, and walked down the road to where the masses were thronging.

A solid wall of huge, violent looking men with dark glasses, semi-automatic binoculars, and RSPB T-shirts blocked the entrance.

"I'm with the organisation," said Max hopefully.

"What's the password, matey?" said RSPB 1, releasing the safety catch.

Max paused a moment, then confidently announced, "Lesser-spotted brown drudge."

"Pass, friend."

With an inward sigh of relief, he went up the slope and onto the plain, the left-hand side of which was fully covered by a sea of multi-coloured stalls and lean-to tents.

Max made his way to the RSPB security tent, where a bearded man in a chainmail shirt and helmet was handing out cross bows.

"Used one of these before?" the man asked an all-in wrestler type with the words "Touch my bird and you're dead" prominently tattooed down his left arm.

"Course, mate. I'm not some National Trust jessie."

"Ok, great. But just remember that they're only a deterrent to stop people coming in via the slope, so no firing unless they're identifiable as members of the council. Then, just use your initiative, right? If you do need to shoot, aim for their wallets. That'll hurt them the most."

"Hi, Jeff, how're you doing?" Max asked. "Inspired choice, the RSPB. Never would have thought of it myself. How did you come up with them?"

"Years ago, when I was in the army, I had a drink with Andy McNab. He told me he tried and failed to get into the RSPB. Too tough for him. So, when I heard about the RSPB objecting to the original venue, I thought they were perfect. I might have slipped in somewhere that it was the council that wanted us to play on Shark Rock, and that Rick was the one who forced the change. He does like birds, doesn't he?"

"Yes, but his particular musical generation of flightless bird lovers is being retired as their bird-handling skills are deemed out of date. Can I get you anything from the stalls?"

"That's kind of you," Jeff said. "I did see this interesting phone extension for sale."

***

The Gold and Silver Circle punters were starting to lay out their Fortnum's picnic rugs on the grass in front of the stage, and the pleasant smell of money wafted over the entire field. The sun was picking up heat, and the first hats from Bates and Stephen Jones started to blossom on middle-aged heads. In contrast, those same pillars of the establishment were poured into faded and torn T-shirts, the last remnants of youthful attendance at concerts by legendary bands on tours of almost mythic status. For all the snobbery and chic attaching to the rest of their expensive branded clothing and festival essentials, any discerning thief looking for valuables would simply have had the shirts off their backs and been done with it.

Right in the centre of the commercial zone, Max found a large hut shaped like an oversized VW camper van, with the name Rick's Café painted on the outside in tasteful dayglow turquoise paint.

"An inspired choice, Glen, at least for obsessive super-fans."

"It is a bit of an in-van joke, I'll admit," joked Glen, peering jovially over the counter, "and it's confused the hell out of Cee, which is always a laugh."

"How's business stacking up?"

"I think this is going to be a cracker of a day. I've priced the Wakeman Breakfast at twenty quid, with your money back if you can clear the plate. I'm going to be well rich, though, as not even a pack of wolves could get through that lot. But, just as a precaution, I've banned Americans and, of course, Rick himself."

"And what's this load of bottles here?"

"Ah, that's another of my little schemes. I've taken some off the shelf gin and replaced the label with 'Rick's Gin,' and stuck a lovely photo-shopped picture of Rick and Ingrid Bergman on the front. I'm banking on the fact that some of crowd are old enough to have seen *Casablanca*."

"Rick might be your best customer for that. By the way, where is Cee? Shouldn't she be helping you out?"

"I've sent her off to pick up a few happy smokes. I know it's not officially legal, but what with our heavy Dutch influence, I thought it would be ok if done discreetly and could make us a tidy little bonus."

"I'm sure it will, and you don't need to worry about the gendarmerie either. None of them will make it past the RSPB, unless they're dressed as Tweety Pie."

Max gave Glen a high five and moved on. Out of the corner of his eye, he saw Cee wending her way through the crowd with a steaming wheelbarrow.

She waved at Max and hurried over. "Glen's going to be so pleased with me! I asked old Bill at the Coast Watch if he knew where I could get some top quality, loose grass, and he gave me all this from round the side of the tower. What a nice, sweet smell, too. I never knew grass could be like this, and I completely get now why concert goers like it so much." She breezed off, leaving Max temporarily open mouthed.

Jeff rushed by, puffing and clinking. "Man down!" he shouted in a deafening Swiss alp-to-alp cry and hurried off.

Max followed him in a vaguely interested way, stopping from time to time to take in what the different stalls had to offer.

An RSPB guard was lying prostrate on the grass bank, moaning and clutching his shoulder.

Jeff stepped through the ropes and shimmied down to him.

"What happened, mate? You look like you've been hit by a truck."

The man gasped. "I tried to stop this huge mountain of a bloke from getting in, and he just attacked me like a wild animal. Defenceless, I was.

No chance at all. Smashed my shoulder, destroyed my crossbow, and threw me aside like a rag doll."

Max turned and faced a large candyfloss.

"I thought he was joking about not coming up the slope, and I just gave him a playful tap," said the candyfloss questioningly. "Here, this is for you."

"Hi, Jessica, uh, erm, lovely. I wondered where you had got to. William seems to think that you've abandoned him."

"I have. I think there's something a bit strange about him."

Max stayed silent.

"His knowledge of Rick's music is way too deep. He even knows about obscure pirated versions of Rick's albums. No manager or accountant would know that. Most of them are barely literate. I hate to say this, Max, but I think William may be a stalker, like that crazy blonde girl from the hotel."

Max attempted to look reflective.

"I'm worried about Rick, but he'll be fine with me close to him."

"What do mean 'with you close to him?' What are you ...," but Jessica had dematerialised, leaving Max distinctly edgy. So edgy, in fact, that he sought out the reassuring bonhomie and laser smile of Gus, who was warming up the steel band in a far corner of the plain, along with Dev.

"How's it going, guys?" enquired Max cheerily.

"Just brilliant!" said Dev. "I've dreamed of playing songs like 'Dan is the Man in the Van,' 'My Pusin' and 'Obeah Wedding' for years, and now the band is encouraging me to sing them, too."

"And can you sing?"

"Is the Pope an Anglican? Of course! I've been practising for years in the shower, and now's my chance. But I need to have a stage name. Plain old Dev Patel isn't going to cut it."

"How about 'Calypso Devil?' That way, you get to keep at least part of your name."

"Genius, Max! Love it! Let me give you a hug."

"Um, I'll take a raincheck on the hug if you don't mind, Dev. But as a personal favour, it'd be great if you could sing 'Sell The Pussy,' Sparrow's harrowing tale of a poor family needing to part with the family's beloved cat."

"Done, Max. I'll dedicate it to cat lovers everywhere."

"Gus, can I have a quick word?"

They stood aside while the band swung into action with a superior take on "Michelle."

"I just wanted to check that you're fine with the rider for the artists? Nothing too outlandish or deviant for you?"

"Oh, no. With Rick, it's quantity that counts. Brian's jelly babies are in, and everyone else seems happy with choices from the regular hot chocolate menu topped up with some Buckie. There was, however, one request for horse pills, and I'm not sure what to make of this request from Zoe Ball?"

"Ooh, no. I should leave that one well alone. It may be ok for Ibitha but not Mead Bay."

A Van Chocolat van stopped beside them on its way around the narrow, cordoned off edge of the main field, and some rosy cheeked elder statesmen of the music world popped their heads out. "Whish one of youze Gurse?"

"That'll be me," said Gus taking a step forward, smiling and threatening the band with temporary retinal damage.

"Plesure ter meet yer. Now whaz that weeve gotter sing?"

"Ah, yes. If it doesn't cause you too much trouble, then the first one is 'I Am a Chocolate Drinker,' and then there's also 'I've Got a Mug of Van Chocolat Hot Chocolate, and I'll Give You a Sip.'"

"Well, the furrst one sallrite I s'pose, but the second one don't scan at oll. Wheel afta work summatout. But don't you worry Gurse, it'll be foine. S'pose we do get ter drink some o' the stuff?"

"Dear me, yes! There's a yard each of my 100% finest waiting for each of you in the Coast Watch Tower."

"A yard of 'ot chocolate! Well, dang and buggery, I s'pose there's a furst time for everything! Lead on, droiver. Ooh, wait a sec. There are toilets an all? We'm getting on a bit, y'know."

"Goodness, yes. With sea view."

The van trundled off and Gus looked slightly sheepishly at Max. "The truth is, that although we've got lots of toilets for the punters, your organisation, well, our organisation, rather forgot about the musicians. So, we've rigged up an open-air job, er, no pun intended, on the other side of the cliff railings behind the stage. The view is to die for."

A voice from one of the houses behind them called out, "Was that Hawkwind?"

"No, slightly more agricultural than Hawkwind."

"That'll be Tull then. Good band, but I've always wanted to see Hawkwind again. Last time they had Vera Lynn with them. I thought maybe she had replaced Lemmy but turns out it was some charity do. Are you one of the organisers of this shindig?"

Max answered, "In an unofficial way. You know that you get free entry and as much hot chocolate as you like, given that your house is on the plain?"

"I knew about the free entry, but not the chocolate. That's a real bonus! I must say that I couldn't believe it when I heard about the festival. Beats having to listen to awful Mead Bay Orchestra murdering the classics. That's what passes for culture around here, would you believe it?"

Max cut the conversation short and hurried away, as a string of Van Chocolat vans appeared, packed full of orchestral equipment.

***

The crowd flowing through the entry was now at its fullest, and Max strongly suspected that Marguerite's estimates were very much on the low side. As he squeezed through the throng back out onto the road by the hotel, he noticed a habit of exhausted monks lying by the roadside, having sold out of their entire stock of Buckie.

"That's the holiday, ah, pilgrimage to Lesbos paid for, lads," wheezed the Abbott. "And as thanks to the Almighty for his beneficence, we will all forgo drinking the local retsina and, um, stick purely to the Chilean Merlot."

Outside the hotel, Stevo and clusters of songwriting course students paced up and down, in various states of nervous distress.

"Oh God, this is just a nightmare," said an ashen Fizz. "I need a drink. Will you come to the bar with me, Max?"

"Anything to help. I recommend a huge spoonful of dark, runny honey and a triple Talisker, knocked straight back. You may call me crazy, but I think it will sort you out."

He rushed into the bar and took things into his own hands. "Here, take it. Honey first, then, one, two three, down the hatch!"

Fizz gasped, and tears ran down her cheeks. "Whoa! Yow-wow! Zabba Dabba Doo! You were absolutely not joking. That was something else entirely. And I've never had honey like that in my life. Guys, guys! Come and try Max's special nerve killer."

They all did.

The barman came back in and asked Max what was going on.

"Sorry, but I helped the musicians to a bit of a pick-me-up. Runny honey and Talisker; a killer combination. How much do I owe you?"

"The drinks are free for the performers, but, ah, we don't have any honey."

"Yes, you do. I just ladled the stuff down everyone's throats. Here's the bottle. See, Finest Hon .... Syrup of Figs. Yesss, well, let's just keep this between you and me, shall we, me old mate?" and he exited humming a snatch of "Run to the Hills." He snuck up the side stairs and found Marguerite still in her office, piling clothes on top of the hotel manager.

"Take those to the Coast Watch Tower and lay them out for Rick. That's all his costumes for the afternoon. The one for the final performance tonight is still being put together and will be delivered by the maker direct. It'd better be good!"

"M, the festival kicks off in an hour, and I wondered if there`s anything else to do?"

"I think we're done, Max, probably absolutely and completely done, but it's too late to run away now. I suggest that you take Stevo and his merry band of misfits backstage in a moment or two. I'm waiting for Rick and Rat to reappear and, if Rick's still in one piece, I'll come over and join you. The plan is that he stays here until shortly before the first show, but you and I can have a few drinks. I've told the orchestra to gather at the hotel entrance late afternoon. I don't want them clogging up the place until much later, and in the meantime, I've asked them to stay rehearsing in the old church."

Max turned to leave, but Marguerite rushed over and planted an enormous kiss on his lips before he could exit.

"There, that's done! I've had so many negative thoughts today that I wanted to do at least one charitable act. Right, off you go."

Max walked outside onto the hotel driveway. "Fizz, Fizz, how are you feeling?"

"Just great, thanks."

"Good to know. Um, I meant to ask where the e-bikes are. I didn't see any for sale on the plain. Changed your mind about selling them today?"

"Oh, no, definitely not. It's just that the Duke of Attenborough's private jet had some engine trouble, and he's running a bit late. Should be here any moment. I think it's extremely kind of him to agree to man the tent, but he was only too happy to help out. It seems he's keen to observe concert goers in their natural habit for a documentary he's making."

A large Paddington Bear ambled by as they were talking.

"Sorry, Hugh, you're still going to have to pay to get in," said Max.

The bear swore somewhat fruitily, headed over to the bank beneath the plain and started to climb up. Fizz started to intervene, but Max grabbed her arm. "Better let nature take its course."

Max turned towards Stevo, who was looking as white as a sheet despite the pick-me-up.

"You really think that this is going to work, Max? Last night was not a good experience, and I'm frankly shitting myself about this afternoon."

Max winced slightly but spoke reassuringly, "It's going to put you on the map, have faith. Now, have you got your costume ready, and did you make contact with the backing band as I suggested?"

"Yes, yes, that's all done. But, you know, I've put so much effort into my career, and with precious little return, that I need some, some, return. Some respect."

"Stevo, you'll be amazed at what you get. And Zoe Ball's going to introduce you, so what could be better?"

"Ok, guys, are we all here, apart from Jeff and Dev who are already on-site?"

"No one's seen Usan since breakfast," said Magnus. "Usan didn't like the stereotyping of the security badge with 'Wakeman' written on it and is having a new one run up."

"Well, we can't wait for Usan. Usan can join us later. Usan's a big, uh, grown-up entity."

A gorilla walked by, heading in the same direction as the bear.

"Hold on a second there!" Max called out after it. "Brian, you can use the main entrance if you've got your badge."

"Thank'ee kindly, sir. Hello, hello, what's this? Here's that young wench I was discussing the finer points of Shakespeare with last night over a few sherbets. Finty? Flinty?"

"Fizz."

"Oh, yes, I've got plenty of that left, my scrumptious. Just you wait until after the show. Ha! Ha! Er, are my jelly babies backstage? Splendid!"

"Is he quite alright?" asked Stevo.

"God, I hope not. We're relying on him to liven things up a bit. That, and your act, of course."

Stevo winced.

The sound of heavily gunned motor bikes could be heard in the distance, the noise escalating second by second until about a dozen Harley Davidsons rolled into view, mounted by riders in black leathers and RSPB insignia. In their midst, on a Harley trike, in all-green leathers with BBC insignia and a prominent Blue Peter badge, sat Attenborough.

"Terribly sorry for being late," he said in world famous tones. "Problem with the jet. Leaking fuel everywhere, I'm afraid. We managed to land at Wrangaton Golf Club, but I'm afraid there's been a bit of collateral damage out on the course. People really shouldn't smoke when they're playing."

Max walked forward, extended his hand and grasped a leather clad mitt.

"Max Ahrenbee, your Dukedom, part of the organisation. Delighted that you could join our little soiree, and best of luck shifting all those e-bikes."

Fizz introduced herself and joined Max in extending a hand, but Attenborough was having none of it, instead clasping her tightly in both arms.

"Countess, such a pleasure to finally make your acquaintance after all those calls with your underling. You can completely rely on me to flog as much of the merchandise as possible; the old chateau roof's leaking more than I like to admit. Now, I thought that I'd better do a swift change into my usual TV safari suit, and then you can get me one of the bikes. Haven't been on a bicycle for years, apart from the Harley of course, but I'm sure it'll all come back to me. I'll ride it into the festival if you agree. Must create the right impression, mustn't we?"

He reached over to his saddle bags and, with some assistance from an RSPB heavy, took them off and laid them at Fizz's feet. He bowed, smiled at her conspiratorially and said out the side of his mouth, "And here's the bats as promised. *Battus Attenboris*, straight from the chateau roof. Delightful little chaps, with a nice little bite. Ought to appeal to a rock crowd, don't you think? Anyway, they're two hundred quid a pop, come with a lifetime guarantee and a 10% single room discount in the chateau off season which is, er, the 3rd of May."

Max decided to wait until Attenborough had changed and then to take him and the musicians into the festival together. This gave him a few minutes respite to survey the comings and goings from the hotel. Having been wholly focused on the organisational side of the festival that morning, Max had not had the time to observe more closely the various characters who had been staying at the hotel the previous night, and whom he had glimpsed briefly on the lawn before breakfast.

He tried hard to identify some of the older figures who were, by their strange loping gait and wide-eyed expressions of benign confusion, obviously musicians from a former era. However, try as he might, Max could not identify one old rocker from another; they had all acquired the same ruined patina and were completely indistinguishable beyond genus.

Attenborough returned in documentary gear and looked almost debonair as he was lifted into position on his e-bike.

"One of you chaps wouldn't mind just grabbing hold of my arm, would you? I'm not quite as young as I used to be, and any wobble might be seen as a sign of drunkenness. Don't want to be mistaken for one of those boozy history presenters who keep following me around."

"Following you around?" Max asked with some surprise.

"Yes, there's a couple of them dogging my footsteps wherever I go. Look! There's one of them now. All black leathers and made up like a panda. Look, behind that monk!"

Max's gaze fixed upon the monk and spotted the small, attractive, leather-clad panda. He walked over.

"Are you stalking the duke by any chance?"

"What me? Oh, gosh no, I mean, yes. Is it that obvious?

"The duke has your number Ramirez. The game's up."

"No, no, please don't give me away. You see, I'm doing a documentary for BBC4 on the history of TV presenters, and Attenborough is the only one left alive who spans all eras of TV, so we're following him around and filming for posterity."

"But why the great secrecy?"

"Well, it's called *Dead TV Greats*. It's been in the works for years, but Attenborough just goes on and on, and we couldn't postpone the filming any longer. Oliver's also working with me on it, and he's also in disguise. He's shaved off all his hair, but it doesn't seem to be working. Look, he's completely surrounded by aging prog rockers."

Max cast around him again and fully understood the situation. It's not often that a mid-1970s Syd Barrett lookalike turns up in public.

"It's ok, I'll keep mum, but in return, would you mind diverting some of your attention for the day away from the duke and hanging around backstage to film a few interviews? Zoe Ball's bouncing around, but it would also be good to have the BBC History Department's angle. There will, after all, be some very old and historically significant figures back there. You can take Syd with you; some of them may think they remember him. It'll help break the ice."

Max returned to the duke. "Ok, all sorted. Case of mistaken identity. They thought you were someone called John Simpson. Apparently, he's an elderly BBC travel presenter who's sent around the world to report on places no one wants to vacation in."

Attenborough harrumphed. "Never heard of him! Probably some Johnny-come-lately who started at the BBC in the 60s."

"1970, actually," Max said.

"Pah! Still wet behind the ears. They should be following me around. I could show them a thing or two."

Max was still digesting this in when he was tapped on the shoulder by a large, hairy hand.

"Er, Max, isn't it? Do you think I might be permitted to start proceedings with a bit of *King Lear*? I thought it might raise the tone a bit. Oh, hello, your Grace! Delighted to see you again. Blessed. Brian. Sir."

Attenborough gazed thoughtfully through the furry undergrowth. "Tanzania wasn't it? 1961. You were being taught sign language by Jane Goodall. I must say you've come on in tremendous leaps and bounds, no pun intended, although your sentence structure is still a bit off."

Sir Brian looked crestfallen. "Um, no, well, actually, it was in London, the Parkinson Show, in 1980. You remember, *Gordon's Alive*!?"

"Is he now? Well, I'm afraid that my memory's not quite what it used to be. Brother of yours?"

"Sir Brian," Max said intervening, "I'm afraid that we won't have time for *King Lear,*" and then added under his breath, "although maybe something out of *Jungle Book*."

Fortunately, Max didn't notice the glint in Sir Brian's eye as he caught this aside. He turned to the songwriting group and immediate followers and announced, "Chaps, we're going in. Just keep your wits about you, relax and enjoy yourselves. Abject panic at this stage will serve no purpose at all apart from feeding the uncontrollable frenzy of a wealthy, middle-aged crowd who realise that they've been taken for a ride, a very long ride culminating in a very long fall off a very high cliff into the mouths of fast-food starved, fully armed, Mid-West, Trump-voting libertarians."

They moved off, with Fizz steadying Attenborough's bike, and RSPB security forming a guard of honour through the entry gates. At the top of the slope, Attenborough waved Fizz off and went to the left, while Max's group swung to the right. The smart money followed the duke, whose Fizzless e-biking was dangerously entertaining, and started to draw the crowds long before he reached, or rather, ran into, the e-bike tent. There, he found a large package awaiting him, full of orange T-shirts with "Atts is Bats" emblazoned on the front, and an arresting photo-shopped photo of a leather clad, bat-like duke on the back, with the chateau website address printed below. A handwritten note from Fizz suggested that each e-bike buyer should get one free, with a £30 cash only payment otherwise. The duke rubbed his hands in glee and started his pitch.

"Get yer e-bikes 'ere! Get yer blee-ee-ding bikes 'ere! Only a grand a bike, and oi'm doing a special deal at five for four grand, so yer can take the 'ole family out for a 'ealthy ride in nature for less than a meal at Gordon Ramsay's gaff. You carn't say fairer than that, can yer? Oi'll even frow in this 'ere classy bat T-shirt for free, and it's worf thirty nicker if it's worf a penny. Did you know that bats is even more intelligent than cats? Stands ter reason, don't it? I mean, B comes before C. 'Course, I'm the smartest of all, 'cause Atts starts with an A. Bet you never thought of it like that before did you, Madam, er, Sir, er, what's that? Usan??"

A frisson of nervous energy swept over Max as he led the others around the edge of the crowd, where a narrow path had been left for vehicles. At the Coast Watch hut, there was an entrance to the backstage marquee, the only gap in a line of high metal dividers that had been stretched from the front edge of the stage. The dividers had been draped in yet more canvas, and William had belatedly tried to cover them in his only remaining red paint. This had not had any time to dry before being hauled into place, and the paint was running down the canvas in rivulets onto the grass, leaving the strong impression of an ongoing backstage massacre.

"Glass of champagne, sir?" said a small child staggering under the weight of a fully loaded tray.

Max took two and looked around for Fizz. He found her deeply engaged in a serious conversation with a man wearing a red beret and dark sunglasses.

"Max, this is Ray. He's our festival sanitary specialist, and he's worried about our cliff-side loos."

Max reached out to shake hands but thought twice about it. "I didn't know that we had a festival sanitary specialist? Do you go to many music concerts?"

"Crikey, yes. I spend my whole time visiting the loos at music venues all around the world. I find that with the amount of beer I drink, they become a sort of home from home."

"And you think that there's a technical problem with our loos here?"

"Nah, not really," he guffawed. "I was just trying to impress this charming young lady with my sanitary tales of yore."

"Well, I think you've made a conquest. Your face is looking very flushed, Fizz."

"Yes, well, thank you, gents. I will now go and visit these famous facilities. It's nice to go without my private escort and seat polisher for a change."

"She has an escort? Now that's what I call posh!"

"Countess of Arnhem."

The sanitary expert whistled through his teeth.

"She wouldn't like me to give her seat a quick buff, would she?"

"That's very kind, but maybe later. I think she's going to be well acquainted with the facilities by nightfall."

Sven peered through the entry and called out to Max, "Can the volleyball players come in to change?"

"Oh, God, I'd forgotten about them! How many of you are there?"

"Thirteen."

"Look Sven, I don't know a huge amount about the game, but thirteen sounds excessive."

"It's three teams of four, plus me. They will play a quick exhibition knock-out competition, and I'm the referee."

"Alright, if you say so. You'd better all squeeze into the Coast Watch building, but kick out anyone who's in there first. We want the exhibition to be strictly limited to the stage only."

A blinding flash of light was followed by Gus, bearing bottles of chocolate liqueur. "Anyone like a glass? It's 70° proof."

Gus disappeared from view almost instantaneously as a murder of musicians descended on him like a group of ravenous crows. Max could see the Rabot teeth flashing at intervals from the centre of the scrum and reflected on whether Gus was giving out some kind of enamel-based SOS signal.

Then, as suddenly as it had gathered, the mob dispersed, leaving a windswept and visibly diminished Gus gasping for air, his hands opening and closing on thin air where there had once been bottles.

"I think you can call that a success, Gus, although you've somewhat underestimated the consumptive powers of the average muso. Can I suggest a bottle each? I'll give you a hand to fetch some more."

They walked out of the backstage area, bumping into some well-known faces on their way in.

Max called out to each of them in turn, "Nice to see you and loved the latest album! Not everyone would risk those lyrics today. Brave."

"You know a lot of people, Max."

"Yes, I do, Gus, but none of these guys."

The quickest way to Gus's main storage van was along the narrow corridor in front of the stage, and a helpful RSPB guard cleared a path through the punters with the wave of his crossbow and the occasional reveal of his mace. By now the crowds were starting to pack in tight, and it was a perilous task for anyone trying to thread their way around sprawling picnickers without stepping on someone's jar of stilton, knocking over their bottle of Sauternes or stubbing out their spliff. Talking of which, Max nearly fell over Cee just in front of the main stage. She was carrying a large tray, like the kind used for serving up ice cream during a theatre show interval, full of loose, green stuff.

"What've you got there, my gel?" asked a high court judge-type wearing a ripped Mötorhead T-shirt.

"Best Reed-Sweet Grass, sir."

"Never heard of it. Is it pucker, and is it expensive?"

"Very," asserted Cee, nodding her head sagely twice.

"Right, then I'll take a kilo please. Does it come with a kiss?"

"Have you not heard of Me2?"

"Me, too," said the off-duty drugs squad officer next to him, smiling enthusiastically.

"Right, that'll be £150 each and then... you can kiss my feet," said Cee gleefully.

"Oo-er," said High Court, "I'll give you an extra fifty quid for that!"

"How's the fungal infection, Cee? Getting any better?"

"Thanks, Max, a little bit. My big toe is still green, but the others have now progressed to yellow. I'll show you after this charming gentleman has kissed them."

The judge gagged and retreated rapidly, treading heavily on the drug officer's size 13 feet, who yelled, "Oi, watch what you're doing, mate." He looked High Court up and down and sniffed disdainfully. "You're just another rich poseur aren't you? I bet you don't even know anything about Mötorhead do you?"

"I do, too! I've seen all their Top of the Pops performances and," he spoke triumphantly, "I've got a signed copy of the *May 25th Live at the BBC* bootleg. Cost me a fortune it's so rare!"

The officer switched up a gear to snorting. "That's nothing, mate, I was at the bloody concert and I've got Lemmy's underpants to prove it."

High Court was unable to hide his awe.

"How the hell?"

"I was there undercover, and we busted the band afterwards. Stripped Lemmy right down to his Speedos. Right name for them and all. Bulging with amphetamines they were."

"And what happened?"

"Well, I'm a decent bloke, so I split the stash with him, and he gave me his underpants as a goodwill gesture. Signed them for me, too. What a gentleman. I've got them on now, want to have a look?"

Cee's feet were suddenly history, a busted digital flush, although she managed to whisk the £50 tip out of High Court's hands unnoticed while he was engrossed in talking lingerie, and swiftly moved on down the line, leaving Max and Gus to push on in the opposite direction towards the van.

Scarcely had they closed the door when a loud banging started on the roof.

"Those gulls are getting to be a real bugger," Max said in vexed tones.

The banging got louder and turned vocal.

"Open the bloody doors before I blow them off, will you!"

"And abusive, too." Max let Marguerite in. "So nice to see you."

"I saw you two slackers from the other side of the plain. What are you doing hiding in here? You don't need to hide be-fore the concert starts. You're safe, be-fore it starts. By the way, Gus, is this thing armour plated? I'm thinking exit strategy."

"If you think I'm going to let my nice, new van be ripped to shreds, you've got another thing coming," Gus said. "It's very expensive; the paint contains real Rabot Estate Trinitario. Anyway, the best way out is going to be by unblocking the footpath behind the stage. But why are you so worried? It's going to be a breeze. Anyway, have a drink now you're here. Let me have your jacket."

Gus reached over and slipped, causing a dozen bottles of chocolate liqueur to cascade onto the floor with an orchestral crash.

The term "death by chocolate" came into Max's head as he slipped for the third time, bringing both Gus and Marguerite down with him.

"Well, thank you so much, Max. There's nothing a girl likes more than being rolled in chocolate liqueur wearing her best party frock."

"What, you mean that wet brown rag you're wearing? Ow! Oww!! Get off, you vicious little chocolate devil. Gus, Gus, Help me!"

But Gus was busy sucking his shirt sleeves.

"Mmm, this is rather good. I could charge a fortune for a chocolate immersion course. Perhaps? Perhaps?"

"Later, Gus, later. Our first priority is how to get backstage with the rest of the bottles without being licked to death en route, pleasant though that might be in the right circumstances."

***

Out in the open, the on-stage speaker system began to crackle into life, and the sound of "In the Summertime" flowed out over the crowd, raising a muted cheer.

Gus, Marguerite and Max inched back towards the relative safety of backstage, assisted this time by a flock of RSPB security guards. The sight of their dripping brown clothes caused a degree of mirth.

"Look, it's Hot Chocolate!"

"No doubt about it!"

"I should coco!" and ending with the slightly less salubrious, "Watch out for those festival toilets, lads!"

"Shall I shoot them, ma'am?" enquired a string-happy guard.

"Only if they don't clap when the bands are on."

"Right, you lot, you heard the organiser. Clap or die! Got it?"

The front row started clapping.

"Not now, you dozy bunch of grockles! There's nothing to clap now, is there? If you clap when no one is on stage, I'll also shoot you. Capiche? Right, now relax and enjoy yourselves. There's going to be some pretty music coming up. Just right for soothing the birds."

Backstage, Marguerite, still dripping, found herself a chair and a microphone.

"Right, now listen up please. Lis-ten Up Puh-lease! OK, shut the f**k up, you bunch of brain-dead tossers!! One more bloody peep out of you, just one peep, and I'm on direct dial to Ronan the Barbarian, and you'll all be put away for the rest of your sad, miserable, debauched little lives!"

She paused and swept her hair back in an arch manner, at the same time winching a terrifying smile into place, like a crossbow string being drawn tight.

"It's such an honour to have so many distinguished musical guests and gate-crashers here today for this totally unique celebration of Rick's music. I can't deny that the short time we have had to organise this event has presented some huge personal and logistical challenges, but the enthusiasm and commitment of everyone involved has been, um, almost annoyingly well focused. Right, I would now just like to take this opportunity to properly execute a few pe... that is to say, I would not be executing my duties properly without naming a few of those people without whom none of this would ever have happened.

"So, firstly, a shout out to Glen Matlock, erstwhile chef-proprietor of the Mead Bay Café, who I'm sure had absolutely no idea what he was letting either us or him in for when he wrote suggesting a Rick Wakeman celebration event at his café. Without Glen's unstinting support, in the form of three or four cooked breakfasts a day, Rick would be half the man he is today. So, go and buy from his stall, although I'd keep off the grass if I were you.

"Next up, a word about our sadly absent PR support, Millennials PR. Their contribution has been quite incalculable, and I'm glad to say that they have been paid back in full for all their help. It was a genuine pleasure settling up with both them and our promoter in person. To Team Wakeman, which includes Max and Fizz here, none of whom I had hoped to meet just a week ago, huge thanks, although for exactly what I haven't quite worked out yet. The Mead View Hotel, where most of you are staying, has provided us with an office and round the clock catering that includes orange pasta and the type of cocktails that put hairs on your palms. Although no one knows what the hotel manager is called, thanks for that Max, he's been like a sacred little lamb in his support of me and the festival's cause.

"Now, none of what you see around you would have been possible at all without the incredible generosity and hard work of local Devon tradesmen. The quality of the props is amazing, and the lighting equipment alone looks like it comes from a Premiership football club. Ok, ok, right, Saviour time! Gus Rabot. Mr. Chocolate. Gus, where are you? Come here my little death ray of sunshine. Without Gus, no sponsorship and no festival. Period, full stop. I am hugely grateful to him for his support, which is why I have become a walking advertisement for his chocolate liqueur. 'If you're going to catch pneumonia, then do it in style' is what my doctor, old Dr. Hutt, used to say.

"Rick is still beautifying himself, kindly supported by the make-up team from Lord of the Rings, but he would like me to add his personal thanks to all of you who have turned up today to perform at the festival. I struggle to find the right words to describe you, so I'll be polite and stick to eclectic and surreal. Please give yourselves all a small hand. Remember, though, that not only is this a celebration of Rick's music, but the profits, if there are any after, er, essential deductions, will help ensure the architectural integrity of Mead Bay and the long-term survival of any number of hitherto unmissed birds. Oh, and on that subject, please don't annoy the security folks with any birdist jokes, or it'll be early dodo for you.

"Fine, that's all done, and if anyone wants to watch, I'm off to suck my clothes dry. Oh, hold on! Wait just one moment! What is this piece of paper that has just been handed to me, with the printer ink still wet? Yes, folks, incredible as it seems, it's The Set List; a thing of mythical status until about thirty seconds ago, and still an object of wonder and, more than likely, totally misleading content. When I saw the only previous draft TBA was dominating the set list, but they seem to have withdrawn at the last moment and been replaced with real acts, some of which I have even heard of. Here goes then.

"At 2:00 we kick-off with that most rock n' roll of acts, the International All-Star Beach Volleyball Team. We hope that they will wake up the crowd with their sporting brilliance and serve as a happy reminder of the fact that Mead Bay was once a leading seaside resort. Refereeing the action, whilst no doubt performing his patented crane dance, will be Sven Anderson. I would introduce Sven, but there's little point as he is already well known to at least fifty percent of you backstage, and in the crowd.

"At 2:45 we have those eternally dedicated cider, and now I understand, chocolate drinkers, The Wurzels. One of the Southwest's most enduring acts. Great to see you, lads. It gave me a real buzz to find out that you were still alive. At 3:30 the Gus Rabot Mostly-Caribbean Steel Band, featuring Calypso Devil will sweep you away with their tribute to the aptly named Mighty Sparrow, an RSPB favourite. At 4:00 we change from calypso to total mystery with Steve 'Tweet Tweet' Roberts and his band. Yes, right, ah, let's pass on quickly to 4:30 and, Christ help us, it gets worse, The Groovy Songsters, a scratch group of international nature currently based in Mead Bay and featuring Fizz d'Arnhem on keyboards and vocals, Jeff The Yeti on alp horn and security, Saff Ponsonby-Cartwright on guitar and vocals, Cee Bea Geaby on spoons and vocal noises, with possible additional accompaniment by Usan. Is that an instrument of torture? God knows what these guys sound like, and he's suddenly pleaded another engagement.

"At 5:00, thank the stars, yes! Deacon Blue. A touch of real class. By the way, this Chocolate Girl outfit is just for you, Ricky. At 5:45 we move from chocolate to cornflakes, with the wonderfully kind and almost local Tori

Amos, who, I might add, has a highly successful career and doesn't need to be here at all. Love you, Tori! At 6:30 we catch our first glimpse of Rick, performing a special set of his favourite songs from the, er, punk era, with the previously unheard of Punk Wakeman Band. I bet none of you knew that Rick liked punk, eh? Well, yes, he had a recent epiphany and believes that liking punk is good for his continued health and well-being. At 7:15 we welcome local boys, Muse. Nuff said. Some of you may even have heard of them?

"At 8:00 we have a thirty-minute break while the stage is set up for *Journey to the Centre of the Earth*. Rick's due on at 8:30, but as our curfew is 11:00, we have some leeway to allow for set changes and any technical hitches. Touch wood, and anything else that might be to hand, it'll all go off without a hitch. Right, that's it, couldn't be simpler, could it? For those of you who are still conscious at the end, there will be a gentle soiree at the Mead View Hotel, starting at 11:59 on the dot, with breakfast served later. Please be careful when offering hard liquor, drugs or a quick leg over to doddery old people at the hotel. Some of them may actually be paying guests."

Marguerite stepped down and squelched her way to the Coast Watch building, Max in tow. The door was locked. "Are you still in there, girls? I want to come in and change."

A deep tremulous voice called out, "Go away! I won't have any more naked women prancing around here. It's a disgrace! The Coast Watch is a serious organisation."

"Clearly the 'watch' bit is Bill," Max said. "As in, why were you watching? I think we need William to have a quiet word with you about your behaviour."

"Nooo, not that!" and the door flung open to reveal a shaking old barnacle.

"Look, go upstairs and lock yourself into the observatory. That way, you'll be safe from both temptation and death."

Bill scuttled upstairs, and Marguerite stepped in. "Oi, what do you think you're doing, Max? Get out!"

"Look, I have no objection at all to naked women prancing about, even if it's only one. Anyway, that is exactly what you will be doing for the rest of the day unless I assist. Ever wondered what you were going to change into?"

"Oh, shoot!"

"Just give me a few minutes to rustle something up for both of us."

Finding someone in the crowd willing to give up clothing proved more challenging than expected. Plenty of shorts were offered up, but Max found it well-nigh on impossible to find a single soul prepared to part with a treasured band T-shirt, no matter how woebegone or fetid. About to give up all hope, Max spotted a tall, distinguished looking gentleman in his late 60s, with tight grey curls and a beatific smile that was slightly obscured by wreathes of sweet smoke that had evidently not been supplied by Cee.

"And how can I help you?" he said, in a warm Dutch accent, as Max sidled up to him somewhat furtively.

Max was about to answer when he noticed that the man had a multi-coloured chart in front of him, covered in squares, lines and arrows, adorned with lots of scribbled mathematical figures.

"Are you a surveyor by any chance?" Max enquired, clothing momentarily forgotten.

The man chortled. "Oh, no, this is just my drawing of the festival site. You see, I have marked down every food and drink stall on the other side of the plain, and every picnic blanket on this side. The tents and stalls are coloured differently by relative bargain value of goods, and the picnic blankets by potential opportunity of obtaining free food, drink or other items. I have also marked each person on each blanket with a colour for gender, although I am guessing slightly as this can be fluid depending on the generation. The weaving parallel lines you see are numbered and show the best routes to access the cheapest stalls, as well as key areas such as the toilets. I have added in the distances to an accuracy of three decimal points, as well as the estimated travel times, based on factors such as traffic circulation, wind speed, barometric pressure and degree of being drunk or stoned. I would like to add a bit more detail about seagull types, but I am running out of coloured pens, and they're not cheap, you know."

Max looked suitably impressed. "Are you sure you're not a surveyor?"

"No, no, just a humble retired teacher."

"Maths?"

"Beat Poetry and Free Form Jazz."

"In that case, can I have a smoke of that? Its properties seem transformative."

"But of course. Here is one I made earlier. Only eight Euros. Now, I believe that you wanted to ask me something?"

Max inhaled and found himself looking down on the plain from way up in the air. A Dutchman's eye view in fact. The map now made perfect sense. All the colours seemed to be smiling and winking at him and all the blankets dancing. A pure white seagull swooped down, almost touching his head. He waved and called out, "Hello, Jessica. Nice plumage," and shot back to reality, coughing violently and trying to clear his head.

"Yes, yes, er, yes, a shirt. My kingdom for a shirt, or rather two shirts."

The Dutchman's eyes narrowed.

"And how much is your kingdom worth?"

Max emptied his pockets. "Will a hundred pounds do? I'm desperate."

"You have a deal. You see I am desperate, too. So desperate that I would have let you have the shirts for £98.47."

Max floated back to the backstage area and knocked on the Coast Watch door. "Marguerite, your knight in shining armour returns."

The door opened, and Max went in, full of smiles.

"You bastard! You absolute and total bloody bastard!! How could you do this to me?? I'm a professional! I have a reputation! Oh God, I hate you sooooo much, Max!!"

A few minutes later, Max and Marguerite crept out walking backwards, wearing shades, and with their arms folded tightly across their chests. But it was just hopeless, absolutely hopeless. The sheer size of James Blunt's angelic face, circled by the glitter- printed words "You're Beautiful" could not be hidden.

"And you paid a hundred quid! A hundred bloody quid! A bloody hundred bloody quid for, for, for ... this!!"

"Look, M, this poor bloke's wife is a huge fan of Blunty, and he's been forced to live a double life of subterfuge and lies ever since she saw him in concert. It's driven him to the very, very edge, and we've saved him. Think about that. Doesn't it make you feel good?"

The hammer blow to his solar plexus suggested perhaps not.

"Fizz, come and talk to us, will you? Thanks, a bit to the right, and closer. Good. Waiter, can we have some champagne? Slightly off the chocolate liqueur for the moment."

Fizz was already looking nervous and twitched noticeably as her phone went off. "Hello, Fizz. Ah, it's you, Duke. So nice to hear from you, and so soon. How's it going? Fizz? Oh, that! It's just an informal Dutch greeting, a bit like 'Top of the morning.' Yes, I know it's afternoon, but that's just the Dutch way. We're economical with words." Fizz listened on intently for a few seconds, trying to screen out the hubble bubble of sound around her. "Can you just repeat that?"

"Yes, certainly," said the duke somewhat scratchily down the line. "The bats, they've gone. The whole damn lot, gone!"

"What! Someone has stolen all the bats? How is that even possible?!"

"No, no, not stolen, bought!"

"Bought!"

"Yes, this 'of the night' character, dressed in black, with slicked back, black hair, came up and asked about them. He seemed incredibly knowledgeable about bats and their blood types and was particularly interested by my telling him there were thousands more of the little buggers in the chateau roof. Even asked me if the chateau was for sale? Gave me his details. Lovely chap. A Mr. Lett."

Fizz hopped around in joy, shaking her arms in the air like a crazed air marshal, while Max and Marguerite looked at her quizzically.

"Bats. All gone. Bats!"

"Who's gone bats? Not the duke, not after all these years, surely?" Max said with real mock concern.

"No! No one's gone bats or, ah, at least I don't think so. Is going bats a new gender thing?" Fizz asked.

Max told her that at least as of that morning, no.

"Ok, ok, so what I meant to say, in my very basic English, is that someone has bought all the bats. And the guy who bought them, a Mr., er, Lett, might even be interested in buying the duke's chateau, just so he can be close to the bats."

"I hope he knows what he's lett-ing himself in for."

"Cut it out, Max," said Marguerite, raising her eyebrows skyward. "Can't you be grown up just for one second?"

Silence reigned.

"Answer me!"

"That was your one second. I hope it was enjoyable."

"Men!" she sighed. "You're basically surplus to requirements."

"Oh, I don't know," Fizz said, "some are very good at drawing up itineraries."

"Count me out, then," Max said swiftly. "I just rely on luck and a sense of smell when I travel. If there's a vineyard within 100 miles, I'll find it."

Marguerite smiled dismissively. "But then you're so uniquely talented, aren't you, Max, honey, even if you usually have to say it yourself."

"You're so right, M, and I sense in your voice the smallest hint of, what is that, admiration, veneration, devotion..."

"Abject mockery."

"Well, fine, I know when I'm not wanted, so I shall go and talk to some, how did you describe them, eclectic and surreal people, who I'm sure appreciate great talent when they see it. You coming, Fizz?"

"No, I feel a sudden urge to look at the view. It's so stimulating that, um, ar, bye!" and she shot off like a bat hot winging it out of an owl convention.

Max surveyed the backstage in search of a worthwhile conversation. The desperate gaze of delectable 90s chantette, Emma Nubnot, caught his attention, and he moved swiftly in her direction, interrupting William's final nude portrait sales pitch.

"And as you're obviously not as young as you once were. Ha! Ha! I can hang some gauze in front of you."

She turned to Max. "You know what I really want? What I really, really want? A cig."

"A cig?"

"Aaaah!"

"Well, Em, as you've just stubbed out William's creative flow, shall we take a stroll? Anyone you'd like to meet?"

"That Gus Rabot is rather dishy, could you introduce me?"

"No sooner said than done, old spi, ah, girl. Just let me pop these over your eyes for protection. Gus!"

Max waved Gus over. "Gus, this is Emma."

"Delighted to meet you, Emma. I was a big fan of your, um, but I'm sure you don't want to hear all that now. Perhaps you'd like to sample some of the goodies I keep in the back of my chocolate van? I cater for all tastes."

"You had me at 'but.' Lead on, Gussie!"

Max stepped back and bumped into a neat and trim figure, sporting a questionable moustache.

"I'm so sorry," they both exclaimed at the same time.

"I loved your hippopotamus!" cried Max with fannish glee.

"Well, thank you very much. It's always a pleasure meeting a connoisseur. I'm afraid it had to go in the end, though. The pool was just not big enough for the both of us."

The sound of fist hitting nose attracted Max's attention, and he glided over to where William lay crumpled on the grass.

"Surely you didn't suggest doing a nude portrait of him?!" cried Max, pointing at a rapidly receding figure in an oversized hat.

William staggered to his feet, dripping blood down his shirt front. "It was only a light-hearted joke. This man told me he was called JK, and I congratulated him for walking the trans talk."

"You're having a great day, William, aren't you? Can I suggest you keep your conversation to the weather and your health for a while? I have your best interests at heart, believe me. I don't want you becoming anaemic."

"Max! Maxy, darling! Just a quick word in your shell-like. You know I really still think a bit of *King Lear* will work. How about if I introduce Rick with,

You see me here, you gods, a poor old man, As full of grief as age; wretched in both.

A bit of drama sets the scene nicely, doesn't it?"

"But Brian, petal, don't you think that might come across as a bit of downer to a venerable musician like Rick, about to put his pitifully battered and bloated body on the line one more time for the sake of charity and self-promotion? It would be like shouting 'Branagh!' to a Shakespearean actor just before they go stage. Discomforting at best."

"Yes, yes, I suppose you're right, but it's just that with such a big audience I feel the need to really show them I've still got it!"

"Look, Brian, sugar puff, I know your reputation, and I know you've still got it. But we most definitely don't want to see it today."

***

There was a sudden buzz of excitement, and into the marquee came a slight, springy figure with skinny jeans, spiky dark hair and a face that looked to be simultaneously that of a schoolboy and Methuselah. "Anyone got any tea?" he barked in a markedly friendly manner.

Marguerite stepped forward, with a large cup. "Hi, Ronnie, so pleased you could make it. How's tricks?"

"Oh, hi, Marguerite!" cried Ronnie crushing her in a huge bear hug. "I wouldn't miss my old mate Rick tinkling the ivories for anything. We once dropped a tab together and thought we'd been to the centre of the Earth. Woke up and the whole place was inhabited by wanker bankers. Turned out, we were at Moorgate tube station. Bad trip, that, I can tell you!"

"I never knew Rick took acid."

"Neither did he. He thought it was one of those parma violet sweets that kids used to eat back in the 70s. You know Rick, anything food related and he's up for it, no questions asked."

"Did you ever think of getting Rick to play along with the band?" chipped in Max from the sidelines.

"I'd have loved it, mate, but there's no way Mick would ever agree to share a stage with a huge bloke wearing a gold lamé cape and doing fifteen-minute keyboard solos. And as for Keith, let's face it, he'd never see his shepherd's pie again, would he?"

Ronnie eyed the people milling around him with keen interest before continuing, "Who in f***k's name did the..."

"He's called William. Likes to break things down to their basic constituent parts. Great admirer of the works of Lidl and Sainsbury."

"Him I've got to meet. Is he some kind of nutter?"

"Ha! Ha! Ha! No. Yes."

"As in no, I shouldn't meet him and yes, he is a nutter?"

"Oooh, I, um, well, ah, look, no violence please, Ronnie. Promise! Just imagine you are dealing with a poor little kitten whose mother has just been turned into guitar strings. You can't expect a normal conversation about saucers of milk, can you?"

Ronnie cackled with amusement. "Jesus, what are you guys on!?"

Max left Ronnie still grinning and went in search of something to eat. It seemed like a very long time since breakfast, and he yearned for a sausage sandwich with a side of fries and some chili mustard. He toyed with the idea of trekking over to Rick's Café, but instantly ruled it out. Not with that T-shirt on. Instead, he knocked hard on the Coast Watch door and summoned Bill. After an age of bolts being unlocked, first upstairs, then down, the door cracked open a fraction of an inch.

"Bill, what food do you have? The countess is relying on you, and I have been asked to sample the fare to check its suitability."

Max followed Bill up the stairs to the observatory where, to his amazement, there was enough food to feed the five thousand.

Bill, spotting Max's astonishment, moved quickly to justify his position.

"What with the concert and the crowds, I thought I might be stuck here all day without being able to leave my post. And, naturally, I also wanted to provide for any, er, esteemed guests who dropped by. There's a tremendous view of the throng from here, and it occurred to me that perhaps one or two might like to come up to watch the proceedings in safety and comfort."

Max could smell profit as well as food. They smelt equally good.

"I'll tell you what, Bill, I've got a little proposition for you. I'll send you up guests at twenty-minute intervals, and if you give them all a drink and a piece of cake, I'll make sure you get £50, er, I mean £10 a head for the Coast Watch. Deal?"

Grabbing a leg of chicken and some orange sponge, which on closer inspection turned out to be an orange sponge, Max vacated the premises and had a discreet word with backstage security. Some vague promises of money exchanged hands, and one of the security men, a passable looking Neanderthal, left and started talking to the crowd, garnering immediate interest.

"Got to get rid of this T-shirt," Max mumbled to himself, and did a quick jig as a small flash of inspiration struck him. He rushed over to where William was now discussing the finer points of abstract art with a bemused Wurzels roadie and grabbed him by the arm.

"How'd you like to paint me, as in right here, right now?! And what I mean is not paint me, but paint on me. This T-shirt, in fact. I want it re-faced, or to be more blunt, obliterated. Get your brushes and give me your finest ever bar code."

Five minutes later, Max, very damp with paint, but otherwise jubilant, intercepted another drink and manoeuvred his way over to a far corner where Sven and the volleyball team were taking part in a last-minute team talk.

"You think people will like us?" enquired Ludmilla hopefully.

Max assured her that it would be the highlight of the day for many in the crowd.

"A lot of people come to concerts just to seem cool, and they don't appreciate the music at all. You, they'll totally get, believe me. Best of luck."

"Max, can you help us with shifting the sand for the volleyball?" barked Marguerite. "And how did you get your shirt sorted out?"

"William."

"So, there is a reason for his existence. Lead me to him immediately. I'm not going onstage until Blunt has been smothered in paint."

Max looked awkward.

"But M, you can't get William to paint on you."

"Why not? It worked for you, didn't it?"

"But, you know," said Max with an embarrassed grimace. He struggled to elaborate, and waved his right hand vaguely in front of her, before giving up and mouthing, "You've got b-r-e-a-s-t-s."

"Oh, my God, Max, yes, yes, you're completely right! Thank you so much for that. And to think that for all these years I've been trying unsuccessfully to tune in to BBC Radio 4."

"Well, ok, if you want to risk it, he's over here. William! Marguerite wants a paint job, too. Oi! William! William! Come back, you coward! Don't worry, M, I'll handle things, figuratively speaking, if you don't object? I've got a great idea, too. Come over here."

Max worked feverishly for a few minutes and stood back to admire his work. "There! All done."

Marguerite looked down. "You've painted a bloody radio on my chest!!"

"Yes, and it's all thanks to you. Do you like the way I've kept Blunty's eyes as dials, works a treat, doesn't it?"

***

The stage was set, or at least the sandpit was filled, and the volleyball players jogged up and down nervously in the wings. A distant church bell chimed two o'clock.

"On you go, Max," said Marguerite nudging him in the ribs hard.

"What do you mean on I go? I'm not playing volleyball!"

"Introduce it. Start proceedings. Get out there!"

"What did we get frigging Blessed for then?"

"He's doing the music acts."

"Well, get Sven to sing then! There's no way on earth that I'm going out there..."

***

"Ladies and Gentlemen! May I have your attention, please! Welcome to Mead Bay and the Van Chocolat sponsored 'Centre of the Earth Festival,' starring everyone's favourite Grumpy Old Man, Rick Wakeman! I can promise you that this will be like no festival you have ever been to before, or your money back. And now, before we dive into our feast of eclectic and surreal musical entertainment, it's time to wake you blanket dwellers up a bit. So, without further ado, here is a reminder of what beach resorts should all be about. I give you the International Beach Volleyball All Stars, refereed by Mr. Sve, Mr. Sve ... Elvis Presley!"

A huge cheer sent a screech of seagulls up into the air as the players, including a fully costumed Sven, took to the stage.

Sven addressed the players. "Ladies, on the third hop, you may begin."

The crowd loved it, all apart from the front row who found themselves engulfed by a full-on desert storm of sand.

"This whisky tastes odd, Daddy," complained a young Scots toddler, two rows back.

"Aye, too much grain in it, Andy," his father astutely replied. "I'll drink it for you, shall I, son? Shame to waste it. You drink the Buckie."

Just off stage, Max's phone lit up. It was Jeff. "There you are, Max, I've been trying to get hold of you for ages. It's all going fine out here. Look, I must tell you, we've shot a bear! Great, isn't it? Just like the good old days. What was that? No, no, just winged it. Difficult angle. It got away through the trees, but I got its red hat, and I'm going to mount it on my trophy wall."

Max started breathing again. "Jeff, look, it's only local councillors you're supposed to shoot, remember, not sad, old, out-of-work bears."

"Point taken, Max. But that wasn't the only reason I called. It's virtually impossible to get to the backstage entrance through the crowd. For security reasons, we're going to need to open a small entrance between the cliff and the left-hand side of the stage. That's the left- hand side looking from the crowd. We'll just loosen one of the painted canvas panels and man the gap with one of the lads. Make sense?"

"Actually, Jeff," Max said, shouting to be heard above the volleyball action, "that's a surprisingly good idea. Please proceed. I'll come and help."

Max crept around the back of the stage and found the blind side was not completely empty. 'Syd' Oliver was holding a somewhat agitated conversation with an elderly rocker.

"I don't remember the Scottish accent, but then I don't remember that much of anything. Too many sherbet dips if you know what I mean. You been living up there a while, then? I could have sworn you'd passed on, much mourned of course, but definitely passed. Is that young lady I saw you with your carer?"

Oliver tried to explain his way out of the misunderstanding, without much success.

"You're a well-known archie-what? Well, you need to give that up, old son. It's not good for you at all. I stopped taking everything about twenty years ago and look at me now. New teeth, new nose, new liver; I feel great."

"Sorry to interrupt you gents," Max said, "but can I ask you to go back round to the main backstage area? We've got to do a bit of essential maintenance work here."

Max escorted them back around the corner and bumped into Marguerite.

"Max, it's nagging me that I can't get hold of anyone at the church. The orchestra is supposed to be doing a final rehearsal on its own, but neither the Farting woman nor Magnus or his Welsh chum are picking up. That makes me feel a bit uneasy."

"It'll be the thickness of the walls, I'm sure. Don't worry, we can send Jeff down a bit later just to catch up with them. Any message? Oh, here's Jeff, you can tell him yourself."

"Tell me what?" Jeff asked, struggling to crawl under the canvas. "This canvas has been anchored down like a ship. It'll need both of us, Max, to pull out the metal peg."

They strained fruitlessly for about five minutes before Max called out in exasperation, "We need to stop and get some frigging gloves, Jeff. My hands are being ripped to shreds here. The guys must have used a jack hammer to drive this thing in with."

Jeff nodded and started to crawl back under the canvas again when, unexpectedly, the metal peg slid out of position and the ethereal figure of Jessica appeared.

"You must have loosened it," she said, handing Jeff the foot long, spiked peg.

"Where have you been?" Max asked. "You've been missing all the fun backstage."

"Oh, here and there, just floating around, you know."

"You've never been a seagull, have you?"

She giggled. "Oh, Max, you are so funny," and made to poke him in the middle.

However, Max, having faced disembowelment before, was too fast for her and folded neatly in two before her hand could engage.

Jeff was highly impressed. "That was amazing! Just like you two've been rehearsing for an action movie. Here, Jessica, try it on me. I'm a pretty quick mover, you know. You had to be in the Special For..."

"Jessica, you just can't go about disabling our security team with your sleight of hand tricks," said Max sternly. "William, yes; it's kind of de rigueur, but security team, no. Come on, Jeff, stop sobbing and let me get you a restorative. Here, sip it very slowly, that way we can see if there are any obvious leaks."

Jeff was helped into a chair and continued to moan.

"What you need is a Nurofen Plus," said Max, and flagged down one of the waiters to put in the request.

"There, you'll feel better in no time. I'm going to take one as well as my hands are still aching like buggery. Nurofen for you, M?"

"Thanks Max, my head is about to split in two. I'm getting too old for this kind of stress."

The sound of sustained applause outside indicated the end of the beach volleyball exhibition, and suddenly, an atoll of bikini clad beach volleyball players burst into the backstage area, stopping all conversation momentarily dead. Sven followed soon after them, grinning from ear to ear.

"That was amazing! Totally amazing! And the icing on the cake is that there's a girl about thirty metres back from the stage that I've never met before."

"I thought you'd passed on," said the elderly rocker, passing by in search of sustenance. "Welcome back. You've been hanging out with Lord Lucan I suppose?"

Sven assessed the situation very quickly. "Oh, yes. We've both been investing heavily in oil, you know. Do you have any spare cash because I could cut you in on a nice little piece of investment action here in Mead Bay. You do? Excellent. Waiter! Could you bring this lovely gentleman a large bottle of absinthe and a pen please?"

He rubbed his hands and looked at Max. "Max, could you do me a favour and ask the young girl I mentioned if she'd like to meet up later? Say Elvis sent you."

"And how do you think I'm going to know which girl it is, Sven? There's hundreds near the stage."

"Just ask who knows Elvis but doesn't know Sven."

"Ok, next on stage, please!"

The Wurzels were leveraged upright, dusted down, and gently assisted into the wings, while Sir Brian Blessed swept by wearing a very tight-fitting ball gown and singing, "I'm just a girl who can't say no!"

Max began to feel very strange, very strange indeed. He could see that white seagull coming closer to him again, with an Elvis-shaped crane hopping just behind it. A battered, old crow seemed to say something about not touching the Goat's Head Soup, and a parrot with a red beret was happy squawking. Max tried shaking his head, but that made it worse, and now the whole world seemed to be turning into a giant kaleidoscopic aviary. Far in the distance, he heard the sound of a familiar cannon booming out the words, "Ladies and Gentlemen, straight from The Hundred Acre Wood, The Woozles!" before everything went very future Britain.

When it became light again, Max found himself sitting on the ground in front of the stage. His state was that of being between two thirds asleep and one third awake; a place where dreams and reality overlap, like a basket full of sleeping dogs. He could neither move nor speak, but he was still able to observe, in the manner of a distant spectator surveying Earth from a different planet. And, out of the corner of his eye, he noticed two kindred spectators in the forms of Jeff and Marguerite, both in a similar state of semi-conscious bliss.

A large man in a dress came on stage and caused a sonic boom. This was soon followed by the soaking-in-a-bath-of-warm-rum sensation that good calypso music delivers. Max drifted off for a while, returning to the present in time to hear the cries for an encore ring out as the calypsonians tried to leave, the cheers when they came back, and the warm hum of approval that lingered after their final departure. The sonic boom returned, and the sounds of calypso were replaced by ... beach volleyball, and somewhere in Max's freewheeling mind, came the vaguest sense of déjà-vu.

He struggled to shift the fog in his head and focus on the stage announcement.

"Ladies and Gentlemen! Ladies and Gentlemen! May I have your attention, please? At this point in time, we were supposed to be hearing the delectable tones of Steve 'Twit Twit' Roberts, but I regret to have to inform you that he has suffered an unfortunate body part malfunction and has had to cry off. To be honest, I think you scared him witless, and now he's shitting himself. Ha! Ha! Who writes this crap, eh? Oh, I do! Well, never mind, let's get on with the show. Will you all please rise and show your appreciation for The Grubby Songsters! I give you The Grubby Songsters! The Grub..."

Sir Brian was halted by a small child who had been pushed from the wings and was now simultaneously pulling at his sleeve and trying to whisper in his ear. He listened and guffawed loudly. He summoned the crowd to intimacy with a hairy mitt and bellowed, "Well, it seems that the shit really now has hit the fan! Most of the Grubby Songsters are also up to their ankles in muddy water and won't be clean any time soon! Ha! Ha! Who writes this stuff? I mean, really? You should all be ashamed of yourselves frightening the performers like that. You're all very naughty! But, fortunately for you, and not that you deserve it, you wicked people, the beach volleyball stars will re-take the front stage while we clean up the mess backstage! Ha! Ha! God, I'm good! So, please welcome back The International Beach Volleyball All-Stars, accompanied as ever on whistle by Sweden's finest, Hopalong Elvis. Applaud, you buggers, applaud!"

Max watched on as the beach volleyball action was transformed over time from high energy to slow motion, as the players tired, and Hopalong Elvis became Stagger Lee Elvis. Sensing their imminent collapse, the ever-resourceful Sir Brian interceded into the game.

"Come on, come on, let me have go! I'll show you carpet crawlers how it's done. Throw me the ball, throw me the ba..!"

The game stopped, much to the relief of the players, and Sir Brian was dragged from the stage, clutching his testimonials and squeaking, "My King Lear. Oh, Sweet Jesus, my poor King Lear. Finished!"

The crowd, thinking that this was part of the entertainment, roared with approval, and awaited the next act.

The stage was once again cleared of sand, and for five minutes, nothing happened at all. Then just as the crowd were getting restless and calling for King Lear, a tall, gloomy looking girl with glasses walked out and took the microphone.

"Hello. My name is Cee. I want you know that I have been kidnapped and forced to come up here. No, really, stop laughing. It's so unfair. How did this happen to me? All I wanted was a quiet life and now this. I work in a café, and I was supposed to be selling drugs today. No, please don't laugh. I've never sold drugs before, and I didn't realise that not all grass is the same. Please, stop! So, I've sold you all grass that was mowed yesterday here on the plain, and I'm just so, so, sorry. What's going on, why are you cheering? Please, no! I charged everyone a lot of money for selling you what amounts to compost. I cheated you, and you may turn green."

By now the crowd was starting to crack up, and Cee's earnest attempts to quell them were simply causing the cracks to widen.

"I didn't even know who Rick Wakeman was until a week ago, and when I was told he had done *Journey to the Centre of the Earth*, I thought he was an explorer."

The crowd started to crumble.

"Like Ralph Fiennes."

And collapse.

"When I studied Glue Theory at university..."

And disintegrate.

A visibly very distressed Cee was forced to take several bows and finally exited the stage, shaking her head in abject bafflement.

A slight pause ensued before a bouncy Zoe Ball entered, dressed as a chocolate log.

"Sir Brian is temporarily indisposed, but the good news is that Steve 'Tweet Tweet' Roberts, with the help of our cosmic medical director, Dr.

May, has now been rebuilt and is ready to perform, ably backed by those denizens of agricultural songstry, The Wurzels!"

Stevo shuffled painfully onto the stage, sporting a breath-taking seagull costume. He shifted agitatedly from foot to foot as the crowd laughed in a filterless manner at his attire.

"Play it straight," was the advice Max had given to Stevo. "It'll be so much more effective." Stevo had had no idea what Max was on about. He was always serious about his work.

"I'm honoured to be here today to support this cause. I like all birds of all shapes and sizes and ...", but the rest was drowned out by raucous laughter.

"This one's called 'Windswept Pigeons on the Champs Elysees.'"

It was quite a while before the crowd quietened enough for Stevo to go on, but finally all was calm.

"Through the grey, swirling mists of a cold, joyless day
I saw windswept pigeons strut on the Champs Elysees.
They raised their sad heads in a desolate way
And called out to each other...
Ooh arrh ooh arrh ay!"

Stevo stopped dead in his tracks, appalled. The crowd roared with delight, and The Wurzels beamed contentedly, happy to be earning a bonus from Max which consisted of a bottle of chocolate liqueur a man for each time the phrase could be inserted into a song.

"No, no, that's not how it goes at all. You're ruining my song! I'm a professional, you know, not some farmyard halfwit! Right, look, let's have another try, shall we? This one's off my last album and it's called 'Dalwhinnie Platform.' It's a love song about a girl I met on a songwriting retreat in Scotland.

"She told me to meet her at the end of platform number three
Just before the land runs out and slides into the sea
She said let's till the land together, for farmers we shall be
Because ...
I've got a brand new combine harvester, and I'll give you the key!"

Stevo exploded.

"You useless bunch of geriatric barn dwellers! How dare you re-write my songs? I've written more good songs than you've had, er, baths. Hot or cold! I'm a highly respected musician. Really very highly respected. And versatile. Not many people got to play with both Kajagoogoo and Black Lace!"

At this point, antagonised beyond all reason by the joyous whoops and hollers coming from the crowd, Stevo picked up his guitar and dashed it on the ground. He then jumped up and down on it repeatedly, costume wings flapping uncontrollably, and made to kick it into the crowd. Alas, he stepped onto some sand left over from the beach volleyball and shot straight off the stage. Thinking it was all part of the act, Stevo was raised shoulder high and passed helplessly back across a cheering plain, shouting popularity-enhancing obscenities all the way.

Max found himself looking at the hotel manager. Or at least, several hotel managers, as the shaking of his shoulders was causing everything to distort.

"Wake up! Wake up Misteraranbee! I try to find to you. Big problem! Come now!"

"Well, hi there, all of you. Can you just leave off the shaking a moment," was what Max thought he said, rather than the, "Welleyeairoloveyou. Canyerjuzzlivovverjayjinamomen," that actually emerged.

He started to close his eyes again when the manager licked his face; an action that not even the effects of the dodgiest Nurofen Plus could compete with.

"Yeeeugh! What are you playing at? Toilet seat polishing for the Dutch aristocracy is one thing, but licking your guests clean is a step too far!! Oh, hello Scabies, what are you doing here?"

"I bring him with me to find you. Come quick. There are big problems in the church."

Max struggled once again to get a grip on reality. What was the man on about? "You run a hotel, not a church," he finally stammered.

"Yes, yes, any fule kno that. There is a big problem at the church. With the orchestra. The police are there."

"The orchestra! How could they possibly be in trouble, apart from murdering the classics? Oh, well, Marguerite, Jeff, get up!"

There were just a few giggles but no action.

"Right, Scabies, you take the hairy one, and I'll handle this one."

Max grabbed Marguerite under the arms, braced himself, and heaved. "Bloody hell, M, are all your bones made of lead?!"

Once upright, Marguerite began to show signs of life. "Ooh, my head, it's so fuzzy. I want to go to sleep."

"Sorry, M, that's right off the agenda."

Max looked around him for a second, had a word with his neighbour and dipped a spoon into a jar. "Here, M, open your mouth and swallow. This will help you wake up."

A stifled scream followed. "You ****** What in the ******!!!!!

"There you go, M, wide awake now, are we? There's nothing like a tablespoon of Marmite to restore the senses. No, don't try to thank me, it's what friends are for. Now let's all go to church together, shall we? Jeff, can you stop crawling on all fours, please, or Scabies will get interested, and I'm doubtful as to your pedigree."

At the edge of the plain, Max could once again hear Brian Blessed's dulcet tones introducing the 'Blue Deacons' and commenting on how it made a change from all the 'Blue Nuns' he'd enjoyed as a lad.

"Look," Max said, "I know we need to get to the church, but can I suggest a five-minute pause for the blackest coffee ever created? None of us are in a fit state to encounter any piggery jokery just yet."

Having consumed a pot of coffee so black it could be chewed like tobacco, the newly woke group walked down to the old church and found the churchyard full of edgy coppers.

"What seems to be the trouble, officer?" Max asked in a childhood fantasy fulfilling moment.

"We received reports of strange and violent shrieks and scraping noises from within the church vicinity and came to investigate. The door is locked, but the sounds are most unnatural, so we're calling for backup. It's a strange place, Mead Bay. We've had devil worship cults before, so you can't be too careful."

Max relaxed and let out a breezy laugh.

"You are aware that it is the Mead Bay Orchestra in there? What you described sounds like a normal rehearsal."

"With respect, sir," said the officer, a weathered looking woman in her 40s, with steely grey hair, grey eyes, grey eye shadow, and grey teeth, "that does not sound like an orchestra rehearsing, no matter how bad they are. There's been some shouting and moaning in there that's well out of order."

"Look, I know these people; they're supposed to be playing at the festival up the road later on. Can I try to talk to them?"

"Well, be it on your own head, sir."

Max advanced to the door and banged against it heavily with his foot. "Mrs. F'Ting-Brightly are you there?"

Silence. Max repeated his call. Cackling followed, and suddenly a voice rang out from the clock tower. Looking up, Max saw Mrs. F'Ting- Brightly waving a broom at him, in some distress.

"Someone spiked our tea! Everyone's gone crazy, and they're planning to overthrow the government. It's total madness in here. Colonel Tripehound is leading them, and he's eaten all the church flowers, the brute. I can't tell you how expensive they are!"

"Why aren't you with them?

"Can't stand tea. Horlicks girl, with just a soupcon of brandy. I managed to barricade myself in here, but I can't hold out much longer."

Max walked back to the officer. "I guess you heard all that?"

"Yes, sir, and if they really are planning to overthrow the government, we'd better leave them to it, don't you think?"

"Your instincts are impeccable, officer, but we need all these people on stage in just a few hours."

"I'm very sorry, sir, but that won't be possible. You see, we're going to need to question everyone here, once the siege is lifted, and anyone who is intoxicated will not be permitted to attend in any event."

"But we need them!" cried Marguerite, suddenly sparking into life with a jolt. "We've got five thousand people waiting to hear Rick Wakeman play bloody *Journey to the Centre of the* bloody *Earth*, and there'll be a bloody riot if we say, 'Sorry, we've only got an oboe player 'cause the rest of the orchestra have been arrested for drinking dodgy tea!!'"

Seeing the steely eyes of the officer turning to a post-graduate level of steel, Marguerite took a deep breath and, with some violent internal struggles, made a stab at speaking in a calmer manner. "Look, don't you understand, officer? These are wealthy, middle-aged, middle class, festival goers. Destructive as f***k, in other words, if they don't get what they came for! And no indiscriminate smashing up of a few bus shelters and the odd, old car. No, these people are smart; they'll clinically dismantle the whole bloody town! This place will look like the inside of the bloody prime minister's head by the time they're finished. Just primeval ooze!!"

Satisfied with her balanced delivery, she stepped back, only to be deafened by Max.

"Jeff, Jeff, what are you doing?!"

"I'm going to get them out. I'll shoot a bolt into the bell tower attached to a piece of a rope and climb up the wall. Then, using the broom as a pike, and Mrs. F'Ting-Brightly as a shield, I'll drive them back and open the church door for the police. I was in the Special Forces, you know?"

"Yes Jeff, but that was over twenty-five years ago; the Special Forces put aside their crossbows and brooms in the mid-90s when they discovered their opponents were using Uzis and thermo-nuclear tracking missiles. All you're trained for now is selling IT security systems to firms of accountants and actuaries. You'll only hurt yourself. Jeff, where did you get that rope? Jeff, don't do it!"

An hour later, the tension was still palpable in the hotel bar, where Max, Jeff and Marguerite were recovering over several large glasses of wine.

"Don't look at me like that, Marguerite," Jeff said, wincing under her withering gaze. "It all went to plan, didn't it? We got the ringleader."

"The fact that your bloody arrow hit the support holding the bell and caused it to drop fifty feet onto where the colonel was standing, was planned I suppose? We're lucky he's still a-bloody-live, and remember, they haven't got him out yet. He's probably going to sue us for the worst case of tinnitus ever recorded outside of the bloody Mötorhead Fan Club!"

"That's a mere bagatelle, dear M," interjected Max smoothly, "when compared to the loss of our entire orchestra, that is to say with the honourable exception of one pensionable oboe player with the hots for Rick. We don't even have any backing singers, as Magnus and Neil were hauled in with the rest. That leaves us with a seagull bedecked guitar player, who is probably still being passed around the crowd, a bass player who has gone AWOL and a drummer who may still terminate the main act. So, Miss Marple, what are we going to do? Do you want to tell Rick, or shall we just high tail it out of here straight away and seek immunity on Sealand?"

Marguerite pulled her face down with her hands, revealing rather unattractive, red eye rims. The enormous appeal of decamping to the Principality of Sealand, with all that fresh air, lack of bureaucratic red tape, and the opportunity to become a duchess, was weighing heavily on her mind. She started to nod her head, and was about to give herself over to the fish-eating aristocratic life, when she found her mouth emitting the words, "No, bugger it, we'll just keep going! Who needs a bloody orchestra anyway?! I mean, they were total crap!"

Max could think of so many reasons why they needed an orchestra that his brain refused to engage with his mouth. "Ahhhmmmumahhh," he gargled.

"Pink Floyd?" asked Jeff hesitatingly, eyes screwed up in concentration.

"Ok, so that's settled then," Marguerite said. "Max, you go to the backstage tent and round up as many musicians as possible. They're mostly old enough to actually be able to play their instruments and to improvise. Tell them it's a surprise for Rick and that they're not to say a word about it to him. Jeff, round up your avian security chums and gently persuade members of the crowd to lend any instruments going. Guitars, banjos, kazoos, whatever. Get a couple of them to raid the old church, too; all the orchestra instruments will still be there. Max, you've got some equipment, don't you? Add that in. Tell everyone that Ronnie Wood will sign everything. Max, why are you still here?"

"Everything you have said is great, M, except that you are going backstage, and I am going to stay here and mind Rick. No, don't look so outraged. You know all these people, whereas they don't know me from Adam, or even Marco. Come on, you know I'm right."

Marguerite gnashed her teeth and emitted a noise like a tiger who has just swallowed a nest of bees. But there was no actual violence, and she made for the door, giving Max a passing kiss that was borderline head-butt.

"Oh, can you send Fizz back here, M, if she's finished looking at the view? Two will be better than one looking after Rick until we bring him backstage."

Marguerite left, taking Jeff with her, and Max was left alone to reflect on just what on earth was going on. Surely there would come a point where all the blind optimism and devious deception in the world was going to fall short? Because, at some point, even Rick was going to find out what was going on. Which reminded him, where was Rick?

***

Max went down to reception and found it empty. He called out Rick's name but to no avail and eventually walked out onto the driveway, where he could see the whole staff gathered, listening intently to the sounds emanating from Tori Amos's set. He spotted the manager, who informed him that Rick and the 'crazy man' were in the annexe where the songwriting course had been taking place. Max hung around, undecided on whether to wait for Fizz or not. Would she be disappointed at not having made it on stage to sing her song? Would she suspect that he was to blame? Would she gain her revenge in some ghastly Dutch manner, whatever that might be? He started to google 'Dutch revenge methods.' The death by tulip enema was particularly unpleasant.

Fizz interrupted his thoughts by skipping into view.

"Hello, hello, hello!" she trilled in a vexingly bright-eyed and bushy-tailed manner.

"I've been purged, and I feel so pure! This must be the lightest I've been for years. I'm a total convert to Talisker and honey."

"And you're not sore about missing your chance for fame and fortune?"

"Bats and e-bikes, Maxy, that's where my fame and fortune's going to come from, not screeching on stage. Thank God I didn't have to go on! Now, tell me, why is Marguerite holding some kind of clandestine meeting backstage, and what happened to you guys anyway?"

As Max explained, Fizz's eyes opened so wide Max could have comfortably stepped in and enjoyed a post-corneal drink.

"And so, that's why I asked M to send you over. We need to mind Rick. You know, keep his spirits up, and just generally lie about everything."

At the far end of the annexe was a large piano, a large piano player, a large bowl of chocolate digestive biscuits, a beaten-up set of drums and a beaten-up bespectacled drummer, who was showing signs of evident frustration.

"No, Ricky boy, do it again, only this time with just one finger on each hand. The Captain never played 'I Just Can't Be Happy Today' like an octopus on speed. Simplicity and attitude, that's the key thing. Ok, again. No!! Can't you count to f*****g one!!"

Rick sighed and took another biscuit. Punk was more complicated than he'd imagined. They tried again.

"Ok, that was better. But just loosen up, and for Christ's sake, make some mistakes! More punk, less polish is the order of the day. Oh, hello, Fez. And you're Max, right? You here to check that His Nibs is still alive?"

"Something like that. Er, can I have a private word?"

Max drew Rat aside and asked a question.

"Of course, I know they're here. Made contact when I flew in from me island. Planned ourselves a nice little reunion at Paignton Zoo after I'd finished this Wakeman business. Now, we'll just do it here instead. Be a bit of fun. Lucrative fun, I hope. That's if Grumpy Old Rick don't f**k it up. Sorry, what's that? Can I keep a secret?"

Max whispered in his ear.

"Are you ok, Rat?" asked Rick. "Had some bad news?"

Rat was red-eyed and wheezing uncontrollably in a Muttleyesque manner.

He just wagged a finger at Rick and, in a voice broken by too much joyous passion, croaked, "Best news ever! You ... wait ... and ... see!" before being cut off by a near terminal coughing fit and falling off his drum stool.

After that, the practice session fell apart, and Scabies entertained the troops with tales of trips around strange French churchyards at full moon. Eventually, a voice called from the door, "Mr. Wakeman, to the stage, please. Mr. Wakeman, to the stage."

Outside, a gleaming Gus stood beside a gleaming Van Chocolat van, with the door open, waiting. Rick was halfway inside when he seemed to get caught on something, and the sound of ripping could be heard. Rick got out and surveyed the damage. Scabies was standing there in front of him with a knife and a crazed glint in his eye.

"Can't have you going on stage to play a punk set dressed like Gandalf, can we?"

And he continued to slash at the cape until it was well and truly shredded.

"Right, that'll do. What do you think? Rat got your tongue? You'll be just fine. Just think angry thoughts, whatever pisses you off. Just imagine you were replaced on *Grumpy Old Men* by Elton."

"No f******g way would they replace me with Elton! Who told you that?"

"I just heard the rumours. You're reckoned to be getting too soft, mate."

"F******g BBC bastards! I'll have them, I will. Elton's got no chance. I'm much, much grumpier than him. And much cheaper!"

Scabies smiled at Max, got in, and closed the door.

A few minutes later, Sir Brian swept onto the stage wrapped in a towel, with his hair gelled high and coloured blue. "Now listen up, scum! It's punky time, and I want you up on your feet and po-going. Up! Up! All of you! That's better. Now, go on, po-go! Dear, oh dear, you are worse than useless. Try again, and this time try putting your back into it. One, two three, go! Well, it's slightly better, I suppose, but not much. Watch me now. One, two, three, go!"

And up went Sir Brian, and down went his towel. Scabies, seeing what looked like his blanket, scurried onto the stage and made a grab for it, and he and Sir Brian were soon engaged in a to-the-death tug of war, while the crowd bayed gladiatorially.

"I've still got it, you know," bellowed Sir Brian, "Oh, no, you've got it! Bugger!"

Scabies left the scene, leaving the crowd with a director's cut view of Sir Brian. However, whilst many great Shakespearean actors, finding themselves at such a disadvantage, would have crept away in shell-shocked and mortified fashion, Sir Brian was made of sterner stuff. Indeed, the 'never say die' spirit that saw him survive many episodes of 60s police series Z Cars and got him within a book publishing deal's distance of the summit of Mount Everest, shone through. With one hand covering the untamed parts of his anatomy, Sir Brian grabbed the mike, ordered the band to strike up and launched into a graphic version of "The Bare Necessities" to naked acclaim.

"Thank you, people, thank you, people, I hope you enjoyed the show. And now, please show your po-going best for Rick Wakeman and his, er, punk chums."

Rick emerged to partisan cheers and stood behind his keyboards.

"Yeah, well, welcome. Or I should say f**k off! I've been a fan of punk music for many hours now, and I'm delighted to welcome on stage some genuinely unpleasant people to help abuse your senses. So, please makes lots of noise for, on guitar, Raymond 'Off the Rails' Burns, on drums, Christopher 'Grail Hunter' Millar, on bass, Paul 'Quintessentially' Gray, on vocals, David 'Nearly Always' Lett and on maracas and manic dancing, Mr. Laurence 'Wild Thing' Burrow. I'm very..."

But this was far too much for Mr. Burns, who stepped forward, and simply shouted into his mike, "Bollocks to all that! We're..." and he suddenly noticed Sir Brian, "The Blessed, and we're not a Prog Rock Band! This one's called 'Smash It Up!'"

Squeezed into the Coast Watch building afterwards, Rick was literally bouncing off the walls with enthusiasm, as he was simultaneously interviewed by Zoe Ball and Panda Ramirez.

"Of course, I denied for years that I was an influence on punk, because I didn't like to take away from their moment in the sun, but I've been known for years behind the scenes as the Grand Wizard of Punk. Me and Iggy..."

Marguerite rolled her eyes at Max. "I think the quicker we get him off to the centre of the Earth the better. I can't take much more of this bollocks."

"Oh, I don't know, I think a collaboration between Rick and The, er, Blessed, could produce something out of this world."

"You've got to be joking! It's difficult enough managing just one daft overgrown schoolboy, let alone five of them!"

"Well, I think that's being a bit harsh on Mr. Lett. He's the epitome of maturity. Most of his clothes date from the 19th century."

Max was interrupted by an unhappy Burns.

"I've worn that beret all these years to stop stupid bastards in the crowd spitting on me, and the moment I take it off, the bloody keyboard player gobs on me. I ask you, what is the world coming to? Look, he's at it again!"

Marguerite intervened in best headmistress style. "Richard Christopher Wakeman, stop that this instant!! I'm so sorry, Ms. Ball, he's got a problem with his dentures."

"That's quite all right, Marguerite, I'm used to the rock geristocracy. Now, Rick, before we go on, I just wanted to say how proud I am of you for hosting this festival. It's such a thrill to see a literal monster of rock like yourself giving back to the community and at the same time throwing away the rule book for how festivals should be organised. It's so contemporary, so spontaneous. I love all the surprises you're giving us. Beach volleyball and comedians, mixed with bona fide legends. It's, what's that phrase used earlier, um, 'eclectic and surreal.' Yes, it really is. And now you've done it again. Imagine planning to play *Journey to the Centre of the Earth* with no orchestra, just with whoever happened to turn up on the night backstage. It's totally genius! Rick? Rick? Oh, God, Marguerite, I think he's swallowed his teeth!"

Rick was laid down on a blanket while Ramirez fanned him with a spare copy of Julian Norwich's latest thriller, straight off her home printing press.

William made an appearance at the door. "A Doctor Cox to see you."

Dr. Cox examined Rick carefully and pronounced an eclipse of Venus as being the problem.

"Just give him some sunglasses to protect his eyes and a mug of warm cocoa. After that, things can only get better."

Max collared Marguerite. "What on earth are we going to do now? He's in a complete state of shock. All what used to be his muscles have gone rigid. In fact, I've not seen anyone that catatonic since I visited the House of Lords as a kid."

"Catatonic is good. We need to keep him that way until he's on, or we'll never get him there at all."

"Ok, I think I've got a plan. Bill, are there any cheery girls upstairs at the moment? One. Ok, that's great, bring her down, but everyone else out, please. Rick needs to relax a while."

***

Outside, the musicians were getting excitable as Muse re-appeared backstage, leaving behind them thunderous applause. Their encore, a variation on a theme of "Uncle Tom Cobley," had surpassed expectations.

Marguerite slipped out for a few moments to help direct activities. The chairs for the orchestra could still be used, and there were enough mikes, but a desperate hunt was on for additional plug connections to cope with many more electrical instruments than had been planned for.

"Listen up, everyone!! I've got one old-fashioned cassette of *Journey* here, and Rick's own portable Philips cassette player. Gather around as best you can and pay attention. It'll be played once, and that's your lot. On stage, take your lead from Rick as best you can. Tori and Ricky, you ok taking lead vocals? And Mr. Lett, can you lead the choir? By choir, that means you, my Wurzelly friends, and Fizz and Dev, yes, you! Is Saff off the toilet yet? Yup, you're in the choir, too. Oh, and you, Nubnot. What? Well, if you think you can, Ramirez. No, Oliver! Burnsy, you fine with lead guitar? And Ronnie on slide? Our bass player has gone AWOL so Quintessentially can handle that, and of course, Millar's on drums. We can improvise a lot of orchestral sounds, but it would be good to have keyboard back-up on that. That's where you come in, Wild Thing. Please flesh out the higher range and Amusing Matt the lower. Any more keyboard players? Reg who? Fine, just join in as best you can, dear. Anyone play the violin? Great to see you, Jim! I thought you were dead. Sven, I take your word that you're good at caressing a bit of hard wood in your hands, but can you play the violin? Emily? Bronte? Fine, you can also play. The rest of you back up the others as appropriate and just try blend in. Steel band? Yes, yes, the more the merrier. Finally, any Millennials here? Ok, you can mime playing, but no singing, right? There's no auto-tune."

With these parting words, Marguerite returned to the Coast Watch building, to find Rick annoyingly compos mentis.

"You're fired, Squiggs! All of you are fired! This is a complete stitch up. I told you I never wanted to come to this horrible town, but you insisted. You insisted! And now this catastrophe, this absolute and total catastrophe, is the result. I'm the King Kong of the keyboards, and you want to throw me off the Empire State Building. Well, no, not this time, Mrs. Patten. I won't stand for it, and no amount of bullying or blackmailing is going to change my mind. I'm no yes man, I'm no man, and, er, that's how it's going to stay, so you can all just bugger off!"

And with that, Rick turned white, as the door from the Coast Watch Tower opened, and Jessica emerged.

"Hello, Rick," she said, in a soft breezy voice. "It's nice and cosy in here, and I just wanted to say..." she stopped abruptly, as Marguerite came into view at the same time as William opened the external door and came in.

"It's the stalker!!" four of them shouted concomitantly.

This had the effect of stunning the room into silence for a second as everyone looked around at each other.

"It's the stalker!!" they re-concominated, pointing at each other animatedly.

"What do you mean I'm the stalker!" they yelled in unison, "You're the stalker!"

"No, you shut up and listen!"

"You should be locked up!"

"No, you should!"

"Who do you think I am??!!"

"Brothers and Sisters," cut in Max soothingly, "calm down a second and turn off your mind. Relax, and float downstream a little. I'm sure it's all very Sybil. I'm convinced, don't ask me how, that this little nuclear spat is based on pure supposition and faulty communication. Let's get it all sorted out now, shall we, because tomorrow never knows."

***

"I still think that woman is a stalker," whispered Marguerite a few minutes later, "but by the look on His Nibs's face, he couldn't care if she was the four horsemen of the apocalypse."

"She does give a mean massage," agreed Max willingly, "and if she keeps it up, it'll be a doddle getting him on stage."

"Imagine anyone thinking I was the stalker, though, it makes my blood boil."

"Hmm, but you are a kind of stalker, though, aren't you, M? You're not after Rick's body, but inheriting a castle or two wouldn't go amiss, would it?"

"Max, that's not stalking, that's just good common bloody sense. By the way, how did Jessica come to think that William bloke might be after Rick? Strikes me he's something a stork dropped from a great height, not a stalker."

"I don't know, M, it's all a bit of a spider's web."

"Yeah, and something tells me the spider responsible is still in the vicinity. I eat spiders for breakfast, Max."

"That I can well believe, M. They're very good for you, too. Nutritious and full of protein."

***

The wind was getting up on the plain, but as it was still very warm, the crowd was pleased rather than concerned. That was less the case behind the scenes, where William's backdrop was billowing, and extra pegs were needed to stop it from flapping around. There also seemed to be a power shortage, which completely baffled the technical team until it was discovered that Sven's oil consultant was on full charge in preparation for his podium dance. The problem then was that no one could get close enough to unplug him without being electrocuted.

"We need to buy a bit of time, Max, can you think of anything?" Fizz asked.

Max could.

"Piss off Max! Piss right off and die!"

"But think 'Riverdance,' Fizz, just with Dutch clogs."

"But I can't play 'Riverdance,' moaned Jeff.

"Well, what can you play, Jeff? Security! Security! Stop that woman leaving and escort her onto the stage. Here, take these, Fizz."

"Where did you get those from?! What kind of man walks around with size 5 ladies Dutch clogs on the off chance some stupid girl might like to do a spontaneous duet with an alp horn player dressed like a medieval knight in front of 5000 people at a rock festival in a run-down seaside resort town in the Southwest of England?!"

"Look at them, Fizz ... they're signed by James Blunt. That Dutch bloke came over all charitable and threw them in with the T-shirts I bought. You should really thank him personally; it's what gave me the idea."

"But I've never clog danced in my life! What am I supposed to do?"

"Just imagine it's my face you're stamping on if that helps, Fizzy."

"Ladies and Gentleman, your attention please. We just have time for one last piece of entertainment before we head to the centre of the Earth. It gives me almost too much pleasure to welcome to the stage, on genuine Swiss mountain alp horn, Jeff Plantagenet, and on, er, Dutch clogs, Fizz d'Arnhem, performing their very own and highly original version of AC/DC's 'Back in Black!'"

"Boy, she must hate you very much," observed Marguerite later, admiringly. "I've never seen clogs sending up sparks on a wooden stage before. Pretty bloody impressive the way she set fire to that posh looking bloke's shirt in the front row. OK, let's get the show on the road, shall we?"

"Everyone on stage please, five minutes to show time, five minutes to show time."

Back in the Coast Watch building, Rick was fast asleep, and Jessica had disappeared.

"Bill, is she up there with you?"

"No, she said she had some errands to do. Left about five minutes ago. I've been watching the countess on stage. Fantastic! Those aristocratic types are full of hidden surprises."

"Wake up, Rick!" Marguerite yelled. "It's no good, Max, we'll have to try something more direct. I'll hold his nose, and you give him the Buckie. One, two, three, now! Perfect. Rick, get your costume on. The crowd's in such a good mood that you might just get away with this."

"Jesus, this cape's colossal, Where's me arms!" Rick yelled.

"May I remind you that you're the one who said he was the King Kong of the keyboards, so what did you expect? Seriously a moment. How are you? Are you going to be ok? I do worry about you, you know? Occasionally. Very occasionally."

"Have no fear. I feel twent, er, fifty again. That massage has revived long extinct parts of my body. What a girl, eh? If every man could have a stalker like that, the world would be a better place. This is going to be the biggest natural high ever. Lead on, McSquiggs!"

Max took to the stage, the warm wind sweeping back his hair, his nostrils full of natural high. Despite the occasion, he was lost in his own thoughts for a moment. A week. All this in one week. This wasn't happening, was it? Surely not? And yet, as he cast his eyes around a packed stage, there, amongst the great and the not quite so great of the music world, were Fizz and Glen, along with Saff, standing proudly in the huge choir, next to a very bemused Cee. Old Bill had joined them, too, along with the hotel manager, a hive of tipsy monks, and all the beach volleyball girls.

Further along, Max located Gus by finding that section of the crowd wearing sunglasses. Gus was warming up in the percussion section by banging together two enormous bars of chocolate, while his helpers were handing out more to the other players. Sven was demonstrating wrist techniques to Mrs. F'Ting-Brightly, who was fingering her oboe coquettishly in return. Placed to the fore and raised up, sat Rick's bejewelled keyboards, whilst, at the very front of the stage, easel in hand, a blood-spattered William was trying to capture the moment for posterity.

Max came out of his reverie and took one final glance around, just enough time to see a small, leather-clad bass player lift up her hat ever so slightly, and wink.

"So, finally, the moment the whole world has been waiting for. On stage tonight we welcome the New Mead Bay Orchestra, the Nearly Always Lett Choir, Sir Brian Blessed and, leading us on our fantastical *Journey to the Centre of the Earth*, that colossus of the keyboards, the one and only Wizard of Prog, Mr. Riiiiick Waaakeman!!"

***

Rick was on fire, the players were on fire, the choir was on fire, and Sir Brian, dressed in full mountaineering gear, was positively volcanic. The crowd was transfixed. This was truly live performance as it should be. And, as the winds grew more powerful, so did the effects of the music, until fever pitch was reached. Rick prepared himself for the triumphant final passage. A dash, a crescendo, a final flourish and a resounding conclusion. He raised his arms high in triumphant celebration and, cape flying, majestically took off into the dusk.

***

The crowd was awestruck, as were those on stage. What an absolutely stunning trick! Positively wizard!!

Reporters rushed away to file their reports while Marguerite, Max and Fizz dashed off stage and stared across the bay, seeing nothing.

"I can help! I can help! I can help!" cried Sir Brian, and he made a dash for the Coast Watch building. While the others watched bemused, the venerably antique thespian started to climb the tower. He soon came into view of the crowd, who shouted boisterous encouragement.

The transition from the wood tower to the orange rubber castle on top was not easy.

"Bloody, wobbly condom!" Sir Brian muttered as he hauled himself gingerly up. Finally, up on top, buffeted by the wind, he pulled out his binoculars and scanned the oceans. The crowd collectively held its breath as Sir Brian rode the rubber with seemingly practised ease and raised his hand. He made to speak, then, appearing to change his mind, lowered it again. Twice more he repeated the action, milking the drama like a herd of prize-winning Frisians. At last, both arms flung aloft, and with a definitive stamp of his boot, he bellowed, "Rick's alive!!" whereupon he was sucked instantaneously into the folds of the rubber castle he had just punctured.

EPILOGUE

YouTube videos of Rick's flight went viral, and the world's press fought tooth and nail to outdo each other with the best flying rock star puns.

The *New York Times* ran a more balanced article headed "From the Earth to the Skies: The Day Prog Rock Took off."

> *On Sunday last week, at an open air festival in Southwest Englandshire, prog rock legend, and self-proclaimed King Kong of the Keyboards, Rick Wakeman, blew away both the crowd and himself with a stunning, one could even say soaring, and positively Arabesque performance of his 70s classic Journey to the Centre of the Earth, accompanied by a veritable musicians Hall of Fame, ably supported by the epic narration of Sir Brian 'Sonic Boom' Blessed, the manic twitching of a dancing oil consultant, and a very strange man painting bar codes with what looked like his own blood. Truly, this was the most incendiary rock concert since Nero's backlit violin soirée, and it has left major rock festivals scratching their heads as to how to compete. Glastonbury's Michael Eavis is reportedly looking at constructing a new floating stage to top what some are already calling the "Wakeman Takes Wing" festival. Incidentally, a spokesman for Monty Python gave the considered view that it would take 1153 African swallows to transport an object the size of Mr. Wakeman.*

Other newspapers marvelled at how Rick had managed to stage such a flying feat, including his textbook landing on Shark Rock, and puzzled over the identity of the slight figure in a wide-brimmed hat who had appeared out of nowhere with a boat stolen from Mead Bay Marina, to pick him up.

Rick was not the only person to receive attention from the press. The onstage reunion of Rat Scabies with The Damned also received its fair share of column inches. Questioned as to how this rapprochement had come about after many years apart, Scabies told the *Moose-Jaw Times Herald*, "I'm splitting the proceeds of the Grail with them." On further prompting, Scabies admitted that he had not yet found the Grail but confirmed that he was "well on his way, and [would] be passing through Acton at one," in urgent pursuit of his enquiries.

The front doorbell of Max's house rang out to the tune of "Take Five" by Dave Brubeck, and the canine Scabies barked hopefully.

"I've brought the champagne," enthused Fizz, booting Scabies playfully out of the way. "Anyone else here yet?"

"Jeff's sorting out the kitchen. Apparently, the dust was affecting his asthma. I told him straight, 'If you don't touch stuff, the dust minds its own business.' What about you? I'm sorry that your course has collapsed, but with The Wurzels asking Stevo to join them on their European Rumpy-Scrumpy Tour, it was inevitable. And that live version of 'Dalwhinnie Platform' is killing it online."

"Oh, don't worry about the course, it's the least of my worries. Thanks to you, I'm much more concerned about lying low until the Dutch police stop looking for the Countess of Arnhem. However, the good news is that I stand to make a lot of money from the e-bikes, and on top of that, the duke has asked me to chair his new 'Battenborough Trust.'"

"That's great news! Hang out here for a while if you like? The Dutch police will never find you anyway. You'll be well below their radar. Ouch!!"

"You hit him, Fizz. That's what he's there for," said Marguerite animatedly, coming down the stairs waving a cassette threateningly.

"I might have bloody known it was you behind Rick's 'Arabesque' performance. This bloody cassette you gave him and all the world is that bloody Jeddah Records knock-off! I've never heard so many ouds and mizmars in one bloody place!"

"Yes, yes, mea culpa, but you've got to admit that the performance was considerably spiced up as a result, and the impromptu whirling dervish dance by The Damned's 'Wild Thing' Burrow was the icing on the cake.

That concert will give Rick a whole new regional audience, in addition to his recently acquitted punk following. Where is His Nibs by the way? I thought he'd be here by now."

"It's that bloody pile of scrap metal of his. Or should I say, pile of rust! He's gone to pick it up from Volksbay Motors, so we'll probably never see him again. Talking of which, Jessica has vanished. I know she seems to do that regularly, but I mean well and truly vanished. I tried to contact her at the hotel, and they said no one by that name had ever registered. Admittedly, the manager was as puzzled as me, but her room came up as a blank on the system, and as she always insisted on paying with cash, there was no other record. So, I decided to track her down through work in Vienna, as she told me enough to be able to guess the company. Well, they'd never employed a Jessica who met her description either. The closest they could come up with was some Canadian woman going by another name, and whose details had also mysteriously disappeared from the system.

"How exciting!" exclaimed Fizz. "Maybe she's a spy?"

"You hardly need to be a spy to spot Rick," Marguerite chortled. "Even from space, you can see him and that little Chinese wall. Much more likely she's a money launderer."

"Or a drug smuggler?" suggested Fizz.

"Or an assassin?!" offered Jeff, helpfully.

"No," Max said thoughtfully, "I think she's just a faulty teleportation from another time. Whichever way you look at it, though, she's left William in a bit of a fix. The police nabbed him after the concert for theft and deliberate criminal damage. Seems that someone in the crowd recognised the sail from his yacht being used as part of the backdrop. It didn't help that old Bill identified him as a cold-blooded Scottish gangland boss, so now he's languishing in the local nick under maximum security and will probably go down for a long stretch. The only consolation is that Ronnie Wood wants to buy his painting of the final performance. It turns out that those deep vertical and horizontal lines he painted are a dead ringer for Keith Richards."

The doorbell rang out again, and a breathless Glen came in, weighed down by a huge box.

"I've brought enough stuff to cook Rick the biggest celebration breakfast ever, even though it is late afternoon. There'll probably be enough for you lot and all. Cee sends her apologies, but she's hiding at home. She can't get rid of people turning up at the café and offering her slots on comedy shows. And each time she looks confused, and you know that's pretty much all of the time, they just keel over laughing. Where's Rick, Marguerite?"

"Gone to pick up his prize piece of junk. He'll never get past the ... what in the bloody hell is that bloody noise?!"

They all rushed upstairs onto the terrace, craning their heads around to look up the road, from where the sound of a horn blasting ear-piercingly loud music was coming ever closer. After a few seconds, a gleaming, brown van appeared, from which a buoyant Rick could be seen waving wildly. The logo "Rick's Van Chocolat" was emblazoned along the side.

"Where's the VW?" Max asked, as Rick squeezed out of the front seat, wearing a rather fetching, canary yellow "Wakeman is Damned" shirt.

"Oh, that old thing? I gave it to some monks, or rather, I should say I sold it to them for fifteen hundred quid," he said grinning delightedly.

"You sold that death trap to a bunch of innocent monks?! Are you mad, Wakeman?!" spat Marguerite venomously.

"Hold on now, Squiggs, just, er, hold on. Firstly, they're not that innocent. How many monks invite a squad of international volleyball players to relax and unwind at their monastery? And, secondly, I was totally open and honest. I told them driving that van would take them much closer to God. There, you can't say fairer than that now, can you?"

"But the new van?" enquired Fizz, pointing at the logo.

"Aha, you spotted that! My old mate Gus has given me this state-of-the-art beauty in return for driving it around the country to gigs. There's even a chocolate mud bath in the back for me and my, er, just for me."

Marguerite looked like she was about to erupt, so Max intervened quickly. "Green sausage anyone? I brought them in specially. Thought they might go nicely as a starter with champagne. Rick, take a plateful. Tabasco or mint sauce with them?"

Glen came in from the kitchen holding a small radio.

"Ok, everyone, the moment has arrived, shall we listen to the countdown? Rick, you do the honours."

Rick leaned over and pressed the on button. Almost immediately, Zoe Ball's sandpapery tones leaped out at them. "The battle in the album charts this week has been the fiercest ever seen, with the top two, both by veteran acts, outselling the rest of the Top 20 combined. So, sit back, relax, grab a glass and join me as we journey up the charts..."

Rick, Marguerite, Fizz, Glen, Jeff and Max did indeed enjoy a glass and did indeed sit back and relax. But, as the chart count inched higher and higher, the drinking got more professional, and tension had each of them perched right forward on the edge of their seats, crowding the radio.

"And new in at number eight, The Retread Gang with *You've Heard it All Before, Only Better*." Zoe paused, took a deep breath and pressed on.

"And now, pop pickers, we see the effects of last weekend's already legendary Mead Bay festival kicking in. At number seven, it's a re-entry from those Teignmouth titans, Muse, with their *Licence to Amuse*. At six, and in the charts for the first time since Julius Caesar presented the chart show, it's *Agriculturally Yours* by The Wurzels. Well done, lads. Rumours are that the boys will also be featuring on the singles charts with 'Dalwhinnie Platform,' their stonking live festival performance with Steve 'Gull-ible' Roberts. At number five, we have another re-entry, this time from Scottish veterans Deacon Blue, and their aptly named *Chocolate Girl Celebration*. At number four, Cornwall's favourite American, Tori Amos, wings her way up the chart with *Soar Away, But Please Mind the Pylons*.

"Ok, here we go, at number three, a new *Best Of* compilation, and their second Top Ten album in succession, it's punk's poster boys The Damned with *Blessed are the Damned*. Right, now we'll take a short break so I can introduce the special guest who is going to assist me with announcing the top two. Those of you with radios, turn the sound down now, and those without radios, don't worry, you'll still be able to hear. Attention please and give it up for the loudest man in the world, the incontrovertibly brilliant and, by the looks of it, substantially naked, Sir Brian Blessed!! Sir Brian, good to see nearly all of you. A real thrill for a woman of my age."

"Thank you, thank you, thank you, yes! I'm absolutely delighted to be here. Shall I do a bit of Shakespeare?"

"A bit of *King Lear* maybe?"

"Ah, well, perhaps not. My King Lear is still hors de combat, hence the, er, loose apparel. But I could do some Falstaff if you like?"

"You're too kind, Sir Brian, but I had rather a long conversation last weekend with a Swedish bloke about his Falstaff, so I think we'll save the Bard for another occasion."

"Right, right. 'Let's press on then, shall we,' as the actress said to the bishop. Yes, yes, yes, at number two, after forty-six glorious years away from the charts, we have Rick Wakeman's *Journey to the Centre of the Earth*, featuring the London Symphony Orchestra and the English Chamber Choir. Well done, Ricky, my boy, well deserved!"

Well deserved it may have been, but there was an audible sigh of disappointment in Max's living room, as the group digested the news. Only Max himself seemed strangely unmoved, as the others moped in silence and looked at the floor. So near and yet so far. Glen moved to switch off the radio, but Max waved him back.

"And now," continued Sir Brian, "the moment you have been waiting for. I believe that this has never happened before, has it, Zoe?"

"No, never."

"So, this is quite an epoch-making moment then. *'If music be the food of love, play on.'* Well, it is, and I will! This week's number one selling long player, by a margin of just one solitary record sale, is .... *Journey to the Centre of the Earth* by Rick Wakeman, featuring the Arabian Desert Orchestra and the Oud Unit Choir. A Jeddah Records production!!"

"I did it, I did it, I did it!!" yelled Rick, exploding from his chair like a rocket blasting off for Mars. "Number one and number two together. I'm a total genius!! I knew this would happen!! I totally knew it!! It's karma and chameleon!! That Arab version was always my favourite, didn't I say so, Squiggs?! Here, give me a bottle of champagne, and I'll down it in one!!"

He did, as did the others, and all at the same time high-fiving and cavorting around the room in a splendidly unhinged manner. Eventually, however, the raving took its toll, and everyone sank back into their seats, still beaming beatifically.

"Er, Squiggs, when did I do the Arab version?"

"You didn't."

"What do you mean I didn't?"

"It's a knock-off. Someone replaced the original backing with a new one."

"But it's still number one, isn't it?"

"Yes, Rick, but your chances of getting any royalties are absolutely stone cold zero. In fact, you've got more chance of actually travelling to the centre of the Earth than meeting up with the owner of Jeddah Records!"

"Well, now," said Max, reaching out for another bottle of champagne, and deftly removing the cork, "that's not strictly true."

"Max!!"

"Max!!"

"Max!!"

"Max!!"

"Max!!"

Printed in Great Britain
by Amazon

42600318R00179